Academic Learning Series: Security+ Certification

Lab Manual

Martin Grasdal

PUBLISHED BY
Microsoft Press
A Division of Microsoft Corporation
One Microsoft Way
Redmond, Washington 98052-6399

Printed and bound in the United States of America.

1 2 3 4 5 6 7 8 9   QWT   9 8 7 6 5 4

Distributed in Canada by H.B. Fenn and Company Ltd.

A CIP catalogue record for this book is available from the British Library.

Microsoft Press books are available through booksellers and distributors worldwide. For further information about international editions, contact your local Microsoft Corporation office or contact Microsoft Press International directly at fax (425)
936-7329. Visit our Web site at www.microsoft.com/learning/. Send comments to *mspinput@microsoft.com*.

Acquisitions Editor: Linda Engelman
Project Editor: Laura Sackerman

SubAssy Part No. X10-47241
Body Part No. X10-35353

CONTENTS

LAB 1

EXAMINING SECURITY THREATS AND VULNERABILITIES

This lab contains the following exercises and activities:

- Exercise 1-1: Identifying Types of Attackers That Might Attack a Network
- Exercise 1-2: Identifying Threats, Vulnerabilities, and Defenses Against Attacks
- Exercise 1-3: Calculating Risk
- Exercise 1-4: Classifying Attacks and Identifying Defensive Measures
- Exercise 1-5: Applying Basic Security Guidelines
- Lab Review Questions
- Lab Challenge 1-1: Comparing Qualitative and Quantitative Risk Analysis

After completing this lab, you will be able to

- Identify types of attackers.
- Identify threats to a network, vulnerabilities of a network, and defensive measures that network security personnel can take to defend against attacks.
- Determine security risks.
- Classify attacks.
- Identify possible defenses to network attacks.
- Apply basic security guidelines.

Estimated completion time: 85 minutes

SCENARIO

Contoso Pharmaceuticals manufactures prescription drugs for a worldwide market. It has 18,000 employees in offices throughout the world. The company hosts its own Web servers for public Internet information and extranet transactions with customers. Despite growing into a large company over the years, Contoso has never had an organized plan for designing its network. As a result, the security structure of the network is inconsistent and, in some places, nonexistent.

The Chief Information Officer (CIO) has directed the security department to explore the ways that the network could be attacked. You have been assigned to a team that will brainstorm about potential threats and vulnerabilities to the network. You will also suggest defense strategies that the company can take to secure the network. You will then present your suggestions and recommendations to a senior management committee (the rest of the class).

EXERCISE 1-1: IDENTIFYING TYPES OF ATTACKERS WHO MIGHT ATTACK A NETWORK

Estimated completion time: 10 minutes

In this exercise, you will work together as a class to discuss the types of attackers who pose a threat to Contoso Pharmaceuticals. In five minutes, list all people who might want to attack Contoso and what their motivation might be.

_____

_____

_____

_____

_____

_____

_____

_____

_____

EXERCISE 1-2: IDENTIFYING THREATS, VULNERABILITIES, AND DEFENSES AGAINST ATTACKS

Estimated completion time: 20 minutes

In this exercise, you will work in small groups. Each group should select one of the attackers listed in Exercise 1-1, "Identifying Types of Attackers Who Might Attack a Network." Then, using the instructions below, complete the table on page 4.

1. In the first column, list all the threats that this type of attacker poses.

2. In the second column, list the vulnerabilities that would allow the attack to occur.

3. In the third column, list the defensive measures that Contoso should take.

   Select from the following list of defensive measures for your entries in the third column of your table.

Defensive Measure	Description
Account security	Create accounts only when needed, grant minimal permissions to get the job done, and remove access when it is no longer required.
Antivirus software	Use applications that automatically remove malicious software such as viruses, worms, and Trojan horses. Keep antivirus software updated to respond to new threats.
Auditing	Monitor the activities of services, users, and administrators to verify compliance with security policies. Archive and review log files.
Digital signature	Use a digital signature. For example, use a digital signature to ensure the integrity of data or verify the identity of a sender.
Encryption	Obscure information so it cannot be understood by an unauthorized person.
Firewall	Install and properly configure a firewall to control and monitor inbound and outbound traffic.
ID (intrusion detection) [also IDS, intrusion detection system]	Use IDS to alert network administrators of activity resembling known attacks.
Password security	Choose passwords that are difficult to guess or break. Change passwords frequently, but not too frequently or users will use unsafe ways to remember passwords. Require unique passwords that follow appropriate standards for complexity and length. Audit for compliance with password security.
Proper configuration	Know what is installed on your system by default. Use the security features built into your applications. Make sure they are configured for the maximum allowable security. Follow the best practices recommended by the manufacturer.

Defensive Measure	Description
Physical security	Restrict physical access to any of the following components: hardware; software; firmware; data media, such as disks, backup tapes, and Zip drives. Control entry to buildings and rooms by locks or access cards. Don't use untrusted systems.
Secure baseline	Create a tested standard for configuring all computers of a specific type. Test and apply different baselines for different resources, such as a secure e-mail server, Web server, file server, or desktop computer. Verify that the system maintains a secure configuration.
Security policies	Create documents that specify all security policies. Use technology to enforce security policies whenever possible.
Software updates	Apply software updates to fix known problems with operating systems or applications. Problems with software can allow attackers to bypass security controls.
User education	Train users to follow safe computing practices.

Attacker:

Threat	Vulnerability	Defense Against the Attack

Threat	Vulnerability	Defense Against the Attack

4. When all groups are finished, present your attack scenarios to the other students in the class as though they were a senior management committee.

QUESTION   *What is the difference between a threat and a vulnerability?*

EXERCISE 1-3: CALCULATING RISK

Estimated completion time: 15 minutes

In this exercise, you will work with the group you formed for the previous exercise to perform a quantitative risk analysis to justify the use of antivirus software for a branch office of Contoso Pharmaceuticals. The branch office needs a direct connection to the Internet so that employees can better perform work-related tasks, such as research on competitors' products. Management is concerned that a direct connection to the Internet will expose the branch office to an increased threat from viruses.

Use the following information to justify the purchase of antivirus software for the branch office:

- Number of computer workstations: 200

- Cost of antivirus licenses for all workstations: $4,000.00

- Estimated amount of time to install antivirus software on each workstation: 0.5 hours

- Average hourly wage of IT support personnel: $20.00 per hour

- Average estimated loss of productivity (in hours) for each user when a workstation is infected with a virus: 2.5 hours

- Estimated monetary loss for each lost hour of productivity: $35.00

- Estimated percentage of workstations affected by a significant virus outbreak before the virus is contained (exposure factor): 65 percent

- Estimated probability that a significant virus outbreak will occur at least once a year in the branch office (annualized rate of occurrence): 75 percent

Complete the following steps to perform a quantitative analysis of the risk. In the following formulas, you must express percentages as a decimal value between 0 and 1; for example, 85% = 0.85.

1. Calculate the single loss expectancy (SLE), using the following formula: asset value x exposure factor = SLE.

   To determine the asset value, consider the amount of monetary loss, such as labor costs, that would occur if the virus had to be cleaned from the workstation. You do not have any data on the value of data that might be lost, so you should not consider it for this exercise.

   To determine the exposure factor, consider how many workstations are likely to be affected before the virus is contained.

2. Calculate the annualized loss expectancy (ALE), using the following formula:

   SLE x annualized rate of occurrence (ARO) = ALE.

   The ALE is simply a way of estimating the loss that could occur on a yearly basis if no defensive measures were put in place.

3. Calculate the cost/benefit of antivirus software, using the following formula:

   ALE – cost of antivirus software implementation = cost/benefit.

   In this step, you are determining whether the cost of implementing a countermeasure is less than or greater than the cost of the asset. If the cost of the countermeasure is less than the loss that would occur in the event of a realized threat, the argument for implementing it is clear. To determine the cost of implementing the countermeasure, you need to take into account the cost of software licenses, labor costs, and other relevant factors. In this case, the only data you have relates to the software license and labor costs.

4. Present your findings to the class, using the results from the previous calculations to justify the purchase of antivirus software.

   QUESTION This exercise demonstrates a quantitative risk analysis. Is this the only kind of analysis you can or should perform to assess risk? If not, what other kind of risk analysis can you perform?

   QUESTION The quantitative analysis in this exercise makes only a limited number of assumptions about the kind of loss that would occur if the branch office were infected by a virus. What other kinds of loss should you include in the quantitative risk analysis of a potential virus infection?

EXERCISE 1-4: CLASSIFYING ATTACKS AND IDENTIFYING DEFENSIVE MEASURES

Estimated completion time: 20 minutes

In this exercise, you will work with your group to complete the empty cells in the following table. To complete the Defensive Measures column, use the information provided in the table for Exercise 1-2, "Identifying Threats, Vulnerabilities, and Defenses Against Attacks." Be prepared to explain how you might implement any of the defensive measures you suggest. The first row of the table has been completed as an example.

Attack Type	Description	Defensive Measures
Buffer overflow	The amount of data is larger than the holding area, or buffer, that the program sets aside for incoming data. When the data is placed into the computer's memory, it might overwrite other data.	Software patch; proper configuration
Web defacing		
Physical		
	A computer program that appears to have a benign or useful function, but that in fact is used for malicious purposes.	
	An attack that prevents a system from performing its intended service.	
Spoofing		
Social engineering		

Attack Type	Description	Defensive Measures
	A computer program that spreads from computer to computer through some installation vector, such as an executable attachment in an e-mail message.	
	A passive attack that monitors network communications, usually as a preparatory step to an active attack.	

QUESTION   Worms are often referred to as a kind of virus. However, worms differ from true viruses in one important aspect. In what way do worms differ from true computer viruses?

EXERCISE 1-5: APPLYING BASIC SECURITY GUIDELINES

Estimated completion time: 20 minutes

Read the scenario below, and then with your group prepare a brief presentation that addresses the weaknesses of the proposal in the scenario according to the four fundamental security guidelines: physical security, trust, privilege level, and documentation. Be prepared to present your findings to the class.

One of the branch offices of Contoso Pharmaceuticals has made a brief proposal for implementing a wireless network to use in meeting rooms and to allow greater mobility for internal laptop users. The IT manager at the branch office is aware that wireless networks are vulnerable to eavesdropping and unauthorized third-party access to the LAN. To mitigate these vulnerabilities, he is proposing that all wireless signals be encrypted using a static Wired Equivalent Privacy (WEP) key that will be distributed to all users on a monthly basis via e-mail. Users will configure their own wireless devices to use the current WEP key. Instructions for configuring WEP keys on the laptops will be included with the e-mail. The proposal states that all wireless network interface cards (NICs) will be configured to use DHCP to make it easier for users to configure their wireless devices,

Your manager has asked you to evaluate the proposal and report to her on its merits. You need to assess the proposal according to the fundamental security guidelines for physical security, trust, privilege level, and documentation.

LAB REVIEW QUESTIONS

1. What is the relationship between a risk, a threat, and a vulnerability?

2. What is the difference between a passive attack and an active attack?

3. What is generally the most effective way to deal with passive attacks: prevent them, or detect and stop them?

4. What do social engineering attacks target: computers, users, applications, or networks?

5. What do spoofing attacks target: computers, users, applications, or networks?

LAB CHALLENGE 1-1: COMPARING QUALITATIVE AND QUANTITATIVE RISK ANALYSIS

Estimated completion time: 20 minutes

You are a security administrator for Contoso Pharmaceuticals. Your manager has asked you to make recommendations on the format and process for a new risk analysis that she wants to recommend that the company perform. Specifically, your manager wants you to assess the pros and cons of quantitative and qualitative risk analysis before she presents her plan to executive management. With your group, list the pros and cons of quantitative and qualitative risk analysis and be prepared to present this list to the class for general discussion.

> **NOTE** A quantitative risk analysis uses objective metrics, such as asset values and actual cost of countermeasures, as you learned in Exercise 1-3, "Calculating Risk." In contrast, a qualitative risk analysis attempts to assess risk and the effectiveness of countermeasures based on informed opinion, sometimes using surveys that ask respondents to rank the seriousness of risk and effectiveness of countermeasures. A qualitative risk analysis can take many forms. For example, it can ask respondents to submit anonymous written comments that are later compiled for analysis.

LAB 2
ESTABLISHING AND MAINTAINING BASELINE SECURITY

This lab contains the following exercises and activities:

- Exercise 2-1: Creating and Applying Security Templates
- Exercise 2-2: Monitoring Baseline Security by Using Security Configuration and Analysis
- Exercise 2-3: Assessing Baseline Security by Using Microsoft Baseline Security Analyzer (MBSA)
- Exercise 2-4: Maintaining Baseline Security by Using Microsoft Software Update Services (SUS)
- Lab Review Questions
- Lab Challenge 2-1: Automating MBSA Scans

After completing this lab, you will be able to

- Create and apply security templates to establish a security baseline.
- Monitor baseline security using Security Configuration And Analysis.
- Monitor baselines by using MBSA.
- Use Windows Automatic Updates and SUS to automate the installation of required patches and hotfixes to maintain a security baseline.

Estimated completion time: 110 minutes

SCENARIO

You are a new network security administrator at Contoso Pharmaceuticals, a worldwide manufacturer of prescription drugs. You must ensure that secure baselines are maintained for all computers. Your first task is to create a security template, based on an existing template, that meets the following requirements:

- Only administrators are allowed to shut down the system.
- The last user name used to log on to the system must not be displayed.
- A warning notice must be displayed when a user attempts to log on.
- The Telnet service must always be disabled and the following permissions must be applied to the service:
  - Administrators: Full Control
  - System: Read, Start, Stop, and Pause
  - Authenticated Users: Read

After the template has been created, you must apply it to the system and then verify that your computer's security settings match the baseline you defined. When you have completed analyzing your security settings, you will examine the effectiveness and utility of MBSA and SUS to help ensure a minimum baseline security for the computer systems under your administrative control.

EXERCISE 2-1: CREATING AND APPLYING SECURITY TEMPLATES

Estimated completion time: 20 minutes

In this exercise, you will create a security template that is based on an existing template. You will then apply this security template.

Adding the Security Configuration And Analysis Template Snap-In to the MMC Console and Creating a Security Template

1. Log on to Contoso as **Admin.x** (where *x* is your assigned student number), with a password of **P@ssw0rd**.

   NOTE In a secure production environment, it is customary to require users to change their password upon first logon. However, to facilitate the delivery of the labs for this course, you are not required to change your password. The password for all accounts that have been created for use in these labs is P@ssw0rd.

   The Manage Your Server Wizard page appears.

2. Click the Don't Display This Page At Logon option, and then close the Manage Your Server Wizard page.

3. Click Start, and then select Run.

4. In the Run dialog box, type **mmc** and then click OK.

5. In the Console1 window, on the File menu, select Add/Remove Snap-In.

6. In the Add/Remove Snap-In dialog box, click Add.

7. In the Add Standalone Snap-In dialog box, under Available Standalone Snap-Ins, select Security Configuration And Analysis, click Add, select Security Templates, and then click Add, as shown below.

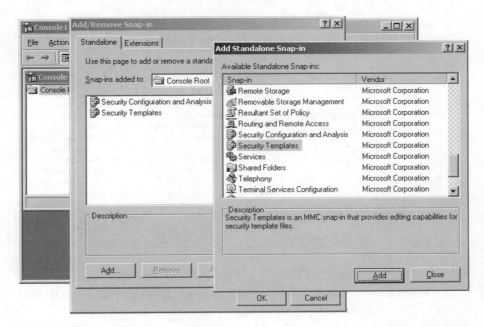

8. In the Add Standalone Snap-In dialog box, click Close, and then click OK to close the Add/Remove Snap-In dialog box.

9. On the File menu, select Save As.

10. In the Save In box, navigate to the desktop.

11. In the File Name box, type **Baseline Tools** and then click Save.

12. In the console tree, expand Security Templates, expand C:\Windows\Security\Templates, and then click Setup Security.

The details pane displays the different categories of Microsoft Windows settings that you can configure by using a security template.

13. In the console tree, right-click Setup Security, and then click Save As.

14. In the Save As dialog box, type **Contoso Security** and then click Save.

15. Leave the Baseline Tools console open for the next set of steps.

Configuring and Applying a Security Template

1. In the console tree of the Baseline Tools console, expand Contoso
   Security, expand Local Policies, and then click User Rights Assignment, as
   shown below.

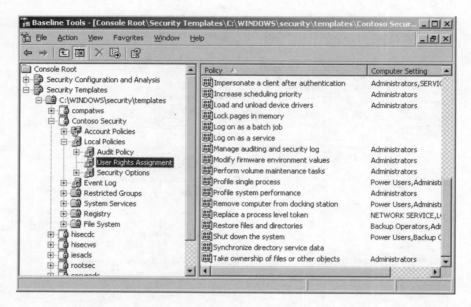

2. In the details pane, double-click Shut Down The System.

3. In the Template Security Policy Setting dialog box, ensure that the Define
   These Policy Settings In The Template check box is selected.

4. Select Backup Operators, and then click Remove.

5. Select Power Users, and then click Remove.

6. Click OK to close the Template Security Policy Setting dialog box.

   In the details pane, notice that only Administrators appears to the right of
   Shut Down The System.

7. In the console tree, click Security Options, and then in the details pane,
   double-click Interactive Logon: Do Not Display Last User Name.

8. In the Interactive Logon: Do Not Display Last User Name dialog box, click
   Enabled, and then click OK.

   In the details pane, notice that Enabled appears to the right of Do Not
   Display Last User Name.

9. In the console tree, click Security Options, and then in the details pane,
   double-click Interactive Logon: Message Text For Users Attempting To
   Log On.

10. In the Interactive Logon: Message Text For Users Attempting To Log On dialog box, ensure that the Define This Policy Setting In The Template check box is selected, type **Unauthorized access is prohibited. If you are not an authorized user, do not attempt to log on** and then click OK.

    QUESTION Why is it a good idea to include a warning for unauthorized users who attempt to log on using stolen or cracked credentials?

11. In the details pane, double-click Interactive Logon: Message Title For Users Attempting To Log On.

12. In the Interactive Logon: Message Title For Users Attempting To Log On dialog box, ensure that the Define This Policy Setting In The Template check box is selected, type **LEGAL NOTICE: Authorized Users Only** and then click OK.

    In the details pane, notice that the message settings that you defined appear.

13. In the console tree, click System Services, and then in the details pane, double-click Telnet.

14. In the Template Security Policy Setting dialog box, ensure that the Define This Policy Setting In The Template check box is selected and that the startup mode is set to Disabled, and then click Edit Security.

15. Click Remove to remove permissions for the Everyone group.

16. Click Add.

17. In the Select Users, Computers, Or Groups dialog box, select Locations, select *computerxx* (where *xx* is the two-digit number assigned to your computer), and then click OK.

18. In the Enter The Object Names To Select box, type **Authenticated Users;System;Administrators** and then click OK.

19. In the Security For Telnet dialog box, click Administrators, and then in the Allow column select the Full Control check box.

20. Click Authenticated Users; then in the Allow column, select the Read check box; and then deselect the Start, Stop And Pause check box.

21. Click System; then in the Allow column, ensure that the Start, Stop And Pause check box is selected; and then select the Read check box. Click OK, and then click OK to close the Telnet Properties dialog box.

    In the details pane, notice that Disabled appears in the Startup column and that Configured appears in the Permissions column next to Telnet.

22. In the console tree, right-click Contoso Security, and then click Save.

23. In the console tree, click Security Configuration And Analysis.

24. Right-click Security Configuration And Analysis, and then click Open Database.

25. In the Open Database dialog box, in the File Name box, type *computerxx* and then click Open.

26. In the Import Template dialog box, click Contoso Security.inf, and then click Open.

In the details pane, Security Configuration And Analysis displays a message indicating that you can now configure or analyze your computer.

27. In the console tree, right-click Security Configuration And Analysis, and then click Configure Computer Now, as shown below.

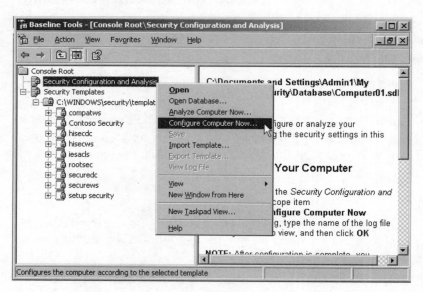

28. In the Configure System dialog box, click OK to accept the default log path and start the configuration.

Security Configuration And Analysis displays the Configuring Computer Security message box, which shows the progress of the configuration process and indicates which areas are being configured.

29. When Security Configuration And Analysis has finished applying the template, close Baseline Tools.

30. When prompted to save the console settings, click Yes.

31. Log off.

Testing the Security Template Configuration

1. With the Welcome To Windows screen open, press CTRL+ALT+DELETE.

   QUESTION   Does the legal notice appear with the title and message that you configured?

2. Click OK.

   QUESTION   Does the user name of the last logged-on user appear in the Log On To Windows dialog box?

3. Log on to Contoso as **studentx** (where *x* is your assigned student number) with a password of **P@ssw0rd**.

4. Click Start, select Control Panel, double-click Administrative Tools, and then double-click Services.

5. In the details pane, click Telnet.

   QUESTION   What is the Telnet service startup type?

   QUESTION   Why can the studentx account view the properties of the Telnet service?

6. Double-click Telnet.

7. In the Telnet Properties (Local Computer) dialog box, in the Startup Type list, select Manual, and then click OK.

   QUESTION   Were you able to change the startup type? Why or why not?

8. In the Services message box, click OK. In the Telnet Properties (Local Computer) dialog box, click Cancel, and then close Services.

9. Attempt to shut down the computer.

   QUESTION   Were you able to shut down the computer? Why or why not?

10. Log off.

EXERCISE 2-2: MONITORING BASELINE SECURITY BY USING SECURITY CONFIGURATION ANALYSIS

Estimated completion time: 10 minutes

Your manager has asked you to identify servers in your organization that do not meet the minimum requirements determined by the Contoso Security baseline template. In this exercise, you will reconfigure your computer with the default Setup Security template. You will then analyze your computer's security settings to determine whether they differ from the Contoso Security baseline that you created.

1. Log on to Contoso as **admin.x** (where *x* is your assigned student number).

2. On the desktop, double-click Baseline Tools.

3. In the console tree, click Security Configuration And Analysis.

4. Right-click Security Configuration And Analysis, and then click Import Template.

5. In the Import Template dialog box, click the Clear This Database Before Importing option, select Setup Security.inf, as shown below, and then click Open.

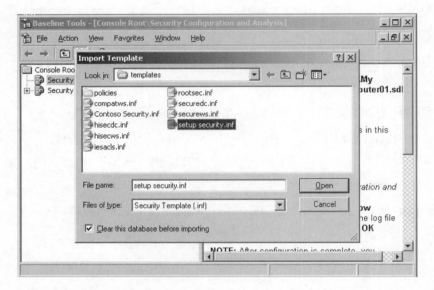

When you select the Clear This Database Before Importing option, you remove any entries in the Security Configuration And Analysis database. When you leave this option at its default setting (cleared), you append imported template settings to the ones that currently reside in the database. In the case of a conflict among settings, the settings in the last template you apply take precedence over earlier settings.

6. In the console tree, right-click Security Configuration And Analysis, and then click Configure Computer Now.

7. In the Configure System dialog box, click OK to accept the default log path and start the configuration.

   The default Setup Security template is applied to your computer, removing the Contoso Security template you applied earlier. The Security Configuration And Analysis utility displays a Configuring Computer Security message box, which shows the progress of the configuration process and indicates which areas are being configured.

   NOTE   In the next steps, you will import the Contoso Security baseline template into the Security Configuration And Analysis database. However, you will not configure your computer with these settings. You will then use the Security Configuration And Analysis tool to compare the settings in the Contoso Security template with the current template configured on your computer. The current template is the Setup Security template, which was configured earlier in the exercise.

8. Right-click Security Configuration And Analysis, and then click Import Template.

9. In the Import Template dialog box, click Contoso Security.inf, and then click Open.

10. In the console tree, right-click Security Configuration And Analysis, and then click Analyze Computer Now.

11. In the Perform Analysis dialog box, click OK to accept the default log path and start the configuration.

   Security Configuration And Analysis displays an Analyzing System Security message box, which shows the progress of the analysis process and indicates which areas are being analyzed.

12. Expand Security Configuration And Analysis, expand Local Policies, and then click Security Options.

13. In the details pane, review the settings for the following options: Interactive Logon: Do Not Display Last User Name; Interactive Logon: Message Text For Users Attempting To Log On; and Interactive Logon: Message Title For Users Attempting To Log On.

   Security Configuration And Analysis displays a red X icon to indicate that the current computer settings for these three options do not match the Security Configuration And Analysis database settings. Remember that you imported the Contoso Security template settings into the database, and that you are now comparing the settings in the database with the current computer configuration. The current computer configuration is now based on the default Setup Security template that was configured in steps 5 and 6. Notice that all other settings that are defined in the database match the computer settings, as indicated by a green check mark. Settings that are not defined in the database are displayed with a blue icon (no highlighting).

14. Close Baseline Tools.

15. When prompted to save the console settings, click No.

EXERCISE 2-3: ASSESSING BASELINE SECURITY BY USING MICROSOFT BASELINE SECURITY ANALYZER (MBSA)

Estimated completion time: 15 minutes

Your manager has asked you to evaluate Microsoft Baseline Security Analyzer (MBSA) as a potential tool for assessing the baseline security of your organization's computer systems. In this exercise, you will familiarize yourself with the basic operation and features of MBSA by using it to check your computer for missing hotfixes and common security vulnerabilities.

1. While still logged on as Admin*x*, click Start and then select Run.

2. In the Run dialog box, type **C:\Lab Manual\Lab 02\MBSASetup-en.msi** and then press ENTER.

3. In the Welcome To The Microsoft Baseline Security Analyzer Setup Version 1.2 page, click Next.

4. On the License Agreement page, read the agreement, click I Accept The License Agreement, and then click Next.

5. On the Destination Folder page, click Next.

6. On the Start Installation page, click Install.

7. On the MBSA Setup dialog box, click OK.

8. On the desktop, double-click the shortcut for MBSA 1.2.

9. Maximize the Baseline Security Analyzer window.

10. Click Scan A Computer.

11. Review the available scanning options, select Learn More About Scanning Options, select the In The Future Do Not Show This Message check box, click OK in the Internet Explorer dialog box, and then read the description of the scanning options.

    QUESTION   What does selecting the Use SUS Server option do?

12. Close Internet Explorer, and then in the Pick a Computer to Scan page of MBSA, clear the Check For SQL Vulnerabilities check box.

   In order to check for security updates, MBSA needs to be able to download a current copy of the Mssecure.xml file from the Internet and place it in the Microsoft Baseline Security Analyzer installation folder. This file contains security update information. If your workstation does not have a connection to the Internet, perform steps 13 through 15. If your workstation does have a connection to the Internet, skip to step 16.

13. Open Windows Explorer, and then browse to C:\Lab Manual\Lab 02.

14. Right-click the Mssecure.xml file, and then click Copy.

15. In Windows Explorer, browse to C:\Program Files\Microsoft Baseline Security Analyzer, and then press CTRL+V to copy Mssecure.xml into the folder.

16. Click Start Scan.

17. When the scan is complete, review the details for each of the potential problems that MBSA identified.

   NOTE If you do not have a connection to the Internet, you will see an exclamation mark and a message indicating an error occurred while trying to scan for Microsoft Office updates. You receive this message because MBSA v1.2 must make an additional connection to the Microsoft Web site and download a number of files that are required to check for Microsoft Office product updates. For more information on this topic, please see the MBSA FAQ at http://www.microsoft.com/technet/security/tools/mbsaqa.mspx and look for the response to the question "How can I download the files necessary to run a scan if my proxy server requires authentication?"

18. In the Score column of the report, move the mouse pointer over a red X so that the mouseover event pop-up description appears.

   QUESTION What does a red X indicate?

19. Move the mouse over the various icons in the Score column.

   QUESTION List the meanings of the icons you see in the Score column.

20. Locate the item that displays Windows Security Updates in the Issue column, and then click Results Details.

   QUESTION What information is displayed in the Results Details page?

21. Close MBSA.

22. Close all open windows.

You might want to have a class discussion on how MBSA might be implemented to assess baseline security and to improve the overall computer security of an organization.

EXERCISE 2-4: MAINTAINING BASELINE SECURITY BY USING MICROSOFT SOFTWARE UPDATE SERVICES (SUS)

Estimated completion time: 35 minutes

As a result of your research into the capabilities of MBSA, you have discovered that many computers in your organization do not have up-to-date patches and service packs installed. You want to evaluate the use of Software Update Services (SUS) as a means to ensure that computers are kept up-to-date with current patches and hotfixes. In this exercise, you will install and configure SUS. You will then configure your computer to automatically download updates from an SUS server that has been installed on the Instructor server.

Installing and Configuring SUS

1. Log on to Contoso as **admin.x** (where *x* is your assigned student number).

2. Click Start, and then select Run.

3. In the Run dialog box, type **C:\Lab Manual\Lab 02\SUS10SP1.exe** and then press ENTER.

4. In the Welcome To The Microsoft Software Update Services Setup Wizard page, click Next.

5. On the End-User License Agreement page, read the agreement, select I Accept The Terms In The License Agreement, and then click Next.

6. On the Choose Setup Type page, click Custom.

7. On the Choose File Locations page, verify that C:\SUS and C:\SUS\Content are listed as the folders to store the Software Update Services Web site files and software updates, and then click Next.

8. On the Language Settings page, select the English Only option, and click Next.

9. On the Handling New Versions Of Previously Approved Updates page, ensure that I Will Manually Approve New Versions Of Approved Updates is selected, and then click Next.

10. Review the information on the Ready To Install page, and then click Install.

    The wizard installs SUS. When the installation has finished, the Completing The Microsoft Software Update Services Setup Wizard page appears.

11. On the Completing The Microsoft Software Update Services Setup Wizard page, click Finish.

   The Software Update Services window appears.

12. If the Internet Explorer dialog box appears, informing you that Microsoft Internet Explorer's Enhanced Security Configuration is enabled, select the In The Future Do Not Show This Message check box, and then click OK.

13. In the Software Update Services window, click Set Options.

14. On the Set Options page, click Do Not Use A Proxy Server To Access The Internet, as shown below.

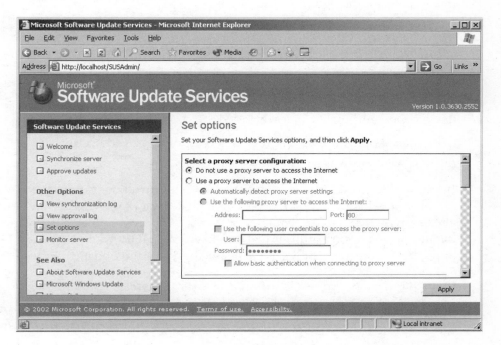

   You should note that you can only specify a proxy server configuration if the SUS server is configured to download updates from the Microsoft Web site. This restriction is intended to prevent SUS servers from pulling updates from rogue update servers on the Internet.

15. Scroll down, and then click Synchronize From A Local Software Update Services Server.

16. In the Synchronize From A Local Software Update Services Server box, type **Instructor01**

17. Select the Synchronize List Of Approved Items Updated From This Location (Replace Mode) check box.

    Normally, when you are setting up SUS for the first time, you download the updates from the Microsoft Web site, test the updates in an isolated lab environment, and then manually approve them. However, because the classroom might not have a connection to the Internet, and to save time in the lab, you configure your SUS server to automatically approve updates that have already been approved on the Instructor01 SUS server.

18. Review all other options without changing them, and then click Apply.

19. In the VBScript dialog box, click OK.

20. Click Synchronize Server.

21. On the Synchronize Server page, click Synchronize Now.

22. When synchronization has finished, click OK in the VBScript dialog box.

23. When synchronization has finished, click View Synchronization Log.

24. Review the items that SUS downloaded.

25. Click View Approval Log, and review the list of approved updates.

26. Click Approve Updates.

    Because you chose to synchronize the list of approved items from the server from which you downloaded the updates, all of the updates are already approved. Notice that the check box to approve updates is dimmed. The reason for this is that you have configured your SUS server to rely on an upstream SUS server (Instructor01) for the update approval.

    QUESTION   In this exercise, you are not downloading updates from Microsoft but from another SUS computer on the network. What are some advantages of this configuration?

27. Click Monitor Server.

28. Review the statistics about available updates, and then close SUS.

Configuring a Local Computer Policy to Enable Automatic Downloading of Updates from an SUS Server

1. Click Start, and then select Run.

2. In the Run dialog box, type **gpedit.msc** and then click OK.

3. In the console tree, expand Local Computer Policy, expand Computer Configuration, expand Administrative Templates, and then expand Windows Components.

4. Select Windows Update, as shown below.

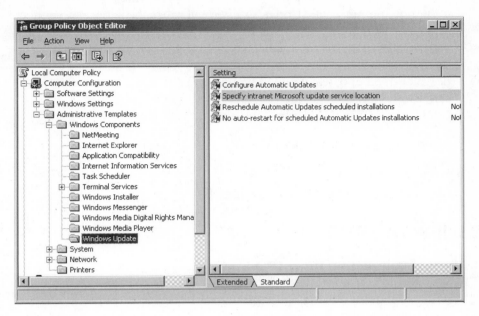

5. In the details pane, double-click Specify Intranet Microsoft Update Service Location.

6. Select the Explain tab.

7. Review the policy explanation, and then select the Policy tab.

8. Click Enabled.

9. In the Set The Intranet Update Service For Detecting Updates box, type **http://computerxx** (where *xx* is the two-digit number assigned to your computer).

10. In the Set The Intranet Statistics Server box, type **http://computerxx** and then click OK.

    The SUS Intranet Statistics are collected in the IIS logs of the specified Intranet Statistics Server.

11. In the details pane, double-click Configure Automatic Updates.

12. In the Configure Automatic Updates Properties dialog box, click Enabled.

13. In the Configure Automatic Updating list, select 2 – Notify For Download And Notify For Install, and then click OK.

14. Close the Group Policy Object Editor.

15. Click Start, select Administrative Tools, and then click Services.

16. In the details pane, right-click Automatic Updates, and then click Restart.

Restarting the Automatic Updates server will cause the service to connect to the SUS server in 5 to 10 minutes to retrieve a list of updates. If you wait for the client to contact the server, you will see an icon in the task bar that notifies you that new updates are available for download. If you download the updates, you will be prompted to install the updates. You can also review the activities of Automatic Updates in C:\Windows\Windows Update.log and in the IIS logs.

NOTE   You should not apply updates to your computer. Doing so might affect the steps in subsequent lab exercises.

17. Close all open windows and then log off.

LAB REVIEW QUESTIONS

Estimated completion time: 10 minutes

1. Why would you want to use the Security Configuration And Analysis tool when you are deploying either group policy or a local policy to change security settings?

2. Your organization's security policy states that after software updates have been tested and approved, they must be installed on user workstations with a minimum amount of end user interaction. How would you configure a Windows Update policy to meet this requirement?

3. You have installed SUS on your network. What do you need to do to make updates available to client computers on the network?

4. You have set up a dedicated workstation to perform MBSA scans of computers on your network. Your organization's security policy states that this computer cannot have a direct connection to the Internet. What do you need to do in order to scan computers for needed security updates?

5. What happens if you import more than one security template into the Security Configuration And Analysis tool?

6. What permissions do you need to run an MBSA scan against a local or remote computer?

LAB CHALLENGE 2-1: AUTOMATING MBSA SCANS

Estimated completion time: 20 minutes

You are the security administrator for Contoso Pharmaceuticals. Your manager has recently heard about MBSA. She would like you to install it on a dedicated workstation to scan computers to verify that approved service packs and other security-related updates have been installed. The dedicated workstation has access to the Internet through a proxy server. Your manager wants the MBSA scan to run during off hours at least once a week, and she wants to view the information in a well-formatted and meaningful report.

You currently have an SUS server on your network that is used to distribute approved updates to your intranet. Using the MBSA components installed on your workstation, create a configuration that allows your workstation to run checks for security patches on all computers in the contoso.com domain in such a way that the scan can be triggered by a schedule and the results of the scan can be imported into a database or spreadsheet.

LAB 3
MONITORING AND MAINTAINING ACCOUNT AND ACCESS CONTROL SECURITY

This lab contains the following exercises and activities:

■ Exercise 3-1: Using MBSA to Detect Account Vulnerabilities

■ Exercise 3-2: Examining and Changing Account Security

■ Exercise 3-3: Confirming Account Security Configuration Changes

■ Exercise 3-4: Using Alternate Credentials to Perform Administrative Tasks

■ Exercise 3-5: Installing the Windows 2003 Administration Tools Pack

■ Exercise 3-6: Examining and Configuring Active Directory Access Control Lists

■ Lab Review Questions

■ Lab Challenge 3-1: Examining Authentication Methods

After completing this lab, you will be able to

■ Use the Microsoft Baseline Security Analyzer (MBSA) tool to discover security configurations on a computer.

■ Use Resultant Set of Policy (RSoP) to view group policy settings that apply to the local computer.

■ Configure the local security policy.

■ Use the Event Viewer to view and analyze logon events.

■ Use the Run As command to perform administrative tasks with alternate credentials.

■ Configure the NTFS file system (NTFS) and share permissions.

■ Install the Active Directory Administration Tools Pack to perform tasks related to the administration of the Active Directory directory service from a member server or workstation.

■ Use the Active Directory Delegate Control Wizard to delegate administrative tasks.

Estimated completion time: 125 minutes

SCENARIO

Your organization deployed a number of workstations and servers using cloned images. After images were deployed, the workstations and servers were joined to the Microsoft Windows 2003 domain. You are concerned that the configuration of the cloned images was not as secure as it should have been. To ensure that your computers are as secure as possible, you need to check for possible security holes on member servers and workstations and then correct problems, if any are found. Once you have corrected the problems, you must verify that you have eliminated them.

EXERCISE 3-1: USING MBSA TO DETECT ACCOUNT VULNERABILITIES

Estimated completion time: 10 minutes

In this exercise, you will use MBSA to check your computer for extra administrator accounts and blank or weak passwords.

> **NOTE**   To complete this exercise, you must have previously installed MBSA in Lab 2, Exercise 2-3, "Assessing Baseline Security by Using Microsoft Baseline Security Analyzer (MBSA)."

1. Log on to Contoso as **Admin.x** (where *x* is your assigned student number).

2. On the desktop, double-click the Microsoft Baseline Security Analyzer icon.

3. In the left pane, select Pick A Computer To Scan.

4. Verify that the name of your computer appears in the Computer Name box.

5. Clear the following options:

   ❑ Check For IIS Vulnerabilities

   ❑ Check For SQL Vulnerabilities

   ❑ Check For Security Updates

6. Click Start Scan and wait while MBSA completes the scan.

7. When the report appears, in the Sort Order box, click Issue Name, and then click Result Details to view the first and subsequent vulnerabilities in the list.

> **QUESTION**   How many accounts on the local computer have administrator rights?

> **QUESTION**   Which accounts have administrative privileges on the local computer?

> **QUESTION**   Did the check of the local Guest Account pass or fail?

> **QUESTION**   Did the Local Account Password test pass?

QUESTION Consult the MBSA help file and list the weak passwords that MBSA can detect.

QUESTION Which accounts failed the test?

8. In the Microsoft Baseline Security Analyzer window, from the Actions menu, select Copy.

9. Click Start, select Run, type **notepad** in the Open box, click OK, and then press CTRL+V to paste the report results into the blank document.

10. Save the file as C:\Lab Manual\Lab 03\Labwork\Computer*xx* MBSA Initial Scan.txt (where *xx* is a unique two-digit number assigned to your computer), and then close Notepad.

11. Close MBSA

EXERCISE 3-2: EXAMINING AND CHANGING ACCOUNT SECURITY

Estimated completion time: 25 minutes

In this exercise, you will view the password requirements for the Windows 2003 domain, configure the local security policy to audit for account management events, remove local accounts, reset a password, and then view the security log. The accounts that should exist in the Administrators group are the local administrator, Contoso\Adminx, and Contoso\Domain Admins.

Using Resultant Set Of Policy to View Policies Applied to the Local Computer

In this section, you will ensure and verify that an appropriate password policy is applied to the computer. Group Policy changes are updated frequently, and security policies for the GPO are completely refreshed every 16 hours, regardless of whether changes have occurred to the GPO. Because not enough time might have elapsed between this lab and Lab 2, "Establishing and Maintaining Baseline Security," in which you applied security templates to change the password policy for the local computer, you will first use Gpupdate to ensure that the default domain group policy is applied to your computer. Then you will use Resultant Set of Policy (RSoP) to determine the policy settings that apply to your computer.

1. Click Start, select Run, type **cmd** in the Open box, and then click OK.

2. At the command prompt, type **gpupdate /force** and then press ENTER.

   The /force switch causes all the policy settings to be applied, rather than only the ones that have changed.

3. Click Start, select Run, type **mmc** in the Open box, and then click OK.

4. In the Console1 window, on the File menu, select Add/Remove Snap-In.

5. In the Add/Remove Snap-In dialog box, click Add.

6. In the Add Standalone Snap-In dialog box, under Available Standalone Snap-Ins, select Resultant Set Of Policy, and then click Add.

7. In the Add Standalone Snap-In dialog box, click Close, and then click OK to close the Add/Remove Snap-In dialog box.

8. In the console tree, right-click Resultant Set Of Policy, and then select Generate RSoP Data, as shown below.

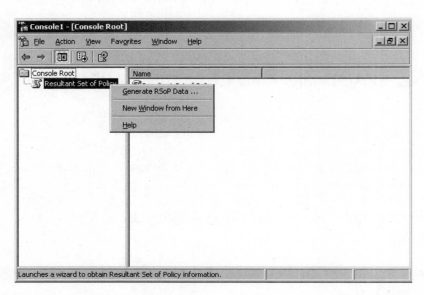

9. In the Welcome To The Resultant Set Of Policy Wizard page, click Next.

10. In the Mode Selection page, verify that the Logging Mode option is selected, and then click Next.

11. In the Computer Selection page, verify that the This Computer option is selected, and then click Next.

12. In the User Selection page, select the Do Not Display User Policy Settings In The Results (Display Computer Policy Settings Only) option, and then click Next.

13. On the Summary Of Selections page, click Next.

While RSoP is gathering information, you will see a progress bar. When RSoP has finished, the Completing The Resultant Set Of Policy Wizard page will appear.

14. On the Completing The Resultant Set Of Policy Wizard page, click Finish.

15. In the console tree, browse to Computer Configuration\Windows Settings\Security Settings\Account Policies, and then select Password Policy, as shown below.

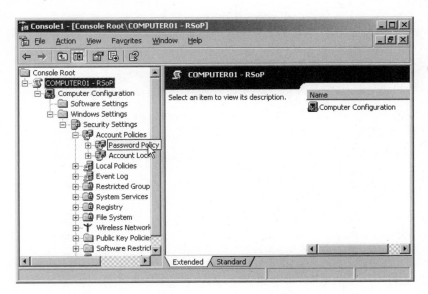

16. In the details pane, double-click Enforce Password History, and then select the Precedence tab.

QUESTION   Where does the Enforce Password History policy setting come from?

17. Double-click the remaining password settings and review their configuration.

QUESTION   List the remaining password setting configurations and where they originated.

18. In the console tree, browse to Computer Configuration\Windows Settings\Security Settings\Local Policies, select Audit Policies, and then review the settings in the details pane.

QUESTION   What is the common setting for all the Audit policies?

19. Close the MMC console, and then click No when prompted to save the settings.

Viewing and Modifying the Local Security Policy

In this section, you will view and modify the local security policies, using the Local Security Policy MMC console.

1. From the Administrative Tools menu, select Local Security Policy.

2. In the console tree, expand Account Policies, and then select Password Policy.

3. Double-click Passwords Must Meet Complexity Requirements.

4. In the Passwords Must Meet Complexity Requirements Properties dialog box, verify that the setting is selected, and then click OK.

   Note that this setting and other password settings are dimmed; you cannot change them using this MMC console.

5. Double-click Minimum Password Length.

6. In the Minimum Password Length Properties dialog box, in the Minimum Password Must Be At Least box, verify that the value is set to 7 characters, and then click OK.

   QUESTION   Why can't you change account policy values through the Local Security Settings MMC console? What tools can you use to change Account Policy values?

7. In the console tree, expand Local Policies, and then select Audit Policy, as shown below.

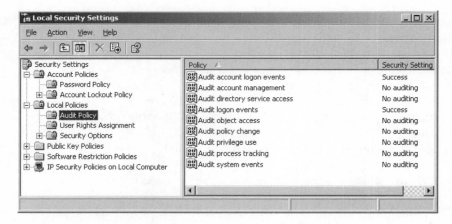

8. In the details pane, double-click Audit Account Management.

9. On the Audit Account Management Properties page, select the Success check box, and then click OK.

10. In the details pane, double-click Audit Privilege Use.

11. In the Audit Privilege Use Properties page, select the Success check box, and then click OK.

> **QUESTION**   *Why can you change these settings, but not the password policy settings, using the Local Security Settings MMC console?*

12. Close Local Security Settings.

Managing Local Accounts and Viewing Security Logs

1. From the Administrative Tools menu, select Computer Management.

2. In the console tree, expand Local Users And Groups, and then click Groups.

3. In the details pane, double-click Administrators.

The Administrators Properties dialog box opens, showing all of the accounts that are members of the Administrators group.

> **QUESTION**   *What extra accounts are in the Administrators group?*

4. Select Sally and Bob, and then click Remove.

5. Click OK to close the Administrators Properties dialog box.

6. In the console tree, click Users.

7. Right-click Bob, and then click Delete.

The Local Users And Groups dialog box appears, confirming the delete command and warning you that if you delete this account, you will not be able to re-create the same account and have the same access.

8. In the Local Users And Groups dialog box, click Yes.

9. Right-click Sally, and then click Delete.

10. In the Local Users And Groups dialog box, click Yes.

11. In the details pane, right-click Guest, and then select Set Password.

12. In the Set Password For Guest dialog box, click Proceed.

13. In the New Password box and the Confirm Password box, type **Password**.

14. Note the error message indicating that the password does not meet the password complexity requirements, and then click OK.

15. In the New Password and the Confirm Password boxes, type **P@ssw0rd.**

16. Click OK to reset the password and close the Set Password For Guest dialog box.

> **QUESTION** Why is **P@ssw0rd** acceptable as a password but **password** is not?

17. Click OK to close the Local Users And Groups dialog box, indicating the password has been successfully set.

> **QUESTION** If the Guest account is disabled, why should you assign a complex password to it?

18. In the details pane, right-click Administrator, and then select Set Password.

19. In the Set Password For Administrator dialog box, click Proceed.

20. In the New Password and Confirm Password boxes, type **P@ssw0rd** and then click OK.

21. Click OK to close the Local Users And Groups dialog box.

22. In the console tree, expand Event Viewer, and then select Security, as shown below:

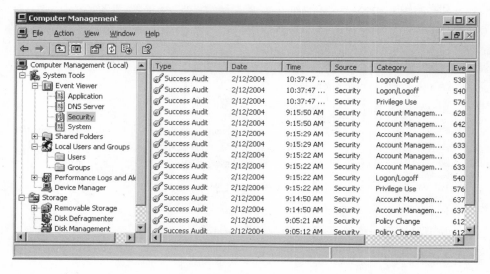

23. In the details pane of the Security Log, double-click the entries that belong to the Account Management category, and then review them.

> **QUESTION** What Account Management events are recorded?

> **QUESTION** Why is it a good idea to configure security auditing for account management events?

24. Close Computer Management.

EXERCISE 3-3: CONFIRMING ACCOUNT SECURITY CONFIGURATION CHANGES

Estimated completion time: 10 minutes

In this exercise, you will run MBSA to verify that your settings are correct.

1. On the desktop, double-click the Microsoft Baseline Security Analyzer icon.

2. In the left pane, select Pick A Computer To Scan.

3. Verify that the name of your computer appears in the Computer Name box.

4. Clear the following boxes:

   ❑ Check For IIS Vulnerabilities

   ❑ Check For SQL Vulnerabilities

   ❑ Check For Security Updates

5. Click Start Scan and wait while MBSA completes the scan.

6. When the report appears, in the Sort Order box, click Issue Name, and then view the first vulnerability in the list.

   QUESTION   How many individual accounts on the local computer have Administrator rights? Which accounts are they?

   QUESTION   Did the check of the local Guest Account pass or fail? Why?

   QUESTION   Did the Local Account Password test pass? Why?

7. In the Microsoft Baseline Security Analyzer window, from the Actions menu, select Copy.

8. Click Start, select Run, type **notepad** in the Open box, and then press OK.

9. In Notepad, press CTRL+V to paste the scan results into a blank document.

10. Save the file as C:\Lab Manual\Lab 03\Labwork\Computerxx MBSA Final Scan.txt (where *xx* is a unique two-digit number assigned to your computer), and then close Notepad.

11. Close all open windows and log off.

EXERCISE 3-4: USING ALTERNATE CREDENTIALS TO PERFORM ADMINISTRATIVE TASKS

Estimated completion time: 20 minutes

In this exercise, you will log on to your workstation with a nonadministrative account and use the Run As command to perform tasks that require administrative permissions.

1. Log on to Contoso as Student*x* (where *x* is your student number) with a password of P@ssw0rd.

2. Right-click the Start menu, and then select Properties.

3. On the Taskbar And Start Menu Properties page, make sure that the Start menu option is selected, and then click Customize.

4. On the Customize Start Menu page, select the Advanced tab.

5. On the Customize Start Menu page, in the Start Menu Items selection box, scroll down to System Administrative Tools and select the Display On The All Programs Menu And The Start Menu option.

6. Click OK on the Customize Start Menu page, and then click OK on the Taskbar And Start Menu Properties page.

7. Click Start, and then select Administrative Tools.

8. From the Administrative Tools menu, select Computer Management.

9. In System Tools, expand Event Viewer, and then click the security event log.

    You will see a warning message indicating that access to the security event log is denied.

10. Click OK to close the warning message.

11. In System Tools, expand Shared Folders, and then select Shares.

    You will see a warning message indicating that you do not have permission to see the list of shares.

    QUESTION   What security groups have permissions to manage shares?

12. Click OK to close the warning message, and then close the Computer Management console.

13. In Administrative Tools, right-click Computer Management, and then select Run As.

14. In the Run As dialog box, select The Following User option; in the User Name box type **Contoso\Admin***x* (where *x* is your assigned number); type the password; and then click OK.

15. Expand Event Viewer, and then select the Security log.

   Security audit events appear in the details pane.

   QUESTION   *Why are you able to view the Security log?*

16. Double-click a number of recent entries in the Security log.

   QUESTION   *Does the Security log show events related to the use of alternate credentials? What authentication methods are reported as being used by security principals when they log on?*

17. Expand Shared Folders.

18. Right-click Shares, and then select New Share.

19. On the Welcome To The Share A Folder Wizard page, click Next.

20. In the Folder Path box, type **C:\Security\Docs** and then click Next.

21. In the Share A Folder Wizard dialog box, click Yes when prompted to create the folder.

22. On the Name, Description, And Settings page, accept the defaults, and then click Next.

23. On the Permissions page, select the Use Custom Share And Folder Permissions option, and then click Customize.

24. In the Share Permissions tab, select the Everyone group, and then click Remove.

25. Click Add.

26. On the Select Users, Computers, Or Groups page, select Locations, select **Computerxx** (where x*x* is the unique two-digit number assigned to your computer), and then click OK.

27. In the Enter Object Names To Select box, type **users** and then click OK.

28. Select the Security tab, and then click Add.

29. In the Enter Object Names To Select box, type **student*x*** (where *x* is your student number), and then click OK.

   If the Multiple Names Found dialog box appears, select your Student*x* account from the Matching Names selection box, and then click OK.

30. With the Studentx object selected in the Group Or User names dialog box, select Modify in the Allow column in the Permissions For Studentx selection box, and then click OK.

31. On the Share A Folder Wizard page, click Finish, and then on the Sharing Was Successful page, click Close.

32. In the Computer Management console, in the console tree, click Shares.

33. In the details pane, double-click Docs.

34. On the Docs Properties page, select the Share Permissions tab.

> **QUESTION** What permissions does the Studentx account have to the newly created \Docs folder when access occurs through the shared folder (\\Computerx\Docs)?

35. On the Docs Properties page, click OK.

36. Close all open windows and log off.

EXERCISE 3-5: INSTALLING WINDOWS 2003 ADMINISTRATION TOOLS PACK

Estimated completion time: 10 minutes

In this exercise, you will install the Windows 2003 Administration Tools Pack on your workstation in order to administer parts of Active Directory.

1. Log on to Contoso as Adminx (where x is your assigned student number).

2. Insert the *Windows 2003 Enterprise Edition Evaluation Edition* CD into the CD-ROM drive.

If the Welcome to the Microsoft Windows 2003 Server screen appears, click Exit.

3. Click Start, select Run, type **<cd-rom drive letter>:\I386\Adminpak.msi** and then click OK.

4. On the Welcome To The Windows Server 2003 Administration Tools Pack Setup Wizard page, click Next.

5. On the Completing The Windows Server 2003 Administration Tools Pack Setup Wizard page, click Finish.

6. Click Start, and then select Administrative Tools.

> **QUESTION** Name at least three utilities that were added to the Administrative Tools menu.

7. Close all open windows and log off.

EXERCISE 3-6: EXAMINING ACTIVE DIRECTORY ACCESS CONTROL LISTS

Estimated completion time: 30 minutes

In this exercise, you will create a desktop shortcut, based on the command-line version of the Run As command. This shortcut will be used to launch an MMC console that will allow you to view and administer Active Directory objects in an Organizational Unit (OU). After viewing permissions on Active Directory objects, you will create a user account in the OU and then use the Delegation Of Control wizard to grant permissions to a user account to reset passwords on user accounts. Finally, you will log on to the Contoso network with the user account that has permissions to reset user account passwords and verify that you can change passwords in the OU.

Creating a Shortcut to Launch Active Directory Management Console Using Alternative Credentials

1. Log on to Contoso as Student*x* (where *x* is your student number).

2. Click Start, select Run, type **notepad** in the Open box, and then click OK.

3. In Notepad, type **runas /user:contoso\admin***x* **"mmc %windir%\ system32\admgmt.msc"** (where *x* is your student number). You must include the quotation marks.

4. Click File, and then click Save As.

5. In the Save In drop-down box, navigate to Desktop, and in the File Name box, type **"AD Management.cmd"** and then click Save.

   IMPORTANT   Make sure you include the quotation marks around the filename, "AD Management.cmd". Otherwise, the file will be saved with a .txt, rather than .cmd, extension.

6. Close Notepad.

Viewing Active Directory Permissions

1. On the Desktop, double-click the AD Management shortcut you created in the previous procedure.

2. At the command prompt, type your password, and then press ENTER.

   After a few seconds, the Active Directory Management console appears.

3. In the Active Directory Management console, select Active Directory Users And Computers, click the View menu, and then select Advanced Features.

4. Expand Active Directory Users And Computers, expand contoso.com, and then expand the ALS OU.

5. Right-click the Employees*xx* OU (where *xx* is the two-digit version of your student number), and then select Properties, as shown below.

6. On the Employees*xx* Properties page, select the Security tab.

NOTE   If you do not see the Security tab, make sure that you completed step 3.

7. In the Group Or User Names box, select the Admin*x* user object (where *x* is your student number) and note its permissions in the Permissions For Admin*x* box.

8. In the Group Or User Names box, select the Student*x* user object (where *x* is your student number), scroll down the list of permissions for Student*x*, note that it has been granted special permissions, and then click Advanced to view the permissions as shown below.

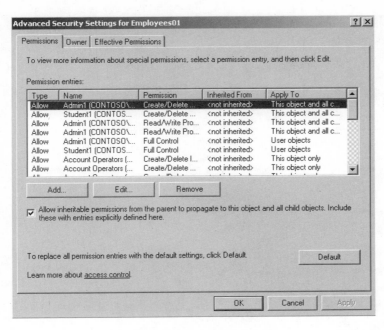

9. In the Advanced Security Settings For Employees*xx* window, click the Name column to sort the entries by name.

   QUESTION How many entries exist for the Admin*x* and Student*x* accounts?

   You might note that the Student*x* account has been delegated Full Control permissions on User Objects. In the next steps, you will examine the effect of those permissions.

10. On the Advanced Security Settings For Employees*xx* window, select the Effective Permissions tab.

11. In the Effective Permissions tab, click Select.

12. In the Enter Object Names To Select box, type **admin*x*** (where *x* is your student number), and then click OK.

    If the Multiple Names Found dialog box appears, select your Admin*x* account from the Matching Names selection box, and then click OK.

13. Review the effective permissions for the Admin*x* account by scrolling down the list of permissions, as shown below.

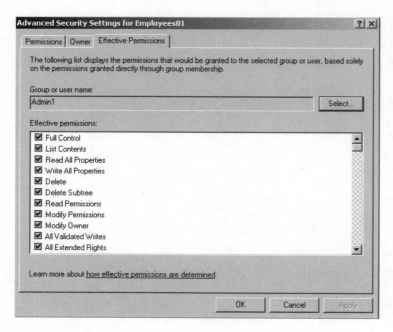

14. In the Effective Permissions tab, click Select.

15. In the Enter Object Names To Select box, type **student***x* (where *x* is your student number), and then click OK.

    If the Multiple Names Found dialog box appears, select your Student*x* account from the Matching Names selection box, and then click OK.

16. Review the effective permissions for the Student*x* account by scrolling down the list of permissions.

    QUESTION   What objects is the Student*x* account allowed to create and delete?

17. In the Effective Permissions tab, on the Advanced Security Settings For Employees*xx* dialog box, click OK.

18. On the Employees*xx* Properties page, click OK.

19. Leave Active Directory Users And Computers open for the following procedures.

Creating a New Active Directory User Object

1. Right-click the Employeesxx OU, select New, and then click User.

2. In the New Object – User page, type **TUser*x*** (where *x* is your student number) in both the Last Name and the User Logon Name boxes, and then click Next.

3. In the Password and Confirm Password boxes, type **P@ssw0rd**, click Next, and then click Finish.

Delegating Authority to Manage User Passwords

1. Right-click the Employeesx OU and then select Delegate Control.

2. On the Welcome To The Delegation Of Control Wizard page, click Next.

3. On the Users Or Groups page, click Add.

4. On the Select Users, Computers, Or Groups page, type **User*x*** in the Enter The Object Names To Select box (where *x* is your student number), and then click OK.

    If the Multiple Names Found dialog box appears, select your User*x* account from the Matching Names selection box, and then click OK.

5. On the Users Or Groups page, click Next.

6. On the Tasks To Delegate page, make sure that Delegate The Following Common Tasks is selected, select the Reset User Passwords And Force Password Change At Next Logon option, and then click Next.

7. On the Delegation Of Control Wizard completion page, click Finish.

8. Close the Active Directory Management Console.

9. Close all open windows, and then log off.

10. Log on to Contoso as **User*x*** (where *x* is your student number), with a password of **P@ssw0rd**.

11. Click Start, and then select Run.

12. In the Run dialog box, type **admgmt.msc** and then press ENTER.

13. In the Active Directory Management console, under Active Directory Users And Computers, expand contoso.com, expand the ALS OU, and then select the Employeesxx OU (where *xx* is the two-digit version of your student number).

14. Right-click the Tuserx user object in the details pane, and then select Disable Account.

    NOTE   An error message should appear, indicating that you do not have sufficient permissions to perform the operation. The Userx account only has permissions to reset passwords and force a password change at next logon.

15. Right-click the Tuserx user object in the details pane, and then select Reset Password.

16. In the Reset Password dialog box, type a new password in the Password and Confirm Password boxes, click OK, and then click OK to close the information dialog box informing you that the password was changed.

17. Close all open windows and log off.

LAB REVIEW QUESTIONS

1. When are password complexity requirements enforced?

2. What are the default password complexity requirements of a Windows 2003 domain?

3. When you use MBSA to scan computers for vulnerabilities, when should you disable scans for weak passwords?

4. What important security principle is implicit in the use of the Run As command?

5. A user belongs to two security groups that have been granted different NTFS permissions to a folder. For example, one security group has the Write permission to a folder and another group has Read and Execute permissions. How are NTFS permissions determined for the user? What happens if one of the groups is explicitly granted the Deny permission to the file or folder?

6. A user has been granted NTFS modify permissions to a folder and Read and Execute permissions to a file within the folder. What are the user's effective permissions to the file?

7. NTFS permissions are an example of what kind of access control?

    a. Discretionary access control (DAC)

    b. Mandatory access control (MAC)

    c. Role-based access control (RBAC)

8. The help desk receives a call from a user who claims that he has lost his password and wants it reset. The help desk technician asks the user a number of questions to verify the user's identity and then resets the password. Subsequently, it is discovered that the help desk technician and company were both victims of fraud perpetrated by an individual who stole an employee's personal information and used it to gain access to the network. How does delegating authority to reset user account passwords to an individual who knows most or all of the users help to mitigate the risk from this kind of attack?

LAB CHALLENGE 3-1: EXAMINING AUTHENTICATION METHODS

Estimated completion time: 20 minutes

You are a security administrator for Contoso Pharmaceuticals. The contoso domain has recently completed a migration from Microsoft Windows NT 4.0 to Windows 2003. The next upgrade project is to replace all legacy Microsoft Windows 95 and Microsoft Windows 98 clients with Microsoft Windows 2000 Professional or Microsoft Windows XP clients. Because the legacy clients will exist for a short time only, the IT group decided not to install the Active Directory Client Extensions Pack on them.

Your manager wants to develop a security plan that will be implemented as soon as the legacy clients have been replaced. In particular, he is concerned that the current authentication mechanisms are unnecessarily weak for an environment that contains only Windows 2000 or higher clients and Windows 2003 domain controllers. For example, he has heard that LAN Manager authentication results in the storage of LAN Manager hashes that can more easily be compromised by a brute-force attack than NTLM hashes can.

Your manager wants you to provide a brief list of recommendations for increasing the security of authentication methods used on the network. He would also like you to review the Network Security Settings under Computer Configuration\Windows Settings\Security in the Local Security Policy of member servers. He wants to know which of these Network Security Settings should be configured, along with the values they should be configured with. Also, he wants you to identify, if possible, one of the standard predefined security templates that ship with Windows 2003 to use as the basis for implementing and enforcing stronger authentication methods.

> **TIP**   In order to complete this Lab Challenge, you might have to refer to the Windows 2003 help files.

LAB 4
USING CRYPTOGRAPHY TO SECURE INFORMATION

This lab contains the following exercises and activities:

- Exercise 4-1: Using EFS for Encryption
- Exercise 4-2: Providing Remote Access for EFS Encrypted Files
- Exercise 4-3: Configuring an EFS Recovery Agent
- Exercise 4-4: Using Encryption for Web Communications
- Lab Review Questions
- Lab Challenge 4-1: Backing Up and Restoring EFS Keys Used to Encrypt and Decrypt Data

After completing this lab, you will be able to

- Use Encrypting File System (EFS) for encryption on a local computer.
- Configure remote encryption.
- Configure digital certificate enrollment for data recovery certificates.
- Configure a recovery agent for an organizational unit (OU).
- Use encryption for Web communications.

Estimated completion time: 120 minutes

SCENARIO

You are a network administrator at Contoso Pharmaceuticals. You are also the IT department representative on Contoso's Computer Security Steering Committee. Recently, the committee has been discussing the need for additional security on data that is classified as confidential or higher. A number of committee members, including you, have recommended using EFS as one method for securing this data. The committee members would like you to review and demonstrate the use of EFS for them.

During the discussions concerning encryption, several committee members said that they need a better understanding of how Web traffic is encrypted when Contoso's partners and customers connect to Contoso's extranet Web site. The committee has also asked you to demonstrate the process of encrypting Web traffic, along with your demonstration of EFS.

> **NOTE**   Several exercises in this lab require that you install software from the *Microsoft Windows 2003 Server Enterprise Edition* CD that accompanies the student lab materials. Before beginning the exercises in this lab, make sure that you have this CD handy. Alternatively, your instructor can copy the Windows 2003 Server source files to a computer so you can use them. In this case, the instructor will give you specific instructions for connecting to the share to install software.

EXERCISE 4-1: USING EFS FOR ENCRYPTION

Estimated completion time: 25 minutes
In this exercise, you will use EFS to encrypt a file. You will then review the EFS information in the file.

Using EFS to Encrypt Files

In this section you will encrypt a file, using Windows Explorer, and verify that you can view its contents.

1. Log on to Contoso as Student$x$ (where x is your assigned student number), with a password of P@ssw0rd.

2. Open Windows Explorer, and then select the C drive.

3. From the File menu, select New, select Folder, type **Encrypted Folder** and then press ENTER.

4. Double-click Encrypted Folder, select the File menu, select New, and then select Text Document.

5. Type **Encrypted File** as the name of the file, and then press ENTER.

6. Double-click Encrypted File to open Notepad, enter some text, select the File menu, select Exit, and then click Yes to save the changes.

7. Right-click Encrypted File, and then select Properties.

8. On the Encrypted File Properties page, click Advanced.

   The Advanced Attributes page appears, as shown below.

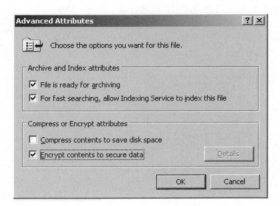

9. On the Advanced Attributes page, select the Encrypt Contents To Secure Data check box, and then click OK. Click OK to close the Encrypted File Properties Dialog box.

   An Encryption Warning dialog box appears, indicating that you have chosen to encrypt a file in a folder that is not encrypted, as shown below.

10. In the Encryption Warning dialog box, read the warning, select the Encrypt The File Only option button, and then click OK.

    NOTE *Normally, you would want to encrypt the folder as well as the file. For this exercise, however, you will encrypt just the file. In the next exercise, you will use the Cipher command to encrypt the folder.*

    Notice that the color of the filename changes to green to provide a visual indication that the file is encrypted.

11. Double-click Encrypted File.

Notice that you can view the contents of the file.

12. Close the file.

Verifying Access Restrictions to an Encrypted File

In this section, you will verify that, by default, only the account that created the file and the designated recovery agent can access an encrypted file.

1. In C:\Encrypted Folder, right-click Encrypted File, and then select Properties.

2. On the Encrypted Files Property page, click Advanced.

3. On the Advanced Attributes page, click Details.

4. On the Encryption Details For C:\Encrypted Folder\Encrypted File page, review the information.

QUESTION   By default, who can transparently access the contents of the encrypted file?

QUESTION   Who or what is listed as the recovery agent for the encrypted file?

You should note that in Windows 2003 and Microsoft Windows XP, you can use this interface to allow other users access to the file. However, as a prerequisite for gaining access to an encrypted file, other users must have first used EFS to encrypt a file and have received a digital certificate that is used for file encryption.

5. On the Inception Details For C:\Encrypted Folder\Encrypted File.txt page, click OK.

6. Click OK on the Advanced Attributes page, and then click OK on the Encrypted File Properties page.

In the next steps, you will verify that another user cannot view the contents of the encrypted file. Because it is not possible to launch Windows Explorer using the Run As command, you will launch Microsoft Internet Explorer using the Run As command, and then open the file from Internet Explorer. You can also launch the command prompt by using alternate credentials and access the file that way.

7. On the taskbar, right-click the icon for Internet Explorer, and then select Run As.

8. In the Run As dialog box, select the The Following User option, enter the logon credentials for Contoso\Admin*x* (where *x* is your assigned student number), and then click OK.

9. In the Internet Explorer Address box, type **C:\Encrypted Folder** and then press ENTER.

10. Double-click Encrypted File.

   Notepad opens, along with a Notepad dialog box informing you that access to the file is denied.

11. Click OK to clear the message, close Notepad, and then close Internet Explorer.

12. Click Start, click Run, type **cmd** in the Open box, and then click OK.

13. Type **cd\Lab Manual\lab 04** and then press ENTER.

14. Type **efsinfo /U /R /C "c:\encrypted folder\encrypted file.txt"** and then press ENTER.

   Efsinfo.exe displays information about the users who can decrypt the file encryption key. This includes the user who encrypted the file and the recovery agent. Efsinfo also displays the thumbprint information for the certificate that contains the public key used in the encryption process. In the next section, "Using the Certificates MMC Snap-In to View Certificate Details," you will compare the output of Efsinfo.exe with the information contained in the properties of the digital certificate that is used to encrypt files.

15. In the space below, record the following information from the output of the Efsinfo.exe command:

   Users who can decrypt file:

   Thumbprint algorithm of user who can decrypt file:

   Recovery agent:

16. Leave the command prompt open so that you can easily compare information displayed in the command with information you will view in the next section.

Using the Certificates MMC Snap-In to View Certificate Details

In this section, you will use the Certificates MMC snap-in to view more extensive details of the digital certificate used for EFS encryption.

1. Click Start, and then select Run.

2. In the Open box, type **mmc** and then click OK.

3. In the Console1 window, on the File menu, select Add/Remove Snap-In.

4. In the Add/Remove Snap-In dialog box, click Add.

5. In the Add Standalone Snap-In dialog box, under Available Standalone Snap-Ins, select Certificates, and then click Add.

6. Click Close to close the Add Standalone Snap-In dialog box, and then click OK to close the Add/Remove Snap-In dialog box.

7. In the console tree, expand Certificates – Current User, expand Personal, and then select Certificates.

8. In the details pane, double-click Student*x* (where *x* is your student number).

9. In the Certificate dialog box, select the Details tab, and then select Public Key in the Field column, as shown below.

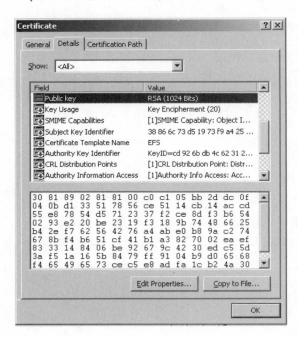

NOTE   The public key used by Windows 2003 to encrypt the file is an RSA key that is 1024 bits long.

10. Under Field, select Thumbprint.

    Compare the thumbprint in the certificate to the thumbprint that is
    displayed in the command prompt window.

    NOTE   A thumbprint is a hash of a certificate. The thumbprints match. This
    signifies that the public key and other information in the certificate match the
    public key and user information that were used to encrypt the file encryption key.
    (Each file is encrypted with a unique file encryption key that is itself encrypted
    with the public key of the user.)

11. Under Field, select Thumbprint Algorithm.

    NOTE   The algorithm that was used to create the thumbprint is Secure Hash
    Algorithm (SHA-1).

12. Select the General tab.

    NOTE   The information at the bottom of the certificate information box
    indicates that you have a private key that corresponds to this certificate.

13. Click OK.

14. On the File menu, select Save As.

15. In the Save As dialog box, navigate to the Desktop, type **Certificate
    Management** in the File Name box, and then click Save.

16. Close the Certificate Management MMC console.

17. Close all open windows.

Using Cipher to Manage Encrypted Files and Folders

In this section, you will use the Cipher.exe program to manage encrypted files
and folders.

1. Open Windows Explorer, and then click C:\Encrypted Folder.

2. On the File menu, select New, select Text Document, type **Unencrypted
   File** and press ENTER.

3. Click Start, select Run, type **cmd** in the Open box, and then click OK.

4. At the command prompt, type **cd\encrypted folder** and then press ENTER.

5. Type **cipher** and then press ENTER.

    QUESTION   Are there any unencrypted files in the folder?

    QUESTION   What attributes in the output of the Cipher command indicate
    whether a file is encrypted?

QUESTION   *If there are any unencrypted files in the folder, why are they unencrypted?*

6. Type **cipher /a /e "c:\encrypted folder*.*"** and then press ENTER.

QUESTION   *Which files in the folder are encrypted?*

QUESTION   *Will new files that are added to the folder be encrypted?*

7. At the command prompt, type **cd** and then press ENTER to change to the root directory.

8. Type **cipher /e "c:\encrypted folder"** and then press ENTER.

If you get an error message indicating the file is being used by a different process, make sure that you do not have the folder open in Windows Explorer.

9. Type **cd c:\encrypted folder** and then press ENTER.

10. Type **cipher**, press ENTER, and review the output of the command.

QUESTION   *What will happen to new files if they are added to the C:\Encrypted Folder directory?*

11. At the command prompt, type **dir > "encryption test.txt"** and then press ENTER.

The output of the Dir command is placed in a newly created file called Encryption Test.txt.

12. At the command prompt, type **cipher**, press ENTER, and review the output.

QUESTION   *Why is Encryption Test.txt encrypted?*

EXERCISE 4-2: PROVIDING REMOTE ACCESS FOR EFS ENCRYPTED FILES

Estimated completion time: 25 minutes

In this exercise, you will configure your computer so that you can create and manage encrypted files on a remote computer. You will first verify that your computer is configured to support remote encryption. Then you will create a folder with appropriate NTFS file system (NTFS) permissions for remote encryption, share the folder with appropriate share permissions, and finally test remote encryption.

You must work with a partner in this exercise. Before beginning this exercise, choose a partner to work with. Make sure your partner has completed Exercise 4-1,

"Using EFS for Encryption," before beginning this exercise. Perform all steps in this exercise on both computers.

> **NOTE** You must have already installed the Windows 2003 Administration Tools Pack. If you have not already done so, please refer to Lab 3, Exercise 3-5, "Installing the Windows 2003 Administration Tools Pack," for specific instructions.

1. Make sure you are logged on to Contoso as Student*x* (where *x* is your assigned student number).

2. Click Start, select Run, type **admgmt.msc** in the Open box, and then click OK.

3. In the Active Directory Management console, expand Active Directory Users And Computers, expand Contoso.com, expand the ALS OU, and then select the Classroom Servers OU.

4. In the details pane of the Classroom Servers OU, right-click the Computer*xx* object (where *xx* is the two-digit version of your student number), and then select Properties, as shown below.

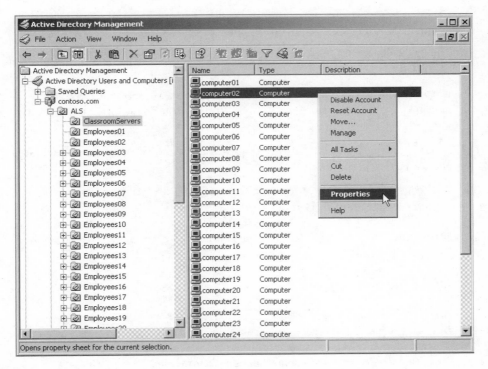

5. On the Computer*xx* Properties page, select the Delegation tab.

6. In the Delegation tab, verify that the Trust This Computer For Delegation To Any Service (Kerberos Only) option is selected.

Note that the delegation options are grayed out and that you cannot change them. By default, only a domain administrator can change these settings on member servers.

NOTE   When member servers are installed, the default setting is Do Not Trust This Computer For Delegation. For remote encryption, the computers must be configured to support delegation. This configuration has been enabled for you as part of the classroom setup.

7. On the Computer*xx* Properties page, click Cancel, and then close the Active Directory Management console.

8. Open Windows Explorer, select the C drive, and from the File menu, select New, select Folder, type **RemoteEFS** and then press ENTER.

9. In Windows Explorer, right-click RemoteEFS, and then click Properties.

10. In the General tab on the RemoteEFS Properties page, select Advanced.

11. In the Advanced Attributes dialog box, select the Encrypt Contents To Secure Data check box, and then click OK.

12. On the RemoteEFS Properties page, select the Security tab, and then click Add.

13. In the Select Users, Computers, Or Groups box, type **Student*y*** (where *y* is your lab partner's student number) in the Enter The Object Names To Select box, and then click OK.

If the Multiple Names Found dialog box appears, select your partner's account, and then click OK.

14. In the Permissions For Student*y* box, in the Allow column, select the Write check box, and then click OK.

QUESTION   Why can the Student*x* account configure NTFS permissions on the RemoteEFS folder?

15. Close Windows Explorer.

NOTE   To complete the steps below, you must have configured the properties of the Start menu to display the Administrative Tools. If you haven't done so, you can open the Computer Management console through Control Panel\Administrative Tools. Or you can enter the **runas /user:contoso\adminx "mmc %windir%\ system32\compmgmt.msc"** command in the Run dialog box, which will cause the command prompt to open and prompt you for a password.

16. Click Start, select Administrative Tools, right-click Computer Management, and then select Run As.

17. In the Run As dialog box, select the The Following User option, then enter the logon credentials for Contoso\Admin*x* (where *x* is your assigned student number), and then click OK.

18. In the Computer Management console, expand System Tools, expand Shared Folders, right-click Shares, and then select New Share.

19. On the Welcome page of the Share A Folder wizard, click Next.

20. In the Folder Path box, type **c:\remoteEFS** and then click Next.

21. On the Name, Descriptions, And Settings page, click Next.

22. On the Permissions page, select the Administrators Have Full Access; Other Users Have Read And Write Access option, and then click Finish.

23. On the Sharing Was Successful page, click Close, and then close Computer Management.

QUESTION   Why did you have to open the Computer Management console with alternate credentials to share the RemoteEFS folder?

NOTE   Wait until your lab partner has completed the above steps before proceeding.

24. Click Start, select Run, type **\\computer*yy*\remoteEFS** (where *yy* is your partner's two-digit student number), and then click OK.

25. Select New from the File menu, and then select Text Document.

26. Type **RemoteEFSTest** and then press ENTER.

27. Double-click the RemoteEFSTest file to open Notepad, enter some text, and then save and close the file.

QUESTION   How do you know that the file has been encrypted? Why was the file encrypted?

EXERCISE 4-3: CONFIGURING AN EFS RECOVERY AGENT

Estimated completion time: 30 minutes

In this exercise, you will configure an EFS recovery agent for an OU to recover EFS encrypted files if a user's EFS encryption keys are lost or corrupted. You will do the following:

- Verify the kinds of certificates that can be issued automatically to user accounts

- Verify that permissions have been correctly configured to allow the issuance of certificates for EFS recovery agents to a security group

- Request an EFS recovery agent certificate for a designated account

- Configure an OU with an EFS recovery agent

Verifying Certificate Template Permissions and Requesting an EFS Recovery Agent Certificate

1. Make sure you are logged on to Contoso as Student*x* (where *x* is your assigned student number).

2. On the Windows desktop, double-click the Certificate Management MMC console you created in Exercise 4-1, "Using EFS for Encryption."

3. In the console tree, expand Certificates – Current User, expand Personal, right-click Certificates, select All Tasks, and then select Request New Certificate, as shown below.

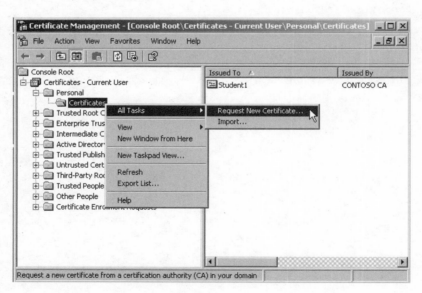

4. On the Welcome page of the Certificate Request wizard, click Next.

5. In the Certificate Types box, note the certificate types that the user account can request. Record the two certificate types that the user account can request in the space below.

Certificate Types:

_____

_____

> **NOTE**   For this exercise, you will use the Certificate Request Wizard to view the certificates that a user can request. You will not actually request a new certificate.

6. On the Certificate Types page, click Cancel.

7. In the Certificate Management console, select Add/Remove Snap-In from the File menu.

8. In the Add/Remove Snap-In dialog box, click Add.

9. In the Add Standalone Snap-In dialog box, under Available Standalone Snap-Ins, select Certificate Templates, and then click Add.

10. Click Close to close the Add Standalone Snap-In dialog box, and then click OK to close the Add/Remove Snap-In dialog box.

11. In the console tree, click Certificate Templates, as shown below.

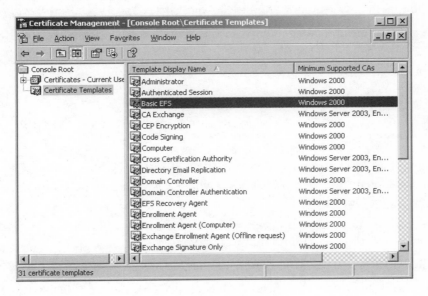

12. In the details pane for the Certificate Templates node, right-click Basic EFS, select Properties, and then select the Security tab.

QUESTION   What is the meaning of the Enroll permission?

13. In the Group Or User Names box, select each of the security groups in turn. Note the permissions that are displayed in the Permissions box.

QUESTION   What effective permissions does the Studentx account have for basic EFS certificates by virtue of belonging to both the Domain Users and the Authenticated Users groups?

14. In the Basic EFS Properties dialog box, click Cancel.

15. In the details pane for the Certificates Templates node, right-click EFS Recovery Agent, select Properties, and then select the Security tab.

16. In the Group Or User Names box, select each security group in turn. Note the permissions that are displayed in the Permissions box.

NOTE   The ClassAdmins group that is listed in the Group Or User Names box was manually created as part of the classroom setup. The group contains all the Adminx accounts used for this lab.

QUESTION   What security groups can request EFS recovery agent certificates?

17. On the EFS Recovery Agent Properties page, click Cancel.

18. Close the Certificate Management console, and then click Yes when prompted to save the console settings.

19. On the desktop, right-click the Certificate Management console, and then click Run As.

NOTE   You must launch the Certificate Management MMC console in the context of the Adminx account for the next series of steps.

20. In the Run As dialog box, select the The Following User option, enter the logon credentials for Contoso\Adminx (where *x* is your assigned student number), and then click OK.

21. In the console tree, expand Certificates – Current User, right-click Personal, select All Tasks, and then select Request New Certificate.

22. On the Welcome page of the Certificate Request wizard, click Next.

23. In the Certificates Type box, click EFS Recovery Agent, and then click Next.

24. On the Certificate Friendly Name And Description page, type **Admin***x* **EFS Recovery Certificate** (where *x* is your student number) in the Friendly Name box, leave the description blank, and then click Next.

25. On the Completing The Certificate Request Wizard page, review the information, click Finish, and then, in the Certificate Request Wizard dialog box, click OK to dismiss the success message.

26. In the console tree, expand Certificates – Current User, expand Personal, and then click Certificates.

27. In the details pane of the Certificates node, double-click the certificate that you requested, review the information in the General and Details tabs, and then click OK.

Leave the Certificate Management console open for the next procedures.

Exporting an EFS Recovery Agent Certificate

In the preceding steps, you were issued an EFS recovery agent certificate that is stored in your personal certificates store. This certificate can subsequently be used to configure your account as a data recovery agent for a domain or an OU. (A data recovery agent is an account that can decrypt a user's encrypted data.) However, before your account can be configured as a data recovery agent using this certificate, you must export the certificate.

In the following steps, you will export an EFS recovery agent certificate to a file that you will later use to configure your account as a data recovery agent for an OU in the Active Directory directory service.

1. In the details pane of the Certificates node, right-click the EFS recovery agent certificate that you requested in the previous procedure, select All Tasks, and then click Export, as shown below.

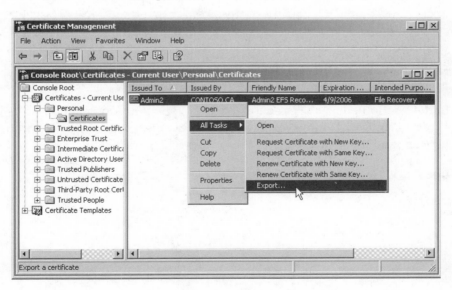

2. On the Welcome page of the Certificate Export wizard, click Next.

3. On the Export Private Key page, ensure that the No, Do Not Export The Private Key check box is selected, and then click Next.

4. On the Export File Format page, ensure that the DER Encoded Binary X.509 (.CER) check box is selected, and then click Next.

5. On the File To Export page, select Browse, and on the Save As page, select the Save In drop-down list, select Desktop, type **DataRecoveryCertificate** in the File Name box, and then click Save.

6. On the File To Export page, click Next.

7. On the Completing The Certificate Export Wizard page, review the information, click Finish, and then click OK.

Configuring an EFS Recovery Agent for an OU

In the following steps, you will configure an EFS recovery agent for an OU by configuring group policy for the OU.

> **NOTE**   It is possible to complete the following steps because the Adminx accounts have been given permission to create and manage group policies on their respective OUs as part of the classroom setup. By default, only Domain Admins and Enterprise Admins can create and manage group policies.

1. Click Start, select Run, type **runas /user:contoso\admin***x* **"mmc admgmt.msc"** (where *x* is your student number) in the Open box, and then click OK.

2. At the command prompt, type the password for Admin*x,* and then press ENTER.

3. In the Active Directory Management console, expand Active Directory Users And Computers, expand contoso.com, expand the ALS OU, right-click the Employees*xx* OU (where *xx* is the unique two-digit version of your student number), and then select Properties.

4. In Employees*xx* Properties, select the Group Policy tab, click New, type **RecoveryAgentPolicy** and press ENTER, and then click Edit.

5. In the Group Policy Object Editor, expand Computer Configuration, expand Windows Settings, expand Security Settings, expand Public Key Policies, and then click to select Encrypting File System.

> **QUESTION**   Are any EFS Group Policies defined for the Employeesx OU?

6. In the console tree, right-click Encrypting File System, and then select Add Data Recovery Agent from the menu, as shown below.

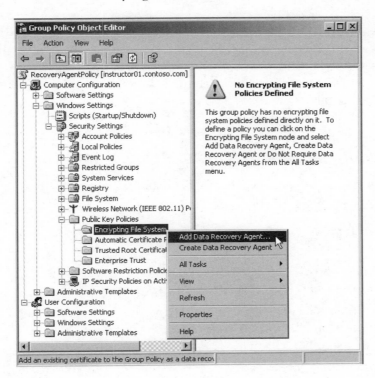

7. On the Welcome page of the Add Recovery Agent Wizard, click Next.

8. On the Select Recovery Agents page, click Browse Folders.

9. In the Open dialog box, click the Look In drop-down list, select Desktop, select the DataRecoveryCertificate.cer file that you created in the previous steps, and then click Open.

10. On the Select Recovery Agents page, click Next.

11. On the Completing The Add Recovery Agent Wizard page, click Finish.

    Because the EFS Recovery Agent policy applies to computers and not users, and because no computer objects are present in the Employees*xx* OU, you cannot use the Admin*x* account to recover data encrypted on your computer.

12. Close the Group Policy Object Editor, and then close the Employees*xx* Properties page.

13. Close the Certificate Management console, and then click No when prompted to save the console settings.

14. Close all other open windows and log off.

EXERCISE 4-4: USING ENCRYPTION FOR WEB COMMUNICATIONS

Estimated completion time: 20 minutes

In this exercise, you will compare Web traffic that uses HTTP with Web traffic that uses HTTP Secure (HTTPS). For this exercise, you must first install Microsoft Network Monitor so that you can view the Web traffic between your lab computer and the instructor's computer.

Installing Network Monitor to Analyze Protocol Traffic

1. Log on to Contoso as Admin*x* (where *x* is your student number).

2. Click Start, select Control Panel, and then click Add Or Remove Programs.

3. On the Add Or Remove Programs page, click Add/Remove Windows Components.

4. In the Components box of the Windows Components page, select Management And Monitoring Tools, and then click Details.

5. In the Subcomponents Of Management And Monitoring Tools box on the Management And Monitoring Tools page, select the Network Monitor Tools check box, and then click OK.

6. On the Windows Components page, click Next, and if prompted, insert the *Windows 2003 Server Enterprise Edition* CD.

    If the Welcome To The Windows Server 2003 splash screen appears, click Exit to close it.

7. On the Completing The Windows Components Wizard page, click Finish.

8. Close Add Or Remove Programs, and then log off.

Comparing HTTP and HTTPS Web Traffic

1. Log on to Contoso as Student*x* (where *x* is your student number).

2. Open Internet Explorer. If you receive a message indicating that enhanced security is enabled for the Web browser, select the In The Future, Do Not Show This Message check box, and then click OK.

3. Click Start, click the Administrative Tools menu, right-click Network Monitor, and then select Run As.

4. In the Run As dialog box, select The Following User, type the following information, and then click OK:

   ❑ User name: **Contoso\Admin.x** (where *x* is your assigned student number)

   ❑ Password: **P@ssw0rd**

5. In the Microsoft Network Monitor dialog box, click OK.

6. In the Select A Network dialog box, expand Local Computer.

7. Under Local Computer, select Local Area Connection, as shown below, and then click OK.

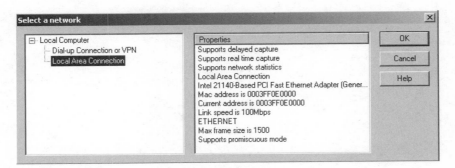

8. From the Capture menu, select Start, as shown below.

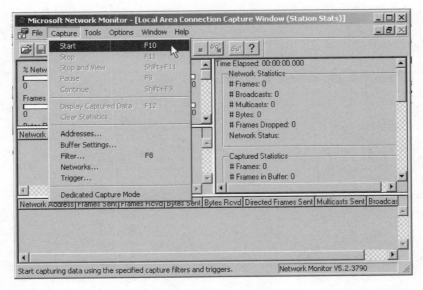

9. Switch to Internet Explorer, type **http://instructor01/default.htm** in the Address box, and then press ENTER.

10. Switch to Network Monitor, and then from the Capture menu, select Stop And View.

11. From the Display menu, select Filter.

12. In the Display Filter dialog box, select Protocol==Any, and then click Edit Expression, as shown below.

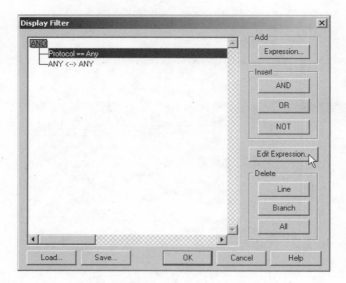

13. In the Expression dialog box, click Disable All.

14. In the Disabled Protocols box, select HTTP, select Enable, and then click OK, as shown below.

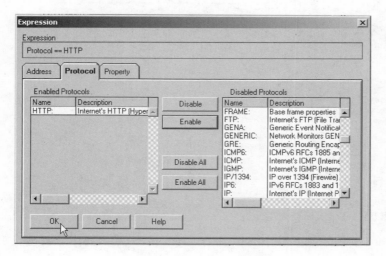

15. In the Display Filter dialog box, click Save.

16. In the Save Display Filter dialog box, type **HTTP** and then click Save.

17. In the Display Filter dialog box, click OK.

18. Double-click the first HTTP frame.

19. In the bottom pane, review the HTTP request, as shown below.

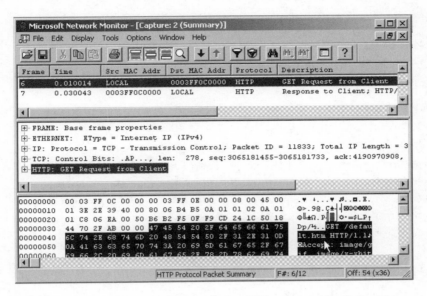

NOTE   Notice that your browser issued a GET command for Default.htm.

20. In the top pane, click the second HTTP frame.

NOTE   Notice that you can read the data in the Default.htm file that the Web server on Instructor01 sent to your browser.

21. From the File menu, select Close.

22. From the Capture menu, select Start.

23. In the Microsoft Network Monitor dialog box, click No.

24. Switch to Internet Explorer, type **https://instructor01/default.htm** in the Address box, and then press ENTER.

25. In the Security Alert dialog box, click OK.

If you receive another security alert indicating that certificate revocation information is not available, click Yes.

NOTE   The security alerts that you see are the result of Web browser security configuration. By default, Windows 2003 enables Internet Explorer Enhanced Security Configuration to provide a higher degree of protection than the Web browser configuration for earlier Microsoft Windows operating systems had.

QUESTION   Once you have connected to a Secure Sockets Layer– (SSL) secured Web site, what visual cue in the Web browser indicates that the traffic between the Web browser client and the Web server is encrypted?

26. Switch to Network Monitor, and then from the Capture menu, select Stop And View.

If you received a warning message that the certificate revocation information was not available, you will see some HTTP traffic related to the request for the certificate revocation list in the capture display. However, you will not see any HTTP traffic related to the request for the default.htm page on Instructor01. If you saw this warning message regarding the certificate revocation list, you should perform the following steps to filter the display so that only HTTPS traffic is visible.

    a. From the Display menu, click Filter.

    b. In the Display Filter dialog box, click Load.

    c. In the Load Display Filter dialog box, select the Look In drop-down list, navigate to C:\Lab Manual\Lab 04, click the Https.df file, and click Open.

    d. In the Display Filter dialog box, click OK.

27. Expand the Description column to view all the information, and then double-click the first TCP frame that displays dst:443 in the TCP row, as shown below.

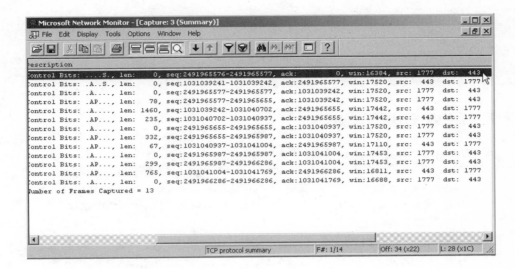

NOTE By default, HTTPS uses Transmission Control Protocol (TCP) port 443 on the Web server. All frames that have a destination or source port of 443 on the Web server are part of an SSL connection between a browser and a Web server.

28. In the top pane, continue clicking subsequent TCP frames; in the bottom pane, review the data in the frames, as shown below.

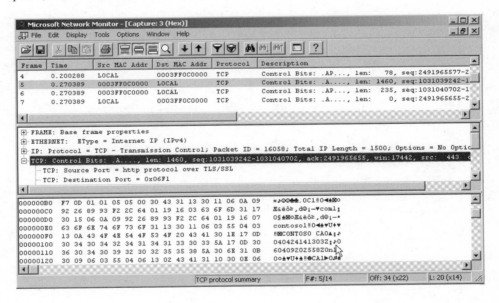

NOTE None of the frames display the HTTP request or the Web page in readable form. All data is encrypted. The only information that is in plain text is some of the data in the certificate that the Web server sends to the browser.

29. Close Network Monitor.

30. When prompted to save the capture, click No, and if prompted to save unsaved entries in the database, click No.

31. Close all windows, and then log off.

LAB REVIEW QUESTIONS

Estimated completion time: 10 minutes

1. You are using EFS to store sensitive data on your network and are concerned that some applications might be leaving temporary files on local hard drives. What should you do to ensure the confidentiality of temporary files?

2. You have enabled a file server to support remote encryption, and users are storing encrypted files through shared folders on the server. In what way is the confidentiality of the data still vulnerable?

3. Why should you configure encryption at the folder level, rather than at the file level?

4. You move an encrypted file to an unencrypted folder that resides on an NTFS volume. Does the file remain encrypted? What would happen if the file were moved to a folder on a file allocation table (FAT) volume?

5. You are reallocating a removable hard drive to another user and are concerned that the portable hard drive might contain sensitive information. What Cipher.exe command-line option should you use to ensure that this data cannot be recovered from the hard drive?

6. You connect to an SSL-enabled e-commerce Web site. How can you view the details of the digital certificate used to establish the SSL-encrypted session?

7. You are using Network Monitor to examine HTTPS traffic. You notice that the port used by the Web server is always TCP port 443, but that the TCP port used by the Web browser client varies.

   QUESTION   What are TCP/IP ports, and what are they used for?

LAB CHALLENGE 4-1: BACKING UP AND RESTORING EFS KEYS USED TO ENCRYPT AND DECRYPT DATA

Estimated completion time: 10 minutes

You are a security administrator for Contoso Pharmaceuticals. A small group of research scientists uses EFS extensively to protect proprietary data. These scientists are about to receive new dual-processor workstations. Because the EFS digital certificates the scientists use to encrypt and decrypt their data are stored with their profiles on the local computer, they will not be able to access their encrypted data if they lose these certificates. One solution to the problem would be to use roaming profiles. However, company policy does not allow the use of roaming profiles.

Although you have configured an EFS recovery agent, the scientists would like to back up their own EFS keys that are found in the EFS certificate and restore them to the new workstations. They have asked you to demonstrate how to back up and restore EFS keys to a different workstation. For this lab challenge, demonstrate how to back up and restore EFS keys for a test user account. You should try to make the demonstration as real as possible by simulating the loss of keys used for EFS encryption. How can you do this?

LAB 5
USING CERTIFICATES

This lab contains the following exercises and activities:

- Exercise 5-1: Examining Root Certificates

- Exercise 5-2: Using Certificates for Web Server Security

- Exercise 5-3: Implementing User Certificate Authentication for Access to Web Sites

- Exercise 5-4: Exporting and Importing a Certificate

- Lab Questions

- Lab Challenge 5-1: Configuring Multiple Web Servers with a Single Certificate

- Lab Challenge 5-2: Automating the Distribution of User Certificates

After completing this lab, you will be able to

- Install a root certificate.

- Install a Web server certificate.

- Configure a Web virtual directory to require client certificates for authentication.

- Request and install a client certificate.

- Export and import certificates.

Estimated completion time: 135 minutes

SCENARIO

Contoso Pharmaceuticals has decided to deploy Microsoft Certificate Services in order to implement its public key infrastructure (PKI) solution. To prepare for the deployment, you will verify that a certificate from the root certification authority (CA) can be easily reinstalled if a user deletes the certificate from his certificate store. Also, you will install a certificate on the demonstration Web server to be used for Secure Sockets Layer (SSL) connections and demonstrate how to use user certificates for authentication. Finally, you will install, back up, and restore a certificate to be used for SSL connections for your Web server.

EXERCISE 5-1: EXAMINING ROOT CERTIFICATES

Estimated completion time: 20 minutes

In this exercise, you will explore the use of root certificates to ensure and verify the identity of remote computers when you connect to them using HTTPS. You will delete a root certificate, examine the effect of deleting the certificate, and then install a root certificate to ensure the identity of the remote computer.

Using the Certificates Snap-In MMC Console to View and Manage Root Certificates

In this section, you will view the root certificate used to ensure the identity of the Instructor01 computer when you connect to it using HTTPS. You will then delete the root certificate used to ensure the identity of the Instructor01 computer. In a subsequent section, you will view the effect of deleting this root certificate.

1. Log on to Contoso as Admin*x* (where *x* is your assigned student number).

2. Open Internet Explorer.

   You should see a message indicating that Internet Explorer Enhanced Security Configuration is enabled.

   If you also see the Internet Explorer dialog box, select the In The Future, Do Not Show This Message check box.

3. In the Address box, type **https://instructor01** and then press ENTER.

4. In the Security Alert dialog box, click OK.

5. On the Microsoft Internet Explorer page, double-click the lock icon, as shown below, to view the details of the certificate.

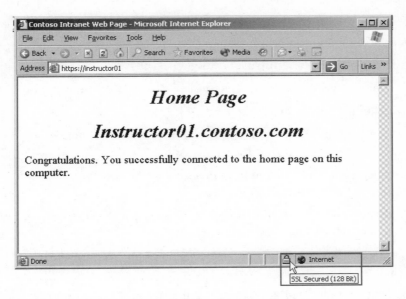

6. On the Certificate page, note the information and answer the following questions:

   QUESTION What is the intended purpose of the certificate?

   QUESTION What entity issued the certificate?

7. On the Certificate page, select the Certification Path tab, as shown below, and note that CONTOSA CA is the root authority for the certificate.

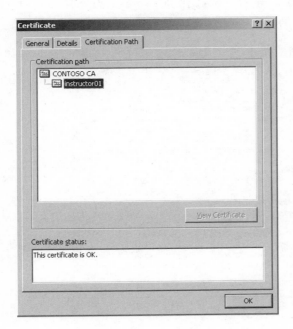

8. Close the Certificate page, and then close Internet Explorer.

9. Click Start, and then select Run.

10. In the Run dialog box, type **mmc** and then click OK.

11. In the Console1 window, select Add/Remove Snap-In from the File menu.

12. In the Add/Remove Snap-In dialog box, click Add.

13. In the Add Standalone Snap-In dialog box, under Available Standalone Snap-Ins, select Certificates, and then click Add.

14. In the Certificates Snap-In dialog box, ensure that the My User Account option is selected, and then click Finish.

15. In the Add Standalone Snap-In dialog box, under Available Standalone Snap-Ins, select Certificates, and then click Add.

16. In the Certificates Snap-In dialog box, select Computer Account, and then click Next.

17. In the Select Computer dialog box, ensure that Local Computer is selected, and then click Finish.

18. Click Close to close the Add Standalone Snap-In dialog box, and then click OK to close the Add/Remove Snap-In dialog box.

19. From the File menu, select Save As.

20. In the Save As dialog box, in the Save In box, select Desktop.

21. In the File Name box, type **admin certificates** and then click Save.

22. In the console tree, expand Certificates - Current User, expand Trusted Root Certification Authorities, and then select Certificates, as shown below.

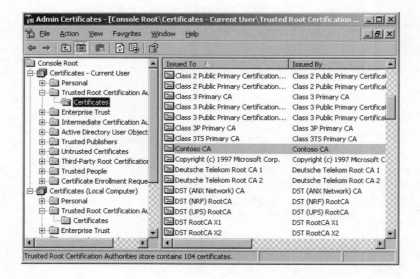

QUESTION   What kinds of entities are represented by the prepopulated certificates in the Trusted Root Certification Authorities certificate store?

23. In the details pane, right-click CONTOSO CA, and then select Delete.

24. In the Certificates dialog box, click Yes.

25. In the console tree, expand Certificates (Local Computer), expand Trusted Root Certification Authorities, and then select Certificates.

QUESTION   Is the CONTOSA CA root certificate in the local computer certificate store?

26. Minimize the Admin Certificates console and leave it open for the next procedure.

Installing a Root Certificate

In the first part of this section, you will connect to an SSL-enabled Web site that uses a digital certificate issued by a CA that is not automatically trusted. You will then add a certificate to the Trusted Root Certification Authorities store to cause the issuing certification authority to be trusted by your browser.

NOTE   By default, the Internet Enhanced Security Configuration feature is enabled on Windows 2003 servers. Because of the high level of security of this configuration, you must reconfigure Internet Explorer so that the following procedure will work. You must complete steps 1–6 for the rest of the steps to work properly.

1. Open Internet Explorer.

   You should see a message indicating that Internet Explorer Enhanced Security Configuration is enabled.

2. From the Internet Explorer Tools menu, select Internet Options.

3. In the Internet Options dialog box, select the Security tab.

4. In the Select A Web Content Zone To Specify Its Security Settings box, select Local Intranet, and then select Sites.

5. On the Local Intranet page, type **https://instructor01** in the Add This Web Site To The Zone box; click Add; and then click Close.

6. On the Internet Options page, click OK, and then close Internet Explorer.

7. Open Internet Explorer and connect to https://instructor01, and then click OK in the Security Alert dialog box informing you that you are about to view pages over a secure connection.

   If you see another Security Alert dialog box informing you that revocation information for the security certificate for this site is not available, click Yes to proceed.

8. In the Security Alert dialog box that indicates that the security certificate was issued by a company you have chosen not to trust, click View Certificate.

   Internet Explorer indicates that the certificate was issued by CONTOSO CA and cannot be verified up to a trusted CA.

9. In the Certificate dialog box, click OK.

10. In the Security Alert dialog box, click Yes.

    Notice that a lock appears at the bottom of the Internet Explorer window, indicating a secure connection with the Web site. If you had responded No when asked whether you wanted to proceed, you would not have connected to the Web site. The default behavior of Internet Explorer is to warn you when it does not trust the certification authority that issued the digital certificate used for HTTPS.

11. Use Internet Explorer to connect to https://instructor01/certsrv.

12. Select Download A CA Certificate, Certificate Chain, Or CRL.

13. On the Download A CA Certificate, Certificate Chain, Or CRL page, select Download CA Certificate Chain.

14. On the Save As page, in the Save In drop-down list, select the C drive, type **ContosoCA** in the File Name box, and then click Save.

15. In the Download Complete box, click Close, and then close Internet Explorer.

16. Maximize the Admin Certificates console.

17. In the console tree, expand Certificates (Local Computer), expand Trusted Root Certification Authorities, and then select Certificates.

18. Right-click Certificates, select All Tasks, and then select Import, as shown below.

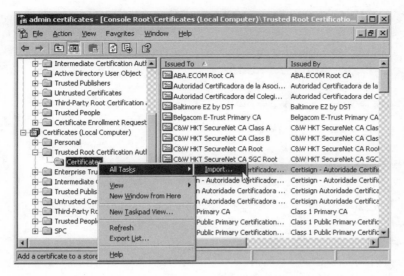

19. On the Welcome To The Certificate Import Wizard page, click Next.

20. On the File To Import page, type **c:\contosoca.p7b** and then click Next.

   If you choose to browse for the file on the File To Import page rather than type the filename, you will need to ensure that you select PKCS #7 Certificates (*.spc, *.p7b) from the Files Of Type drop-down list.

21. On the Certificate Store page, accept the default, and then click Next.

22. On the Completing The Certificate Import Wizard page, review the information, and then click Finish.

23. In the Certificate Import Wizard dialog box, click OK.

24. In the Admin Certificate console, right-click Certificates (Local Computer), select Refresh, and then verify that the Contoso CA certificate is in the details pane.

25. Open Internet Explorer and connect to https://instructor01.

26. Click OK in the Security Alert dialog box informing you that you are about to view pages over a secure connection.

   Notice that you are not warned about a problem with the certificate. This indicates that Internet Explorer trusted the Web server's certificate because it trusts the CA that issued it. The reason that Internet Explorer trusts the CA that issued the certificate is that you imported the CA's certificate into the trusted root certificate store of Internet Explorer.

27. Close the Admin Certificates MMC console, and click No when prompted to save the console settings.

28. Minimize Internet Explorer.

EXERCISE 5-2: USING CERTIFICATES FOR WEB SERVER SECURITY

Estimated completion time: 20 minutes

In this exercise, you will install a Web server certificate on your computer. You will then establish a secure Web session with your computer.

Generating a Certificate Signing Request (CSR)

1. While logged in as Contoso\Admin*x* (where *x* is your assigned student number), from the Administrative Tools menu, select Internet Information Services (IIS) Manager.

2. In Internet Information Services (IIS) Manager, expand Computer*xx* (where *xx* is the two-digit version of your student number), expand Web Sites, and then select Default Web Site.

3. Right-click Default Web Site, and then select Properties, as shown below.

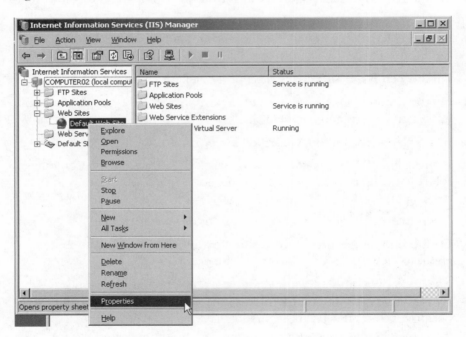

4. In the Default Web Site Properties dialog box, in the Directory Security tab, select Server Certificate.

5. On the Web Server Certificate Wizard page, click Next.

6. On the Server Certificate page, ensure that Create A New Certificate is selected, and then click Next.

7. On the Delayed Or Immediate Request page, ensure that Prepare The Request Now, But Send It Later is selected, and then click Next.

   QUESTION   *What must you do before you can select the Send The Request Immediately To An Online Certification Authority option?*

8. On the Name And Security Settings page, type **Computer*xx* Web Certificate** (where *xx* is the two-digit version of your student number) in the Name box; in the Bit Length box, select 2048; and then click Next.

   QUESTION   *What is the maximum bit length you can select?*

9. On the Organization Information page, type **Contoso** in the Organization box, type **IT Group** in the Organizational Unit box, and then click Next.

10. On the Your Site's Common Name page, ensure that the name of your computer appears in the Common Name box, and then click Next.

11. On the Geographical Information page, type the appropriate information for your location (do not use abbreviations for the State/Province or City field), and then click Next.

12. On the Certificate Request File Name page, ensure that the File Name box contains C:\Certreq.txt, and then click Next.

13. On the Request File Summary page, review the information, and then click Next.

14. On the Completing The Web Server Certificate Wizard page, click Finish.

15. In the Default Web Site Properties dialog box, click OK to close it.

16. Minimize Internet Information Services (IIS) Manager, and leave it open to complete steps in the next section.

Using Web-Based Enrollment to Request a Web Certificate

1. Click Start, select Run, type **notepad c:\certreq.txt** in the Open box, and then click OK.

2. In Notepad, press CRTL+A to select all of the text, and then press CTRL+C to copy the text to the clipboard.

   NOTE   *Make sure that all of the text in the Certreq.txt file is selected, including the lines that indicate the beginning and the end of the certificate request.*

3. Close Notepad.

4. Restore Internet Explorer and connect to https://instructor01/certsrv.

5. On the Welcome page, under Select A Task, click Request a Certificate.

NOTE Make sure that you submit the request (steps 6–12) only once. If you request a second certificate, you will not be able to install the second certificate on the Web server, and you will have to delete the pending request and start Exercise 5-2 from the beginning.

6. On the Request A Certificate page, click Advanced Certificate Request.

7. On the Advanced Certificate Request page, select Submit A Certificate Request Using A Base64-Encoded CMC Or PKCS #10 File, Or Submit A Renewal Request By Using A Base 64-Encoded PKCS #7 File.

8. On the Submit A Certificate Request Or Renewal Request page, place the cursor in the Saved Request box and press CTRL+V to paste the certificate request from the clipboard.

9. In the Certificate Template box, select Web Server, as shown below, and then click Submit.

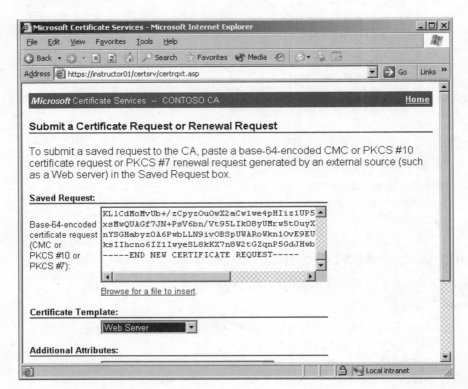

10. On the Certificate Issued page, ensure that DER Encoded is selected, and then click Download Certificate.

11. In the File Download dialog box, click Save.

12. In the Save As dialog box, ensure that Local Disk (C:) appears in the Save In drop-down list and that Certnew.cer appears in the File Name box, and then click Save.

13. In the Download Complete dialog box, click Close.

Installing a Web Server Certificate

1. Minimize Internet Explorer.

2. Maximize Internet Information Services (IIS) Manager, right-click the Default Web Site, and then select Properties.

3. In the Default Web Site Properties dialog box, in the Directory Security tab, select Server Certificate.

4. On the Welcome To The Web Server Certificate Wizard page, click Next.

5. On the Pending Certificate Request page, ensure that Process The Pending Request And Install The Certificate is selected, and then click Next.

6. On the Process A Pending Request page, in the Path And File Name box, ensure that C:\Certnew.cer appears, and then click Next.

7. On the SSL Port page, ensure that 443 appears, and then click Next.

8. On the Certificate Summary page, review the details of the certificate, and then click Next.

9. On the Completing The Web Server Certificate Wizard page, click Finish.

10. In the Default Web Site Properties dialog box, click OK.

11. Minimize Internet Information Services (IIS) Manager, and leave it open for the next exercise.

12. Restore Internet Explorer, and then connect to https://computer*xx* (where *xx* is the two-digit version of your student number).

    Internet Explorer displays the home page on your computer. The lock icon at the bottom right of the Internet Explorer window confirms that you are viewing the page over a secure connection.

13. Close Internet Explorer.

EXERCISE 5-3: IMPLEMENTING USER CERTIFICATE AUTHENTICATION FOR ACCESS TO WEB SITES

Estimated completion time: 25 minutes

In this exercise, you will configure the Web server to require that a user present a digital certificate to authenticate to the Web site before being granted access.

Creating a Virtual Directory for Certificate-Based Authentication

In this section, you will create a Web site virtual directory and configure it to require that users present client certificates.

1. Maximize Internet Information Services (IIS) Manager, right-click Default Web Site, select New, and then select Virtual Directory, as shown below.

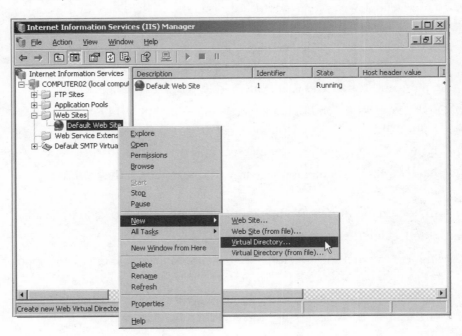

2. On the Welcome To The Virtual Directory Creation Wizard page, click Next.

3. In the Alias box, type **CertSecure** and then click Next.

4. On the Web Site Content Directory page, click Browse.

5. In the Browse For Folder dialog box, select Local Disk (C:), select Make New Folder, type **CertSecure** for the folder name, and then click OK.

6. On the Web Site Content Directory page, click Next.

7. On the Virtual Directory Access Permissions page, accept the defaults, and then click Next.

8. On the You Have Successfully Completed The Virtual Directory Creation Wizard page, click Finish.

9. In the Internet Information Services (IIS) Manager console, right-click the CertSecure virtual directory, and then click Properties.

10. On the CertSecure Properties page, select the Directory Security tab.

11. In the Secure Communications pane, click Edit.

12. On the Secure Communications page, select the Require Secure Channel (SSL) check box, select the Require Client Certificates option, as shown below, and then click OK.

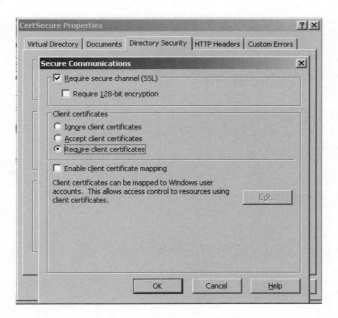

13. Click OK to close the CertSecure Properties dialog box.

   QUESTION   What is the effect of the configuration in step 12?

14. Minimize Internet Information Services (IIS) Manager.

15. Click Start, select Run, and in the Open box, type **notepad c:\certsecure\default.htm** then click OK.

16. In the Notepad dialog box, click Yes to create a new file.

17. In Notepad, type the following HTML code:

    \<html\>

    \<head\>

    \<title\>Computer*xx* SSL Virtual Directory\</title\>

    \</head\>

    \<body\>

    This virtual directory is accessible only if you authenticate with a valid digital certificate.

    \</body\>

    \</html\>

18. When you have finished typing the HTML code, save the file and close Notepad.

19. Open Internet Explorer and connect to https://computer*xx*/certsecure (where *xx* is the two-digit version of your student number).

    The Client Authentication dialog box appears, allowing you to choose a digital certificate to present to the Web site; however, you have no digital certificate to present.

20. Click OK in the Client Authentication dialog page.

    A Web page appears, informing you that the page requires a client certificate.

21. Close all windows and log off.

Requesting and Installing a Client Certificate

In the following section, you will request and install a client certificate, using Web-based enrollment.

1. Log on to Contoso as user*x* (where *x* is your student number).

2. Open Internet Explorer.

    You should see a message indicating that Internet Explorer Enhanced Security Configuration is enabled.

    If you also see the Internet Explorer dialog box, select the In The Future, Do Not Show This Message check box, and then click OK.

NOTE Because Internet Explorer Enhanced Security Configuration is enabled, you must complete steps 3–7 to request a certificate from the certificate services Web enrollment site on Instructor01.

3. From the Internet Explorer Tools menu, select Internet Options.

4. In the Internet Options dialog box, select the Security tab,

5. In the Select A Web Content Zone To Specify Its Security Settings box, select Local Intranet, and then click Sites.

6. On the Local Intranet page, type **https://instructor01** in the Add This Web Site To The Zone box, click Add, and then click Close.

7. On the Internet Options page, click OK, and then close Internet Explorer.

8. Open Internet Explorer, and then connect to https://instructor01/certsrv.

9. Click OK in the Security Alert dialog box.

   If the Connect To Instructor01.contoso.com logon dialog box appears, log on as Contoso\user.x (where x is your student number).

10. On the Microsoft Certificate Services Welcome Web page, under Select A Task, click Request A Certificate.

11. Under the Select The Certificate Type section, click User Certificate.

12. On the User Certificate – Identifying Information page, click Submit.

13. In the Potential Scripting Violation dialog box, review the warning, and then click Yes.

14. On the Certificate Issued page, click Install This Certificate.

15. In the Potential Scripting Violation dialog box, review the warning, and then click Yes.

16. In Internet Explorer, select the Tools menu, and then select Internet Options.

17. Select the Content tab, and then select Certificates.

18. In the Certificates dialog box, in the Personal tab, click the Intended Purpose drop-down list, and then select Client Authentication.

19. Double-click the certificate issued to User.x.

   When you double-click the certificate, you should see that one of the purposes of the certificate is to prove identity to a remote computer, as shown below.

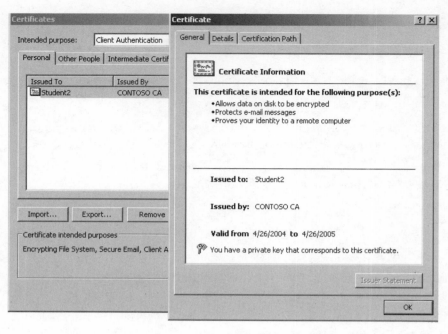

20. On the Certificate page, select the Details tab, and then review the values for the fields.

Note that the Subject and Subject Alternative Name fields contain information about the user account. In particular, the Subject Alternative Name field contains the value for the User Principle Name (UPN), which can also be used to log on to a Microsoft Windows domain.

21. When you are finished reviewing the details of the client certificate, click OK to close the Certificate page, click Close to close the Certificates dialog box, and then click OK to close the Internet Options dialog box.

22. Connect to https://computer.xx/certsecure (where *xx* is the two-digit version of your student number).

23. In the Client Authentication dialog box, ensure that the User.x certificate is selected, as shown below, and then click OK.

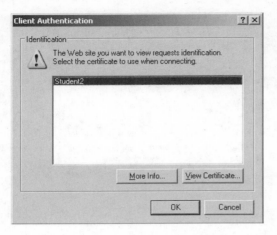

You have successfully connected to the virtual directory.

24. Close all windows and log off.

EXERCISE 5-4: EXPORTING AND IMPORTING A CERTIFICATE

Estimated completion time: 20 minutes

In this exercise, you will recover a Web server certificate. You will first export the Web server certificate and then delete the original certificate from the Web server. You will then import the backup certificate to ensure that you can reinstall the exported certificate during disaster recovery.

Exporting a Web Server Certificate

1. Log on to Contoso as Admin*x* (where *x* is your student number).

2. On the desktop, click the Admin Certificates console you created earlier in this lab.

3. In the console tree, expand Certificates (Local Computer), expand Personal, and then click Certificates.

4. In the details pane, right-click Computer*xx* (where *xx* is the two-digit version of your student number), select All Tasks, and then select Export, as shown below.

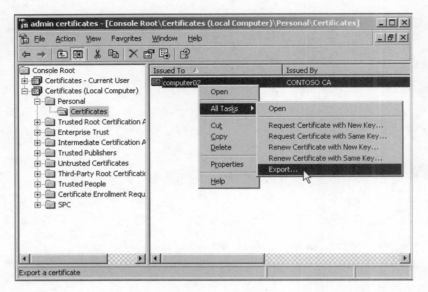

5. On the Welcome To The Certificate Export Wizard page, click Next.

6. On the Export Private Key page, select Yes, Export The Private Key, and then click Next.

   QUESTION   *Why is it necessary to export the private key?*

7. On the Export File Format page, ensure that Personal Information Exchange – PKCS #12 (.PFX) is selected, ensure that Enable Strong Protection is selected, and then click Next.

   When you enable strong protection, the file containing the certificate information will be protected with a password.

   QUESTION   *Why is it a good idea to enable strong protection when you export this certificate?*

8. On the Password page, in the Password and Confirm Password boxes, type **P@ssCert** and then click Next.

9. On the File To Export page, in the File Name box, type **c:\webcert.pfx** and then click Next.

10. On the Completing The Certificate Export Wizard page, click Finish.

11. In the Certificate Export Wizard dialog box, click OK.

12. In the details pane, right-click Computer*xx*, and then select Delete.

13. In the Certificates dialog box, click Yes.

14. Minimize the Admin Certificates console.

15. Click Start, select Administrative Tools, and then select Internet Information Services (IIS) Manager.

16. In the console tree, expand Computerxx (Local Computer), expand Web Sites, right-click Default Web Site, and then select Properties.

17. In the Default Web Site Properties dialog box, in the Directory Security tab, select View Certificate.

    NOTE *Internet Services Manager cannot display the certificate because you removed it from the computer's certificate store. You will need to configure IIS to not use this certificate.*

18. Select Server Certificate.

19. On the Welcome To The Web Server Certificate Wizard page, click Next.

20. On the Modify The Current Certificate Agreement page, select Remove The Current Certificate, and then click Next.

21. On the Remove A Certificate page, click Next.

22. On the Completing The Web Server Certificate Wizard page, click Finish.

Importing a Web Server Certificate

1. Restore the Admin Certificates console.

2. Under Certificates (Local Computer)\Personal, right-click Certificates, select All Tasks, and then select Import, as shown below.

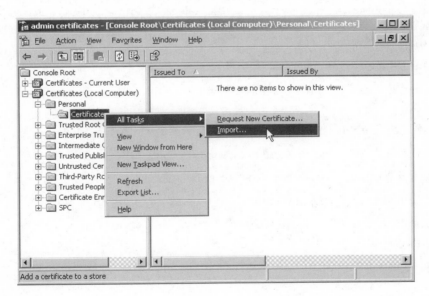

3. On the Certificate Import Wizard page, click Next.

4. On the File To Import page, in the File Name box, type **c:\webcert.pfx** and then click Next.

If you click browse to locate the certificate, you need to ensure that, in the Open dialog box, in the Files Of Type drop-down list, you select Personal Information Exchange (*.pfx;*.p12).

5. On the Password page, in the Password box, type **P@ssCert.**

6. Select the Mark The Key As Exportable check box, and then click Next.

7. On the Certificate Store page, leave the default settings, and then click Next.

8. On the Completing The Certificate Import Wizard page, click Finish.

9. In the Certificate Import Wizard dialog box, click OK.

10. Close the Admin Certificates console without saving changes.

You have restored the certificate into the computer certificate store. You must now configure IIS to use this certificate for your computer's default Web site.

11. In the Default Web Site Properties dialog box, in the Directory Security tab, select Server Certificate.

12. On the Welcome To The Web Server Certificate Wizard page, click Next.

13. On the Server Certificate page, select Assign An Existing Certificate, and then click Next.

14. On the Available Certificates page, in the Select A Certificate box, select Computer*xx* (where *xx* is the two-digit version of your student number), and then click Next.

15. On the SSL Port page, click Next.

16. On the Certificate Summary page, review the certificate details, and then click Next.

17. On the Completing The Web Server Certificate Wizard page, click Finish.

18. In the Default Web Site Properties dialog box, click OK.

19. Close Internet Information Services (IIS) Manager.

20. Open Internet Explorer, and connect to https://computer*xx*.

By connecting to your computer using HTTPS, you verify that you have restored the digital certificate.

21. Close all open windows, and then log off.

LAB REVIEW QUESTIONS

Estimated completion time: 10 minutes

1. Your single intranet Web server should be load balanced with another Web server to increase availability and fault tolerance. The single intranet Web server uses a digital certificate to encrypt Web traffic. What should you do to encrypt Web traffic on the second, load-balanced server?

2. You have configured an intranet Web server with a digital certificate and have used the internal Domain Name System (DNS) name—intranet—as the common name for the certificate. The Web server is also accessible from the Internet for customer access. The external DNS name of the Web server is www.contoso.com. Why is the configuration of the digital certificate a problem?

3. Where can you view the common name used for a Web certificate after you connect to an SSL-enabled Web site?

4. Your organization wants to set up an SSL-enabled Web site that the public can access from the Internet. Your manager suggested that the organization could save money by using Microsoft Certificate Services instead of purchasing a third-party digital certificate from a commercial CA. What is the primary disadvantage of this suggestion?

5. One of your employees tells you he understands that a digital certificate contains a public key that is used for encryption, but he is somewhat confused about the difference between a public key and a certificate. How do you explain the difference?

LAB CHALLENGE 5-1: CONFIGURING MULTIPLE WEB SERVERS WITH A SINGLE CERTIFICATE

Estimated completion time: 20 minutes

Your company is implementing load-balanced Web servers to serve in the extranet for its employees and business partners. The DNS address of the extranet Web site is extranet.contoso.com. All traffic between the Web servers and the Web browser clients is supposed to be encrypted using digital certificates. Because this is not a publicly accessible Web site, your company has determined that it is appropriate to use an internal Microsoft certificate server to issue the certificates for the SSL encryption.

For this lab challenge, you will work with a lab partner to simulate a load-balanced Web site that uses a digital certificate for the fully qualified DNS name extranet.contoso.com. Although the servers will not in fact be load balanced, as a result of this lab challenge, they should use the same digital certificate. This means that regardless of whether the DNS name extranet.contoso.com resolves to the IP address of your computer or your partner's computer, external users can connect without warning messages.

When you have successfully completed this lab and, if required, demonstrated the results to your instructor, remove the digital certificate and restore the digital certificate from the file you created in Exercise 5-4, "Exporting and Importing a Certificate."

LAB CHALLENGE 5-2: AUTOMATING THE DISTRIBUTION OF USER CERTIFICATES

Estimated completion time: 20 minutes

Currently, your organization is making limited use of user certificates for authenticating to intranet and extranet Web sites. However, the security team is recommending that your organization make more extensive use of user certificates. Your manager is concerned that the Web-based enrollment she has seen for user certificate acquisition is not a good solution. The organization has close to a thousand employees who might need user certificates, and she is concerned that the help desk will not be able to handle any problems that users will experience. Ideally, she would like to configure Windows 2003 Certificate Services so that user certificates are distributed automatically and transparently to authenticated users.

She has asked you to research the possibility of configuring Certificate Services to provide autoenrollment of user certificates. She also wants you to briefly summarize the general requirements and steps to enable autoenrollment of user certificates.

LAB 6

SECURING THE NETWORK INFRASTRUCTURE THROUGH AN UNDERSTANDING OF TCP/IP TRAFFIC

- ■ **This lab contains the following exercises and activities:**
- ■ Exercise 6-1: Examining ARP and ICMP Traffic
- ■ Exercise 6-2: Examining the ARP Cache
- ■ Exercise 6-3: Examining DNS Traffic
- ■ Exercise 6-4: Examining FTP Traffic
- ■ Exercise 6-5: Classifying Attacks by OSI Layer
- ■ Lab Review Questions
- ■ Lab Challenge 6-1: Comparing and Contrasting FTP Traffic
- ■ Lab Challenge 6-2: Exploring Threats to Instant Messaging Traffic

After completing this lab, you will be able to

- ■ Use Microsoft Network Monitor to capture and view network traffic.
- ■ Analyze TCP/IP traffic.
- ■ Identify Ethernet frame traffic.
- ■ Identify Address Resolution Protocol (ARP) resolution traffic.
- ■ Identify ports used for User Datagram Protocol (UDP) and Transmission Control Protocol (TCP) communications.
- ■ Identify IP fragments.
- ■ Identify the datagrams related to the establishment of a TCP connection between two hosts.
- ■ Identify the use of primary and secondary ports used in complex protocols such as FTP.
- ■ Identify data payloads of application layer protocols, such as Domain Name System (DNS) and Hypertext Transfer Protocol (HTTP).

Estimated completion time: 165 minutes

SCENARIO

You have recently joined the IT security group at Contoso Pharmaceuticals. You realize that in order to be an effective member of this group, you need to become more familiar with the underlying mechanisms of TCP/IP and with analyzing TCP/IP traffic by using Network Monitor.

In this lab, you will analyze TCP/IP traffic, starting with the lower layers of the OSI model and progressing to higher layers.

Before You Begin

Many of the lab exercises that follow require you to generate network traffic between your computer and a lab partner's computer; you will capture and analyze this traffic using Network Monitor. To simplify the traffic that you capture for analysis and to follow the steps in the exercises, only one lab partner at a time should be generating traffic for analysis. For example, if a lab exercise contains steps that require you to ping your partner's computers and capture that traffic using Network Monitor, you should be the only one performing those steps or otherwise generating traffic between your computer and another. When you have completed capturing the traffic, your lab partner can then perform the set of steps you just completed. As an alternative to performing sets of steps sequentially, you can double up on one computer and perform the exercises together.

The C:\Lab Manual\Lab 06 folder contains a number of saved captures that correspond to the lab exercises. Instead of capturing traffic that you generate, you can load those saved captures into Network Monitor and use them as the basis for the lab exercises, if your instructor approves.

For Exercise 6-3, "Examining DNS Traffic," to work properly, the instructor must reconfigure the DNS server to allow DNS zone transfers to occur to the student computers in the lab. This means that the instructor has to relax the security on the classroom DNS server somewhat. After you finish the lab, the instructor can restore the more secure configuration of DNS for zone transfer traffic.

EXERCISE 6-1: EXAMINING ARP AND ICMP TRAFFIC

Estimated completion time: 25 minutes

In this exercise, you will use Network Monitor to gain a better understanding of the Address Resolution Protocol (ARP), Internet Control Message Protocol (ICMP), and IP. ARP and ICMP are implemented at the lower layers of the OSI model. ARP is responsible for resolving IP addresses to Media Access Control (MAC) addresses so that devices such as computers and routers on the same subnet can communicate with each other. ICMP is used to send control messages between devices. Ping, an application-layer protocol, uses ICMP.

Analyzing ARP and ICMP Traffic

1. Log on to Contoso as Admin$x$ (where x is your student number).

   NOTE The next step requires that you have installed Network Monitor according to the instructions in Lab 4. If you have not already installed Network Monitor, please see the specific instructions for doing so in Lab 4, Exercise 4-4, "Using Encryption for Web Communications."

2. Click Start, select Administrative Tools, and then select Network Monitor.

3. With Network Monitor open, click Start, select Run, type **cmd** in the Open box, and then click OK.

4. At the command prompt, type **ping computeryy** (where yy is the two-digit version of your lab partner's student number), and then press ENTER.

5. In the space below, record your lab partner's TCP/IP address.
   Lab partner's TCP/IP address:

6. At the command prompt, type **arp -?** and then press ENTER.

   The Arp command help appears, showing the command-line options usage. Note the usage of the -a, -d, and -s switches.

7. At the command prompt, type **arp –d** and then press ENTER.

   This clears the ARP cache so that you can view ARP traffic by using Network Monitor.

8. Leave the command prompt window open, and then switch to Network Monitor.

> **NOTE** Only one lab partner at a time should perform steps 9–12 below. When the first partner has finished capturing data, inform your lab partner so that he or she can proceed with step 9. Alternatively, both lab partners can sit at a single computer to capture and analyze the network data. Or, as an additional alternative to capturing the data, you can open the C:\Lab Manual\Lab 06\ ICMPa.cap file from the File menu of Network Monitor. If you choose to use the capture file, proceed to step 13.

9. From the Capture menu, select Start.

10. Switch to the command prompt window, type **ping** *w.x.y.z* (where *w.x.y.z* is your lab partner's TCP/IP address), and then press ENTER.

11. Wait for the Ping command to finish, and then switch to Network Monitor.

12. From the Capture menu, select Stop And View.

13. In the Microsoft Network Monitor capture summary, double-click the first instance of ARP_RARP traffic, as indicated by the entry in the Description column that displays "ARP: Request."

This opens the zoom pane so you can view the capture details, as shown below.

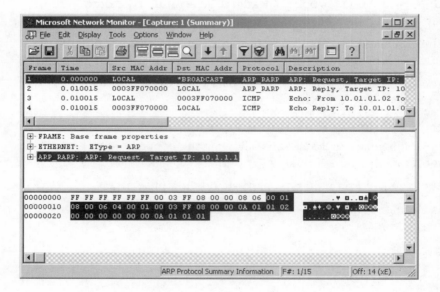

14. Expand the FRAME, ETHERNET, and ARP elements in the middle pane, as shown below.

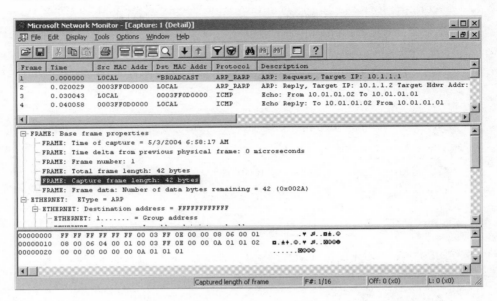

15. Review the details of the captured frame, and then record the following information from the middle pane in the space below.

FRAME: Total frame length:

ETHERNET: Ethernet destination address:

ETHERNET: Ethernet source address:

ETHERNET: Ethernet type:

ARP_RARP: Sender's hardware address:

ARP_RARP: Sender's protocol address:

ARP_RARP: Target's hardware address:

ARP_RARP: Target's protocol address:

16. Select the second instance of ARP_RARP traffic, indicated by the entry in the Description column that displays "ARP: Reply," and in the space below, record the following information from the details of the middle pane.

FRAME: Total frame length:

ETHERNET: Ethernet destination address:

ETHERNET: Ethernet source address:

ETHERNET: Ethernet type:

ARP_RARP: Sender's hardware address:

ARP_RARP: Sender's protocol address:

ARP_RARP: Target's hardware address:

ARP_RARP: Target's protocol address:

QUESTION   Why is the frame length different for the request and the reply?

QUESTION   What is the relationship between an Ethernet address and a hardware address?

QUESTION   What is another name for the hardware address?

QUESTION   What are the sizes of the hardware and IP addresses?

QUESTION   What is indicated by a hardware address of FF FF FF FF FF FF?

QUESTION   What is the purpose of an ARP request?

17. In the Microsoft Network Monitor capture summary, select the first instance of ICMP traffic, as indicated by the entry in the Description column that displays "ECHO: From"; expand the IP and ICMP elements in the middle pane; and record the values for the following in the space below.

FRAME: Total frame length:

ETHERNET: Ethernet destination address:

ETHERNET: Ethernet source address:

ETHERNET: Ethernet type:

IP: Protocol:

IP: Fragmentation summary:

IP: Time to live:

IP: Source address:

IP: Destination address:

18. Select the second instance of ICMP traffic, as indicated by the entry in the Description column that displays "ECHO: Reply"; then record the values for the following in the space below.

FRAME: Total frame length:

ETHERNET: Ethernet destination address:

ETHERNET: Ethernet source address:

ETHERNET: Ethernet type:

IP: Protocol:

IP: Fragmentation summary:

IP: Time to live:

IP: Source address:

IP: Destination address:

QUESTION   How many ICMP frames are generated (total) as a result of using the Ping command? Hint: In the top pane, count the number of rows that display "ICMP" in the Protocol column.

QUESTION   Why do the Ethernet source and destination addresses need to be present?

QUESTION   At what layer of the OSI model is ICMP implemented?

QUESTION   What is the meaning of an IP fragmentation summary value of 0?

QUESTION   What does the IP Time To Live value indicate?

19. Close the capture summary screen, making sure you do not close Network Monitor.

NOTE   Only one lab partner at a time should perform steps 20–24 below. When you have finished capturing data, inform your lab partner so that he or she can proceed with step 20. Alternatively, both lab partners can sit at a single computer to capture the network data. Or, as an additional alternative to capturing the data, you can open the C:\Lab Manual\Lab 06\ICMPb.cap file from the File menu of Network Monitor. If you choose to use the capture file, proceed to the explanation and question immediately below step 24.

20. On the Microsoft Network Monitor screen, select Start from the Capture menu.

21. Click No when prompted to save the capture.

22. Switch to the command prompt, type **ping *w.x.y.z* -l 10000** (where *w.x.y.z* is your lab partner's TCP/IP address), and then press ENTER.

The Ping *w.x.y.z* -l 10000 command sends an ICMP packet with a 10,000-byte buffer.

23. Wait for the Ping command to finish, and then switch to Network Monitor.

24. From the Capture menu, select Stop And View.

In the Microsoft Network Monitor capture summary, note that a number of IP packets follow immediately after the ICMP packets and that "Protocol = ICMP" appears in the Description column, as shown in the figure below.

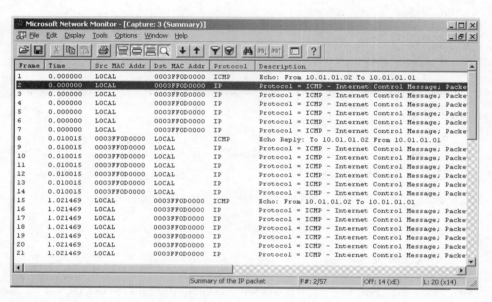

QUESTION   How many packets are associated with the first Echo: From packet?

25. In the Microsoft Network Monitor capture summary, double-click the first instance of ICMP traffic, as indicated by the entry in the Description column that displays "ECHO: From"; expand the elements in the middle pane as appropriate; and then record the values for the following in the space below.

FRAME: Total frame length:

IP: Total length:

IP: Fragmentation summary:

IP: Fragment offset:

QUESTION What does the Total Frame Length value represent?

QUESTION Why does the IP Fragmentation summary list a value other than 0?

QUESTION What does the Fragment Offset value in this packet indicate?

26. Select the remaining IP packets associated with the Echo: From packet; record the total IP length for each of them; and then add the values.

QUESTION What is the sum of the Total IP Length values?

27. Close the capture window and leave both Network Monitor and the command prompt open for the next exercise.

EXERCISE 6-2: EXAMINING THE ARP CACHE

Estimated completion time: 10 minutes

In this exercise, you will simulate an attack that poisons the ARP cache. This will help you understand how to devise appropriate countermeasures against such attacks. The first step in this exercise is to ensure that your computer is configured with a default gateway. Once you have done this, you will add an incorrect static mapping for the default gateway in the ARP cache and view the results. By adding an incorrect static mapping to the ARP cache, you simulate the effect of an ARP cache poisoning attack.

Verifying the Default Gateway Configuration

1. Click Start, select Control Panel, select Network Connections, and then select Local Area Connection.

2. On the Local Area Connection Status page, select Properties.

3. In the This Connection Uses The Following Items box, select Internet Protocol (TCP/IP), and then click Properties.

4. On the Internet Protocol (TCP/IP) Properties page, note whether an IP address is entered for the Default Gateway configuration.

   a. If an entry exists for the default gateway, record the IP address, click OK, click Close, and then click Close again. Then proceed with step 5.

   b. If there is no entry for a default gateway, type *w.x.y*.**200** (where *w.x.y* are the first three digits of your IP address) in the Default Gateway box, click OK twice, and then click Close. Then proceed with step 5.

5. Switch to the command prompt, type **arp –d** and then press ENTER.

This command clears the ARP cache.

6. Leave the command prompt window open, and then switch to Network Monitor.

> **NOTE**   Both lab partners can perform steps 7–11 at the same time. Or, as an alternative to capturing the data, you can open the C:\Lab Manual\Lab 06\ARP.cap file from the File menu of Network Monitor.

7. From the Capture menu, select Start.

8. Click No when prompted to save the capture.

9. Switch to the command prompt window, type **ping 172.16.100.30** and then press ENTER.

> **NOTE**   The 172.16.100.30 address is on a different subnet from the classroom network. The ping process will fail unless the instructor's computer is configured as a router that can reach a 172.16.0.0/16 network containing a host with a 172.16.100.30 address.

10. Wait for the ping process to finish, and then switch to Network Monitor.

11. From the Capture menu, select Stop And View.

12. Examine the ARP protocol traffic in the capture summary, and in the space below record the MAC address of the configured default gateway of your computer.

MAC address of default gateway:

> **QUESTION**   Why is the ARP traffic querying for the hardware address of the configured default gateway, rather than trying to resolve the 172.16.100.30 IP address to a MAC address?

13. Close the capture window, and leave Network Monitor open for the next procedure.

Viewing the Effects of Static Entry on the ARP Cache

1. Switch to the command prompt, type **arp –a** and then press ENTER.

The output of the command lists the contents of the ARP cache. Each IP address will have a corresponding 12-digit hexadecimal physical address.

You should see an entry for the IP address of your configured default gateway.

2. Type **arp –d** and then press ENTER.

3. Type **arp –s *w.x.y.z* 00-aa-00-62-c6-09** (where *w.x.y.z* is the IP address of your default gateway), and then press ENTER.

   In this step, you are creating an incorrect static ARP cache entry for the IP address of your configured default gateway.

4. Type **arp –a** and then press ENTER to confirm that the static ARP entry was added.

5. Leave the command prompt window open, and then switch to Network Monitor.

   NOTE   Both lab partners can perform steps 6–11 below at the same time. Or, as an alternative to capturing the data, you can open the C:\Lab Manual\Lab 06\ARP_Poison.cap file from the File menu of Network Monitor.

6. From the Capture menu, select Start.

7. Click No when prompted to save the capture.

8. Switch to the command prompt window, type **ping 172.16.100.30** and then press ENTER.

   The ping will fail.

9. Type **ping *w.x.y.z*** (where *w.x.y.z* is the IP address of your default gateway) and press ENTER.

   The ping process will fail.

10. Wait for the ping process to finish, and then switch to Network Monitor.

    Leave the command prompt open.

11. From the Capture menu, select Stop And View.

    QUESTION   Why don't you see any ARP traffic in the capture summary?

    QUESTION   Why don't you see any ICMP responses from the configured default gateway?

    QUESTION   If your computer had an incorrect entry for the default gateway in its ARP cache, would it be able to communicate with computers on a remote network? Why or why not?

IMPORTANT   It is important that you perform the following steps to remove the incorrect entry from your ARP cache so that your computer can communicate properly on the network.

12. Close the capture window, and leave Network Monitor open.

13. Switch to the command prompt, type **arp –d** and then press ENTER.

    This step clears the ARP cache and the static mapping you created. You must perform this step or other exercises and labs will not work correctly.

14. Type **arp –a** and then press ENTER to confirm that your ARP cache is empty.

15. Type **ping** *w.x.y.z* and then press ENTER.

    The ping process should be successful. Make sure you can ping the address of your configured default gateway.

    Leave the command prompt and Network Monitor open for the next exercise.

EXERCISE 6-3: EXAMINING DNS TRAFFIC

Estimated completion time: 25 minutes

In this exercise, you will examine traffic related to the DNS protocol. You will first examine traffic related to DNS name resolution, and then you will examine traffic related to DNS zone transfers.

Analyzing DNS Query Traffic

In this section, you will use Network Monitor to analyze typical DNS traffic.

1. Switch to the command prompt, type **ipconfig /flushdns** and then press ENTER.

    This command removes entries from your DNS cache. This is necessary to ensure that DNS queries occur over the network to the configured DNS server.

    NOTE   Only one lab partner at a time should perform steps 2–6 below. When you have finished capturing data, inform your lab partner so that he or she can proceed with step 2. Alternatively, both lab partners can sit at a single computer to capture the network data. Or, as an additional alternative to capturing the data, you can open the C:\Lab Manual\Lab 06\DNSa.cap file from the File menu of Network Monitor. If you choose to use the capture file, proceed to step 7 below.

2. Switch to Network Monitor, and then select Start from the Capture menu.

3. Click No when prompted to save the capture.

4. Switch to the command prompt, type **ping computer*yy*** (where *yy* is the two-digit version of your lab partner's student number), and then press ENTER.

5. When the ping process finishes, switch to Network Monitor.

6. From the Capture menu, select Stop And View.

7. In the Microsoft Network Monitor capture summary, double-click the first instance of DNS traffic, as indicated by the entry in the Description column that displays "Std Qry For."

   Expand the elements in the middle pane as appropriate, and use the details of the captured frame to answer the following questions:

   QUESTION   What transport layer protocol is used for DNS queries?

   QUESTION   What is the destination port number for DNS queries?

   QUESTION   Why is the source port listed as Unknown in the summary information?

   QUESTION   What entries are listed under the DNS Question section of the packet, and what is their significance?

8. In the Microsoft Network Monitor capture summary, select the second instance of DNS traffic, as indicated by the entry in the Description column that displays "Std Qry Resp."

   Use the details of the captured frame to answer the following questions.

   QUESTION   What is the destination port for the DNS query response?

   QUESTION   What is the source port for the DNS query response?

   QUESTION   What additional DNS section does the reply contain?

   QUESTION   What is the significance of the DNS Time To Live value?

9. Close the capture window.

   Leave Network Monitor and the command prompt open for the next procedure.

Analyzing DNS Zone Transfer Traffic

1. Switch to the command prompt, type **ipconfig /flushdns** and then press ENTER.

   This command removes entries from your DNS cache to ensure that DNS queries occur over the network to the configured DNS server.

2. Type **nslookup** and then press ENTER.

   NOTE   *Only one lab partner at a time should perform steps 3–7 below. When you have finished capturing data, inform your lab partner so that he or she can proceed with step 3. Alternatively, both lab partners can sit at a single computer to capture the network data. Or, as an additional alternative to capturing the data, you can open the C:\Lab Manual\Lab 06\DNSb.cap file from the File menu of Network Monitor. If you choose to use the capture file, proceed to step 8 below.*

3. Switch to Network Monitor, and then select Start from the Capture menu.

4. Click No when prompted to save the capture.

5. Switch to the command prompt, and at the Nslookup prompt, type **ls –d contoso.com** and then press ENTER.

   This command causes all the DNS Resource Records in the contoso.com domain to be transferred to your computer, using the same mechanism that a secondary DNS server would use to update its copy of the domain records with those stored in the configured master DNS server.

6. Wait until the zone records for contoso.com have finished downloading, type **exit** at the Nslookup prompt, and then press ENTER.

7. Switch to Network Monitor, and then select Stop And View from the Capture menu.

8. In the Microsoft Network Monitor capture window, double-click the first instance of DNS traffic, as indicated by the entry in the Protocol column that displays "DNS."

   Use the details of the captured frame to answer the following questions.

   QUESTION   *What transport layer protocol is used for DNS in this instance?*

   QUESTION   *What is the destination port for the transport layer protocol?*

9. Immediately above the DNS frame that you examined in step 8, select the frame that displays "Control Bits: ….S." in the Description column, as shown below.

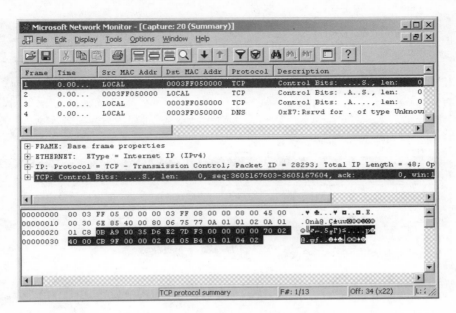

This frame displays the first frame involved in setting up a TCP connection with a remote host using a mechanism known as a three-way handshake. A three-way handshake is the mechanism that TCP uses to establish a virtual connection with a remote host by synchronizing sequence numbers and providing control information. In a three-way handshake, the source computer (client) will send a synchronization (SYN) request to the remote computer (server) at a particular TCP port. The server acknowledges the request by sending a synchronization acknowledgement (SYN-ACK) message back to the client. Finally, the client responds with an acknowledgement (ACK), and then application-layer data transmission begins.

10. In the center frame of the Network Monitor capture window, expand TCP: Control Bits, and then record the values for the following fields in the space below.

TCP: Sequence Number:

TCP: Acknowledgement Number:

The figure below shows you where to locate the Sequence Number and Acknowledgement Number fields.

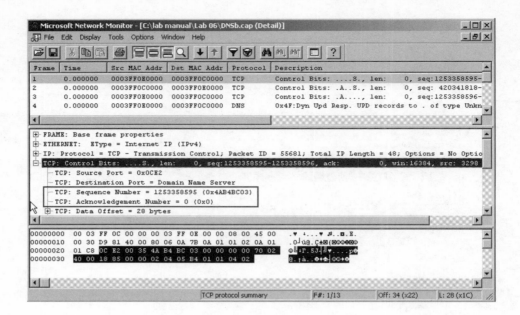

QUESTION   In the captured frame, what does "S" stand for? Hint: Look in the TCP Flags entries for a field where the bit is set to 1.

QUESTION   What is the purpose of the TCP Option Type and the TCP Option Length?

11. Select the next TCP frame immediately below the one you examined in step 10 that displays "Control Bits: .A..S." in the Description column, expand the appropriate objects, and then record the values for the following fields in the space below.

    TCP: Sequence Number:

    TCP: Acknowledgement Number:

    QUESTION   In the captured frame, what does "A" stand for? Hint: Look in the TCP Flags entries for a field where the bit is set to 1.

12. Select the next TCP frame immediately below the one you examined in step 11 that displays "Control Bits: .A...." in the Description column, expand the appropriate objects, and then record the values for the following fields in the space below.

    TCP: Sequence Number:

    TCP: Acknowledgement Number:

13. Click the first instance of a DNS frame immediately below the TCP frame you examined in step 12 and note the TCP: Sequence Number.

14. Select the remaining DNS frames in sequence, and note their TCP: Sequence Number and TCP: Acknowledgement Number.

You should note that a SYN flood attack exploits the mechanism that TCP uses to establish a session between two computers. In a SYN flood attack, the client computer sends a SYN request to the server, and the server subsequently sends a SYN-ACK to the client. However, instead of responding with an ACK, the client sends another SYN request to the server. This causes multiple half-open connections on the server, as the server waits for responses that never arrive to the SYN-ACK messages. If enough resources are consumed by the half-open connections, the result is a denial of service (DoS) attack.

QUESTION   What is the purpose of the TCP frames you examined in steps 10–12?

QUESTION   Collectively, the frames you examined in steps 10–12 are commonly referred to as what?

15. Select the last instance of DNS traffic, as indicated by the entry in the Description column that displays "Std Qry Resp," and expand the DNS elements in the middle pane, as shown below.

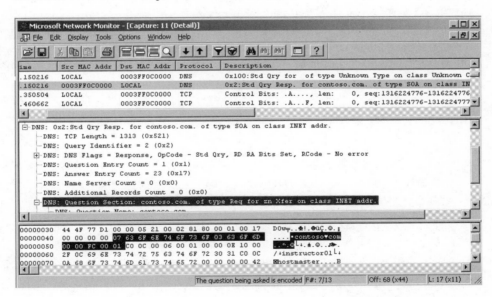

Review the details of the captured frame and then answer the following questions.

QUESTION   What is the DNS Question Type?

QUESTION   What DNS records are listed in the DNS Answer section?

16. Close the capture window.

Leave the command prompt and Network Monitor open for the next exercise.

17. Inform the instructor that you have completed this section of the lab so that the instructor can reset the DNS service to its original configuration.

EXERCISE 6-4: EXAMINING FTP TRAFFIC

Estimated completion time: 25 minutes

In this exercise, you will use Network Monitor to analyze FTP traffic to get a better understanding of the FTP protocol. FTP is a relatively complex protocol in that it makes use of secondary TCP connections to transfer data. First, an FTP client will connect to the FTP port (TCP port 21) on the FTP server. When the client makes a request to either copy data to or from the FTP server, additional TCP ports will be opened to perform the data transfer. How the TCP ports used for data transfer are determined depends on whether the client issues a PORT or a PASV FTP command to the server to initiate the data transfer. If the client issues a PORT command, it will inform the FTP server what ports on the FTP client to send the data to. With the PORT command, the FTP server will always send the data to the client from TCP port 20 to the TCP port the FTP client has opened for the data transfer. In this exercise, you will examine an FTP session where the FTP client uses the PORT command. Lab Challenge 6-1, "Comparing and Contrasting FTP Traffic," provides an opportunity for you to compare and contrast the FTP PORT and PASV commands.

Analyzing FTP Traffic

NOTE   *Only one lab partner at a time should perform steps 1–8 below. When you are finished capturing data, inform your lab partner so that he or she can proceed with step 1. Alternatively, both lab partners can sit at a single computer to capture the network data. Or, as an additional alternative to capturing the data, you can open the C:\Lab Manual\Lab 06\FTP_PORT.cap file from the File menu of Network Monitor. If you choose to use the capture file, proceed to step 9 below.*

1. Switch to Network Monitor, and then select Start from the Capture menu.

2. Click No when prompted to save the capture.

3. Switch to the command prompt, type **ftp computer*yy*** (where *yy* is the two-digit version of your lab partner's student number), and then press ENTER.

4. When prompted for a user name, type **ftp** and then press ENTER.

5. When prompted for a password, type **student.x@contoso.com** (where *x* is your student number), and then press ENTER.

6. At the FTP prompt, type **ls** and then press ENTER.

7. At the FTP prompt, type **quit** and then press ENTER.

8. Switch to Network Monitor, and then select Stop And View from the Capture menu.

9. In the capture summary, locate the first frame that displays "FTP" in the Description column.

10. Immediately above the FTP frame, double-click the first frame that displays "TCP" in the Protocol column and "Control Bits: ....S" in the Description column, as shown below.

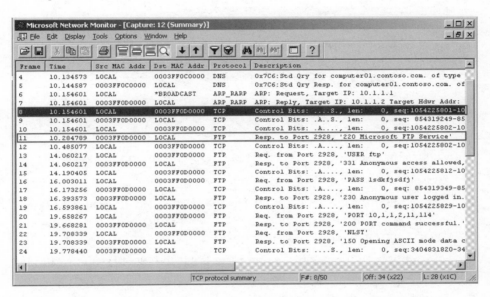

This frame is the beginning of the three-way handshake to establish the TCP connection for FTP.

QUESTION   What are the source and destination ports that are listed in this frame?

11. In the capture summary, double-click the first frame that displays "FTP" in the Protocol column.

QUESTION   What is the relationship between the source and destination ports listed in this frame and the source and destination ports listed in the frame you looked at in step 10?

12. Locate the first FTP frame that displays "PORT *w,x,y,z,a,b*" in the Description column (where *w,x,y,z* represents your lab partner's IP address and *a,b* are two trailing numbers that represent a TCP port number), as shown below, and then record the values for *a* and *b*.

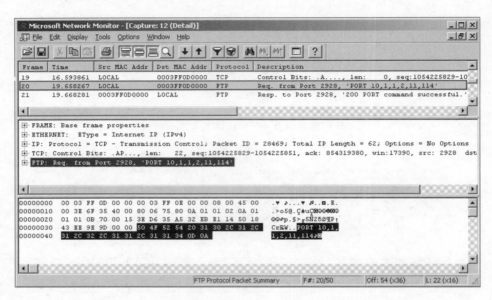

13. Click Start, select Run, type **calc** in the Open box, and then click OK.

14. From the Calculator View menu, select Scientific.

15. Ensure that the Dec option is selected, enter the decimal value for *a* that you recorded in step 12, select the Bin option to convert the number to binary, and then record the 4-bit binary value below.

For example, if the decimal value for *a* is 11, the binary value would be 1011.

Binary value:

16. Select the Dec option, enter the decimal value for *b* that you recorded in step 12, select the Bin option to convert the number to binary, and then record the binary value below.

For example, if the decimal value for *b* is 114, the 8-bit binary value would be 01110010. Note that the calculator might display fewer than 8 bits. If this is the case, make sure you add the appropriate number of zeros to the left-hand side. For example, if you convert 114 to binary, the calculator will display only 7 bits (1110010).

Binary value:

17. Append the 8-bit binary value for *b* to the right of the binary value for *a*, and then record the resulting 12-bit binary number.

For example, if the 4-bit binary value for *a* is 1011 and the 8-bit binary value for *b* is 01110010, the resulting 12-bit binary number is 101101110010.

Binary number:

18. In the calculator, ensure that the Bin option is selected, press C to clear the display, enter the 12-digit binary number that you recorded in step 17, select Dec, and then record the resulting decimal value below.

For example, the 12-bit binary value 101101110010 is equivalent to a decimal value of 2930.

Decimal value:

NOTE   Another way to calculate this value is to use the following formula: $(a*256)+b=$ port number (where *a* and *b* are the decimal values).

19. Switch to Network Monitor, and then select the frame that displays "Data transfer to client" in the Description column, as shown below.

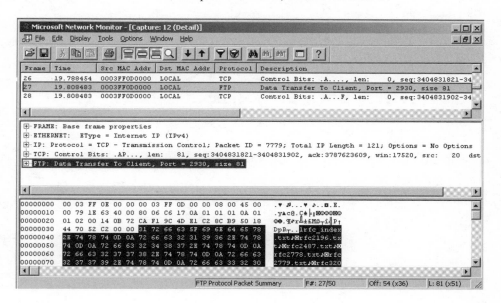

QUESTION   What are the source and destination ports in this frame?

QUESTION   How did the remote FTP service know which port to use to transfer the data to the client computer?

20. Close all open windows and log off.

EXERCISE 6-5: CLASSIFYING ATTACKS BY OSI LAYER

Estimated completion time: 15 minutes

In this exercise, you will work with your lab partner to complete the following paper-based exercise.

In the table below, the column on the left indicates a particular kind of attack. For this exercise, complete the column on the right by indicating the primary layer of the OSI model where the attack occurs and a brief description of the attack. Be prepared to discuss the reasons for your classification. Beginning at the bottom, the seven layers of the OSI model are physical, data-link, network, transport, session, presentation, and application.

Attack	OSI Layer
Eavesdropping (sniffing)	
Ping of death attack	
ARP poisoning	
Malformed URLs	
Port scan attack	
SYN flood attack	
Source route attack	
ICMP flood attack	
Spam attack	
Overlapping fragment attack	

LAB REVIEW QUESTIONS

Estimated completion time: 15 minutes

1. Why must switches be protected in physically secure areas?

2. As a result of a hardware failure, you had to replace a network interface adapter on a computer that is connected to the network through a switch. Now the computer cannot communicate on the network, even though the IP address configuration is correct. What is the problem?

3. Briefly describe the difference between UDP and TCP.

4. Why is it necessary to fragment IP data in some instances?

5. Why is it a security risk to allow a DNS server to accept incoming connections on TCP port 53 from any host?

6. Your organization wants to buy a new firewall to protect servers and applications that are running in your demilitarized zone (DMZ) and are available to users on the Internet. Some of these applications use secondary ports. What features should you look for in a firewall in relation to these applications?

7. You have an FTP client behind a simple Network Address Translation (NAT) device. You can connect to remote FTP servers, but you cannot transfer data from the FTP server. What is the likely reason for this problem?

LAB CHALLENGE 6-1: COMPARING AND CONTRASTING FTP TRAFFIC

Estimated completion time: 25 minutes

Your organization has implemented an internal FTP server for use on the intranet. Your manager has been viewing network captures of FTP traffic on the intranet and has noticed two kinds of FTP traffic: the FTP traffic that occurs when users connect using Ftp.exe from the command prompt, and the FTP traffic that occurs when users connect to the FTP site using Microsoft Internet Explorer.

Your manager has asked you to confirm her findings and to explain the differences in FTP traffic when users connect to the FTP site using Ftp.exe from the command prompt and using Internet Explorer. She also wants you to determine whether one method (Ftp.exe or Internet Explorer) is more secure than the other.

For this lab challenge, you need to use Network Monitor to capture FTP traffic generated when you use Internet Explorer to connect to an FTP site. To connect to an FTP site using Internet Explorer, open Internet Explorer, type **ftp://*hostname*** (where *hostname* is either the host name or fully qualified domain name of the remote FTP server) in the Address box, and press ENTER. When you have finished capturing the traffic, analyze it and be prepared to discuss the differences between FTP data transfers using the PORT and PASV commands.

Your instructor might want to evaluate your analysis of FTP PASV traffic. If this is the case, save the captured FTP traffic in Network Monitor as C:\Lab Manual\ Lab 06\Labwork\ *YourLastName*_6-1_PASV.cap (where *YourLastName* is your last name). Then, open Notepad, and write a couple of brief paragraphs explaining how the PASV command differs from the PORT command and why one method is more secure than the other. Where possible, make references to actual frames recorded in your saved capture. When you have finished your analysis, save the file as C:\Lab Manual\Lab 06\Labwork\ *YourLastName*_6-1_PASV_analysis.txt. Your instructor will provide specific instructions for submitting the files for evaluation.

LAB CHALLENGE 6-2: EXPLORING THREATS TO INSTANT MESSAGING TRAFFIC

Estimated completion time: 25 minutes

Although not officially approved at Contoso Pharmaceuticals, instant messaging (IM) has become very popular. Many employees use IM as an alternative to e-mail to communicate with other employees and with other users outside the company. You need to evaluate the security risks inherent in IM traffic. You have captured some IM traffic between two clients and have saved the capture in a file named C:\Lab Manual\Lab 06\ IM_passwords.cap.

For this lab challenge, you need to open this file in Network Monitor, analyze the traffic, and answer the following questions. Your instructor might want to evaluate your responses to these questions. If this is the case, open C:\Lab Manual\Lab 06\ Labwork\Lab Challenge 6-2 Questions.doc, record your answers in the file, and save the file as C:\Lab Manual\Lab 06\Labwork\ *YourLastName*_LC6-2_answers.doc (where *YourLastName* is your last name). Your instructor will provide specific instructions for submitting the file for evaluation. After you have finished answering the questions, your instructor might want to conduct a classroom discussion on your analysis of IM traffic.

1. What protocol is being used to pass the IM text?

2. What question is being asked in the first frame of the captured traffic?

3. Do any of the frames contain users' e-mail addresses? If so, what frames contain e-mail addresses?

4. Describe how to use the Find feature on the Network Monitor toolbar to search for text strings in the HTTP data.

5. What frame contains the answer to the question posed in the first frame? What is the answer to the question?

6. What question is being asked in frame 14?

7. What is the answer?

8. What particular challenge does this kind of traffic present for the firewall administrator?

9. Assuming the organization has a sufficiently advanced firewall, what HTTP fields can a firewall administrator use to prevent this kind of IM traffic from traversing the firewall?

TROUBLESHOOTING PROBLEMS WITH GROUP POLICY

PART 1: REVIEW

You are a network administrator who has complete administrative authority for a departmental organizational unit (OU) in the contoso.com domain. This OU contains only user and group objects. You are also responsible for the security, monitoring, and maintenance of a Microsoft Windows 2003 Server that is used by your department. The Windows 2003 Server provides file and print services and Software Update Services (SUS) for the department. The server is physically located in your department. However, the Active Directory server object is in another OU, named Computers. This OU is managed by another IT group. You do not have administrative control over the Computers OU.

As a result of a departmental security review that was coordinated with the head office, you have been asked to create a new and more restrictive security template that will be applied to the server object in the Computers OU by another administrator. The template should be based on the default Server Setup Security template (%windir%\security\templates\setup security.inf) that is included with Windows 2003 Server.

To perform this part of the lab, you should open the Setup Security.inf template, save it as Studentx Security.inf (where x is your student number), and make the appropriate changes to this file. You should not modify the Setup Security.inf template file.

CAUTION   *Do not configure your computer with the Studentx Security.inf template file you create.*

The security template must meet the following requirements:

1. The Security log must record the following events:

   ❑ The success and failure of logon attempts

   ❑ The success and failure of attempts to manage accounts

   ❑ The success and failure of directory service access

   ❑ The success of use of privilege

   ❑ The success and failure of object access

   ❑ The success of system processes

2. Only authenticated users and administrators can access the server from the network.

3. Only administrators, backup operators, and power users can log on locally to the server.

4. Guests and anonymous logons cannot access the server from the network.

5. Only administrators can shut down the system locally and remotely.

6. No unsigned drivers can be installed under any circumstances.

7. Domain member secure channel communications must be digitally encrypted and signed.

8. Warning messages must be displayed for users attempting to log on to a system.

9. LAN Manager hash values cannot be stored.

10. The LAN Manager authentication level must be configured to accept NT LAN Manager (NTLM) v2 only.

11. The minimum session security for NTLM SSP-based clients and servers must be configured to the most secure level.

12. The virtual memory pagefile must be cleared upon shutdown.

Once you have completed your template, make sure you save the changes to Studentx Security.inf, copy the file to C:\Lab Manual\Troubleshooting LabA\Labwork, and rename it to *YourLastName*_TSLA.inf (where *YourLastName* is your last name). Your instructor might want you to submit the template file for evaluation. If this is the case, your instructor will provide you with specific instructions for submitting the file.

PART 2: TROUBLESHOOTING SETUP

In this part of the lab, the instructor will give you specific instructions that will introduce a number of problems on your computers related to the application of a group policy.

PART 3: TROUBLESHOOTING APPLICATION OF GROUP POLICY

You have submitted your template to the administrator responsible for the OU where the computer objects are located. The administrator informs you that he has imported the template into a group policy object for the OU and has asked you to verify the correct application of the template through the group policy object. In this part of the lab, you will evaluate the group policy that was applied by the administrator responsible for the OU. You will determine the following:

- The differences between the security template you created in the first part of this lab and the one that is implemented through a group policy in this part of the lab

- Whether the computer can provide the appropriate services for the departmental users

Documentation is crucial. You will be evaluated not only on your ability to correctly identify any problems and recommend solutions, but also on the processes you used to come to your conclusions. Keep a detailed journal of the tools you used and the processes involved in troubleshooting and resolving problems with the group policy. Your journal should also note the reasons for the solutions you propose. You can use the worksheet provided in the Troubleshooting Lab A folder as the basis of this journal, or you can use the worksheet as an alternative to the journal. Your instructor might require that you submit your journal or worksheet for evaluation. If this is the case, your instructor will provide you with instructions for submitting the journal or worksheet.

TIP To help you troubleshoot problems created by the application of a new group policy, you should keep in mind the tools related to group policy that you have learned about in previous labs.

LAB 7
SECURING
COMMUNICATIONS

This lab contains the following exercises and activities:

- Exercise 7-1: Configuring RRAS for Remote Communications

- Exercise 7-2: Comparing PPTP with L2TP/IPSec

- Exercise 7-3: Using RADIUS Authentication

- Exercise 7-4: Examining Wireless Settings for 802.1x Authentication

- Exercise 7-5: Using IPSec

- Lab Review Questions

- Lab Challenge 7-1: Configuring Remote Access Policies

After completing this lab, you will be able to

- Configure a Routing and Remote Access Service (RRAS) server to accept Point-to-Point Tunneling Protocol (PPTP) or L2TP over IPSec (L2TP/IPSec) connection requests.

- Create and configure remote access policies.

- Request and install computer certificates for L2TP/IPSec.

- Configure client virtual private network (VPN) connection objects to connect using PPTP.

- Configure client VPN connections objects to connect using L2TP/IPSec.

- Install and configure Internet Authentication Service (IAS) to provide centralized Remote Authentication Dial-In User Service (RADIUS) authentication for remote access servers.

- Configure remote access policies and wireless client settings for wireless 802.1x authentication.

- Create and configure Internet Protocol Security (IPSec) policies.

Estimated completion time: 170 minutes

SCENARIO

Security is a high priority for Contoso Pharmaceuticals. Management is particularly concerned about the security of network communications, which includes LAN, wireless, and VPN traffic. Management has asked you to take several steps regarding the security of network communications. First, they want you to compare the advantages and disadvantages of PPTP vs. L2TP/IPSec. Secondly, they are concerned by the number of RRAS servers in the network and want you to consolidate authentication and logging on to centralized RADIUS servers. Third, they want you to evaluate the configuration of wireless clients for 802.1x authentications, although no decision has yet been made to purchase 802.1x-capable wireless access points. Finally, they are extremely concerned about the security of highly sensitive and proprietary information on a server used by a small group of researchers. Management wants you to reduce the risk of eavesdropping on network traffic to and from this server.

> **IMPORTANT**   All the exercises in the lab require that you work with a lab partner. Before beginning the lab, please make sure you have a lab partner.

EXERCISE 7-1: CONFIGURING RRAS FOR REMOTE COMMUNICATIONS

Estimated completion time: 35 minutes

In this exercise, you will install and configure RRAS on your computer. You will then create a remote access policy that will grant dial-in permissions to a Microsoft Windows group that you create at the beginning of this exercise. You will also configure a VPN client connection object that will force the establishment of a PPTP connection with the RRAS server.

Verifying Server Permissions for Enabling RRAS on a Member Server

In this section, you will verify that your computer has the appropriate level of permissions to read user account properties in the Active Directory directory service.

> **NOTE**   By default, member servers configured as RRAS servers cannot access the dial-in properties of user accounts and cannot authenticate domain accounts. If the member server provides dial-in access to domain accounts rather than local accounts, it must be able to read Active Directory information.

1. Log on to Contoso as Admin*x* (where *x* is your student number).

2. Click Start, select Administrative Tools, and then click Active Directory Users And Computers.

3. In Active Directory Users And Computers, expand Contoso.com, click Users, and then double-click the RAS And IAS Servers security group.

4. In the RAS And IAS Servers Properties page, select the Members tab.

   You should see Domain Computers listed as a member of this group. By default, the RAS And IAS Server group is empty. The domain computer's group was added to the this group as part of the classroom setup.

5. In the Members box, double-click Domain Computers.

6. On the Domain Computers Properties page, select the Members tab.

7. Verify that your computer is listed in this group.

   QUESTION By virtue of this configuration, all member servers in the classroom are members of the RAS And IAS Servers group. Why would this configuration be inappropriate in a production environment?

8. Click Cancel in the Domain Computers Properties dialog box, and then click Cancel in the RAS And IAS Servers Properties dialog box.

   Leave Active Directory Users And Computers open for the next section.

Creating a User Account and Group to Test VPN Access

In this section, you will create a user account and group that will be used to test RRAS and VPN configurations.

1. In Active Directory Users And Computers, expand the ALS OU, right-click the Employees*xx* OU (where *xx* is the two-digit version of your student number), select New, and then click User.

2. In the New Object – User dialog box, type **Vpn User***x* (where *x* is your student number) in the Full Name box; type **vpnuser***x* in the User Logon Name box; and then click Next.

3. In the Password and Confirm Password boxes, type **P@ssw0rd**, clear the User Must Change Password At Next Logon check box, click Next, and then click Finish.

4. Right-click the Employees*x* OU, select New, and then click Group.

5. In the New Object – Group dialog box, type **Vpn Access Group***x* and then click OK.

6. Double-click the VPN Access Group*x* you created in the previous step, select the Members tab, and then click Add.

7. In the Select Users, Contacts, Computers Or Groups dialog box, in the Enter The Object Names To Select box, type **vpn user*x*** and then click OK.

   If the Multiple Names Found dialog box appears, select your vpn user*x* account from the Matching Names box, and click OK.

8. Click OK to close the VPN Access Group*x* Properties dialog box.

9. Minimize Active Directory Users And Computers, and leave it open.

Configuring RRAS for Inbound VPN Connections

In this section, you will configure RRAS on your computer to accept VPN connections.

1. Click Start, select Administrative Tools, and then select Routing And Remote Access.

2. In the Routing And Remote Access console, right-click Computer*xx* (Local) (where *xx* is the two-digit version of your student number), and then select Configure And Enable Routing And Remote Access, as shown below.

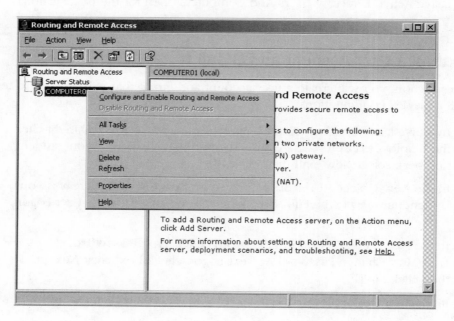

3. In the Welcome To The Routing And Remote Access Server Setup Wizard page, click Next.

4. In the Configuration page, click the Custom Configuration option, and then click Next.

    NOTE   *Normally, an RRAS VPN server has two network adapters: one for the internal network, and another for the external network. On a computer that has two adapters, you can select the Remote Access (Dial-Up Or VPN) option. However, the computers used in this classroom have only one adapter, so you cannot select this option.*

5. In the Custom Configuration screen, select the VPN Access check box, and then click Next.

6. In the Completing The Routing And Remote Access Server Setup Wizard page, click Finish.

7. In the Routing And Remote Access dialog box, click Yes to start the service.

    After a few moments, the service starts, and a green up arrow appears on the computer icon in the Routing And Remote Access console.

    You should note that you are only able to configure and start RRAS by virtue of the classroom setup. Normally, only domain administrators have the authority to configure an RRAS server in a Microsoft Windows 2003 domain.

8. In the Routing And Remote Access console, right-click Computer*xx* (Local), and then click Properties.

9. On the Computer*xx* (local) Properties page, select the Security tab.

10. In the Authentication Provider drop-down list, ensure that Windows Authentication is selected, and then click Authentication Methods.

11. In the Authentication Methods page, ensure that the Microsoft Encrypted Authentication Version 2 (MS-CHAP v2) check box is selected, and then immediately below it, clear the Microsoft Encrypted Authentication (MS-CHAP) check box, as shown below.

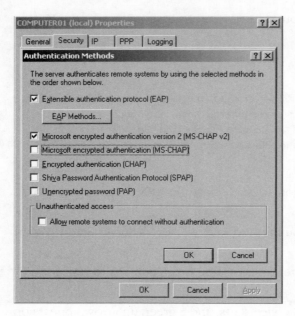

12. Click OK.

13. Select the IP tab.

14. In the IP Address Assignment area, click the Static Address Pool option, and then click Add.

15. In the New Address Range dialog box, enter the following IP addresses:

    ❑ In the Start IP Address box, type **192.168.x.10** (where *x* is your student number).

    ❑ In the End IP Address box, type **192.168.x.20**.

16. Click OK to close the New Address Range dialog box, and then click OK to close the Computer*xx* (Local) Properties dialog box.

17. Minimize the RRAS console.

Configuring a VPN Client Connection Object

In this section, you will configure a VPN connection object in the Network Connections folder to connect to your partner's computer. You will then connect to your partner's computer to test the RRAS server and VPN client settings.

1. Click Start, select Control Panel, select Network Connections, and then select New Connection Wizard.

2. In the Welcome To The New Connection Wizard page, click Next.

3. In the Network Connection Type page, select the Connect To The Network At My Workplace option, and then click Next.

4. In the Network Connection page, click the Virtual Private Connection option, and then click Next.

5. In the Connection Name dialog box, type **computeryy** (where *yy* is the two-digit version of your partner's student number) in the Company Name box, and then click Next.

6. In the VPN Server Selection dialog box, type **computeryy** in the Host Name Or IP Address box, and then click Next.

7. In the Connection Availability dialog box, accept the default selection (My Use Only), and then click Next.

8. In the Completing The New Connection Wizard page, click Finish.

> **NOTE**   *The Connect Computeryy dialog box appears, prompting you to establish a VPN connection with the remote computer. Before testing the connection, you will explore and change some of the default properties of the VPN connection object.*

9. In the Connect Computer*yy* dialog box, click Properties.

10. On the Connection Computer*yy* Properties page, select the Security tab.

> **QUESTION**   *What are the default security settings for the VPN connection object?*

11. In the Security tab, select the Advanced (Custom Settings) option, and then click Settings.

12. In the Advanced Security Settings dialog box, click the Data Encryption drop-down list and examine the choices, but do not change any of the settings.

> **QUESTION**   *What is the most secure setting for data encryption?*

13. In the Logon Security area, clear the check box for Microsoft CHAP (MS-CHAP), ensure that the Microsoft CHAP Version 2 (MS-CHAP v2) check box is selected, and then click OK.

14. Select the Networking tab.

15. Select the Type Of VPN drop-down list, select PPTP VPN, and then click OK.

> **NOTE**   *Given the current configuration of the classroom computers, they should connect to the remote server using PPTP. However, step 15 ensures that the VPN connection that occurs does in fact use PPTP.*

16. In the Connect To Computer01 dialog box, type **vpnuser*x*** (where *x* is your student number) in the User Name box, type **P@ssw0rd** in the Password box, and then click Connect.

The connection attempt fails.

QUESTION   *What error message did you receive?*

NOTE   *Wait until your partner has attempted to connect to your RRAS server before proceeding with the next steps.*

17. In the Error Connecting To Computer*yy* dialog box, click Close.

18. Click Start, select Run, type **eventvwr** in the Open box, and then click OK.

19. In Event Viewer, click the System log, and then double-click the system event that displays 20189 in the Event ID column.

QUESTION   *What configuration changes do you need to make to enable remote access permissions for the user account?*

20. Close Event Viewer.

Examining Remote Access Permissions and Configuring Remote Access Policies

In this section, you will explore settings related to remote access permissions for user accounts.

1. Switch to Active Directory Users And Computers, and then navigate to the Employees*xx* OU (where *xx* is the two-digit version of your student number).

2. Right-click VPNUser*x* (where *x* is your student number), and then click Properties.

3. On the VPNUser*x* Properties page, select the Dial-In tab.

The Dial-In page fails to load.

QUESTION   *Why did the Dial-In page fail to load?*

4. Click OK to clear the Dial-In Page Error dialog box, and then click OK to close the VPNUser*x* Properties dialog box.

5. Minimize Active Directory Users And Computers.

6. Review the following figure that shows the default dial-in settings for user accounts, and then answer the questions that follow.

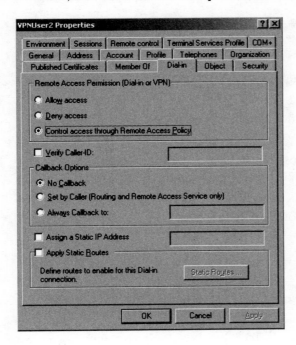

> **QUESTION**   Without changing the default settings of the dial-in user account, how would you grant the user remote access permissions?

> **QUESTION**   The dial-in properties include a setting for assigning a static IP address. Why would it be useful to assign a static IP address to a remote user?

7. Switch to the Routing And Remote Access console.

8. In the Routing And Remote Access tree pane, click Remote Access Policies.

9. In the details pane, double-click the Connections To Microsoft Routing And Remote Access Server policy.

> **QUESTION**   What is the action if the connection request matches the policy conditions?

10. Click Cancel.

11. In the details pane, double-click the Connections To Other Access Servers policy.

    QUESTION   *What are the policy conditions for denying remote access?*

12. Click Cancel.

13. Right-click Remote Access Policies, and then click New Remote Access Policy.

14. In the Welcome To The New Remote Access Policy Wizard page, click Next.

15. In the Policy Configuration Method dialog box, accept the default settings, type **Access By Windows Group** in the Policy Name box, and then click Next.

16. In the Access Method dialog box, ensure that VPN is selected, and then click Next.

17. In the User Or Group Access dialog box, ensure that the Group option is selected, and then click Add.

18. In the Select Groups dialog box, select Locations, select Contoso.com, and then click OK.

19. In the Enter The Object Names To Select box, type **vpn access group***y* (where *y* is your partner's student number), click OK, and then click Next.

    If the Multiple Names Found dialog box appears, select your lab partner's VPN access group*y* account from the Matching Names box, and click OK.

20. In the Authentication Methods dialog box, ensure that Microsoft Encrypted Authentication Version 2 (MS CHAP v2) is selected, and then click Next.

21. In the Policy Encryption Level dialog box, accept the defaults, and then click Next.

22. In the Completing The New Remote Access Policy Wizard dialog box, click Finish.

    NOTE   *Wait until your partner has completed step 22 before proceeding.*

23. Click Start, select Connect To, click Computer*yy* (where *yy* is two-digit version of your partner's student number), type **vpnuser***x* (where *x* is your student number) in the User Name box, type **P@ssw0rd** in the Password box, and then click Connect.

    QUESTION   *What can you infer about how remote access policies are processed?*

24. Click Start, select Run, type **cmd** in the Open box, and then click OK.

25. At the command prompt, type **ipconfig /all** and then press ENTER.

> **QUESTION** How many IP addresses are on your computer? What are they?

26. At the command prompt, type **route print** and then press ENTER.

27. At the bottom of the output of the Route.exe command, identify the IP address that is listed as the default gateway.

> **QUESTION** What IP address is listed as the default gateway?

28. Close the command prompt.

29. In the system tray, right-click the connection icon for the VPN connection, and then click Status.

30. On the Computer*yy* Status page, select the Details tab, and then review the information.

> **QUESTION** What authentication method is being used? What is the encryption strength?

31. Select the General tab, and then click Disconnect.

EXERCISE 7-2: COMPARING PPTP WITH L2TP/IPSEC

Estimated completion time: 30 minutes

In this exercise, you will compare PPTP with Layer 2 Tunneling Protocol (L2TP). You will first capture and save a PPTP session by using Microsoft Network Monitor. Then, you and your partner will reconfigure your computers to establish an L2TP connection and capture and save the L2TP session by using Network Monitor. Finally, you will compare the PPTP and L2TP sessions that you captured.

Capturing PPTP Traffic by Using Network Monitor

In this section, you will capture and save a PPTP session by using Network Monitor.

> **TIP** To make it easier to analyze the PPTP traffic, only one lab partner at a time should perform the following steps.

1. Click Start, select Administrative Tools, and then select Network Monitor.

2. Click Start, select Connect To, click Computer*yy* (where *yy* is the two-digit version of your partner's student number), type **vpnuser*x*** (where *x* is your student number) in the User Name box, and then type **P@ssw0rd** in the Password box.

   IMPORTANT   Do not click Connect until you have started the Network Monitor capture.

3. Switch to Network Monitor, and then select Start from the Capture menu.

4. Switch to the Connect Computer*yy* dialog box on the task bar, and then click Connect.

   IMPORTANT   Wait until the VPN connection is fully established before proceeding with the next step.

5. Switch to Network Monitor, and then select Stop And View from the Capture menu.

6. In the Microsoft Network Monitor capture summary screen, from the File menu, select Save As.

7. In the Save As dialog box, select C:\Lab Manual\Lab 07\Labwork from the Save In drop-down list, type **Lab07_PPTP** in the File Name box, and then click Save.

8. Close the capture window, and minimize Network Monitor.

9. Disconnect the PPTP VPN connection to your partner's server.

Installing Computer Certificates on the L2TP Client and Server

A prerequisite for configuring L2TP is to install digital computer certificates on the L2TP client and server. These certificates are necessary to provide IPSec encryption for the L2TP VPN connection.

1. On the desktop, double-click the Admin Certificates MMC console.

   NOTE   The steps for creating the Admin Certificates MMC console are in Lab 5, Exercise 5-1, "Examining Root Certificates."

2. In the Admin Certificates console, expand Certificates (Local Computer), expand Personal, and then click Certificates.

   NOTE   The certificate store contains a certificate created in a Lab 5, Exercise 5-2, "Using Certificates for Web Server Security."

3. In the details pane on the right-hand side of the MMC console, note the entries in the Intended Purposes and Certificate Template columns.

   QUESTION   What entries are in the Intended Purposes and Certificate Template columns?

   NOTE   The digital certificate used for L2TP/IPSec must include Client Authentication as an intended purpose. Because the current certificate cannot be used for client authentication, you must request a new certificate. However, if there are two certificates in the Personal certificate store for the computer account, it is possible that, during the IPSec negotiation for L2TP, the automatic certificate selection process might select the wrong certificate, and the L2TP connection attempt will fail.

   To ensure that the automatic certificate selection process will choose the correct certificate, you must first remove the current certificate and then request a new certificate that contains both the Server Authentication and Client Authentication purposes.

4. In the details pane, right-click the certificate, select Delete, and then click Yes when prompted to confirm the deletion in the Certificates dialog box.

5. In the tree pane of the console, below the Personal node, right-click Certificates, select All Tasks, and then click Request New Certificate.

   NOTE   If you see a dialog box indicating that you cannot request a certificate because you do not have sufficient permissions or because the certification authority (CA) is not available, the likely reason is that Trusted Root CAs for the local computer is missing the CONTOSO CA certificate. If this is case, follow the steps in the section, "Installing a Root Certificate," of Exercise 5-1, "Examining Root Certificates" of Lab 5. Pay particular attention to step 18 of this section to ensure that you install the root certificate to the local computer certificate store.

6. In the Welcome To The Certificate Request Wizard page, click Next.

7. In the Certificate Types page, click Next.

8. In the Certificate Friendly Name And Description page, type **L2TP/IPSec Certificate** in the Friendly Name box, and then click Next.

9. In the Completing The Certificate Request Wizard page, review the information, click Finish, and then click OK.

   QUESTION   What are the intended purposes of the newly created certificate?

10. Minimize the Admin Certificates console.

Configuring the VPN Client Connection Object for L2TP/IPSec and Adding the IP Security Monitor Snap-In to the MMC Console

In this section, you will reconfigure the VPN connection object you created in the previous exercise to use L2TP rather than PPTP. You will also create a custom MMC console to monitor IPSec sessions.

1. Click Start, select Connect To, right-click the Computer*yy* connection object (where *yy* is the two-digit version of your partner's student number), and then click Properties.

2. In the Computer*yy* Properties dialog box, select the Networking tab, select the Type Of VPN drop-down list, select L2TP IPSec VPN, and then click OK.

3. Click Start, select Run, type **mmc** in the Open dialog box, and then click OK.

4. From the File menu, select Add/Remove Snap-In.

5. In the Add/Remove Snap-In dialog box, click Add.

6. In the Add Standalone Snap-In dialog box, select the IP Security Monitor snap-in, click Add, and then click Close.

7. In the Add/Remove Snap-In dialog box, click OK.

8. From the File menu, select Save As.

9. Select the Save In drop-down list, select Desktop, type **IP Sec Tools** in the File Name box, and then click Save.

10. Minimize the IP Sec Tools console.

Capturing L2TP Traffic by Using Network Monitor

In this section, you will capture L2TP/IPSec traffic by using Network Monitor.

> **TIP** To make it easier to analyze the captured L2TP/IPSec traffic, only one lab partner at a time should perform steps 1–6. In step 1 below, you prepare to establish a VPN connection with your lab partner's computer, but you do not actually connect to the computer until after you have started capturing traffic in Network Monitor.

1. Click Start, select Connect To, select Computer*yy* (where *yy* is the two-digit version of your partner's student number), type **vpnuserx** (where *x*

is your student number) in the User Name box, and then type **P@ssw0rd** in the Password box.

IMPORTANT   *Do not click Connect until you have started the Network Monitor capture.*

2. Switch to Network Monitor, and then select Start from the Capture menu.

3. Switch to the Connect Computer*yy* dialog box on the task bar, and then click Connect.

   IMPORTANT   *Wait until the VPN connection is fully established before proceeding with the next step.*

4. Switch to Network Monitor, and then select Stop And View from the Capture menu.

5. In the Microsoft Network Monitor capture summary screen, select Save As from the File menu.

6. In the Save As dialog box, select C:\Lab Manual\Lab 07\Labwork from the Save In drop-down list, type **Lab07_L2TP** in the File Name box, and then click Save.

7. Minimize Network Monitor.

8. Disconnect the L2TP VPN connection to your partner's server.

Examining L2TP/IPSec Security Associations by Using IP Security Monitor

In this section, you will reestablish an L2TP/IPSec VPN connection with your lab partner's computer and then examine IPSec information by using the IP Security Monitor MMC snap-in.

1. Click Start, select Connect To, select Computer*yy* (where *yy* is the two-digit version of your partner's student number), type **vpnuser*x*** (where *x* is your student number) in the User Name box, type **P@ssw0rd** in the Password box, and then click Connect.

2. When the VPN connection has been established, switch to the IPSec Tools MMC console you created earlier.

3. In the tree pane, expand IP Security Monitor, expand Computer*xx* (where *xx* is the two-digit version of your student number), expand Main Mode, and then click Security Associations, as shown below.

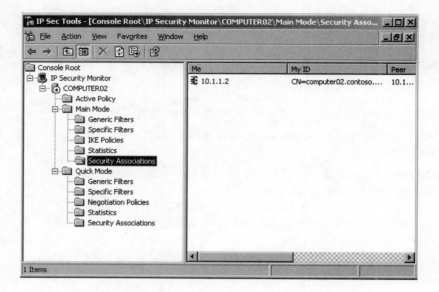

QUESTION   What is listed in the Authentication column in the details pane?

QUESTION   What security method is used for encryption?

QUESTION   What security method is used for integrity?

4. In the tree pane, expand Quick Mode, and click Security Associations.

QUESTION   What protocol and ports are used?

QUESTION   What security method is listed for Encapsulating Security Payload (ESP) confidentiality?

QUESTION   What security method is used for ESP integrity?

5. Disconnect the L2TP VPN connection to your partner's server.

Comparing PPTP and L2TP/IPSec Traffic

In this section, you will compare the PPTP and L2TP/IPSec traffic you captured and saved earlier. However, if you prefer, you can perform this section of the lab using the sample Network Monitor capture files provided for you in the Lab Manual\ Lab 07 folder, as an alternative to using the files you created. The files are named Pptp.cap and L2tp.cap.

You will first examine PPTP traffic and then examine L2TP/IPSec traffic.

1. Switch to Network Monitor.

2. From the File menu, select Open, select the Lab07_pptp.cap file you created earlier, and then click Open.

3. In the Microsoft Network Monitor capture summary, locate and double-click the first row (Ethernet frame) that displays PPTP in the Protocol column.

   QUESTION   What transport protocol and what destination port number are used for PPTP?

4. Locate and select the first frame that displays LCP in the Protocol column, and then highlight IP Protocol in the middle pane.

   QUESTION   What IP protocol type is used in this frame? Hint: Look at the description immediately to the right of "IP: Protocol ="

5. Locate and click the first frame that displays PPPCHAP in the Protocol column; then in the middle pane, expand the PPPCHAP row; and then click the PPPCHAP: Data row.

   In the bottom pane, note the information that is highlighted.

   QUESTION   What information is sent in clear text in this frame?

6. Locate and examine other instances of frames that display PPPCHAP in the Protocol column.

   QUESTION   What other information is sent in clear text in these frames?

7. Locate and examine the frames that display PPP in the Protocol column and MPPE/MMPC in the Description column.

   QUESTION   What do these frames represent?

8. From the Microsoft Network Monitor File menu, select Open.

9. In the Open dialog box, click Lab06_L2TP.cap, and then click Open.

10. In the Microsoft Network Monitor capture summary, locate and double-click the first frame that displays ISAKMP in the Protocol column.

    QUESTION   What transport protocol and destination and source port number are used for ISAKMP?

11. In the same frame that you selected in step 10 above, in the middle pane, expand the ISAKMP row, and scroll down to the bottom of the middle pane.

    QUESTION   What are the ISAKMP payload types listed in this frame?

12. Examine other frames that display ISAKMP in the Protocol column.

    QUESTION   Name at least four other ISAKMP payload types.

13. Locate and click the first frame that displays ESP in the Protocol column.

    QUESTION   What does ESP stand for, as indicated in the IP datagram?

    QUESTION   What is contained within the ESP payload?

14. Scan the remaining frames in the capture of L2TP data.

    QUESTION   Do you see any frames indicating the use of the Challenge Handshake Authentication Protocol (CHAP) or the Point-to-Point Protocol (PPP)?

15. Close the capture summaries, and then minimize Network Monitor.

EXERCISE 7-3: USING RADIUS AUTHENTICATION

Estimated completion time: 20 minutes

In this exercise, you will configure Internet Authentication Service (IAS) on your computer to provide centralized authentication and accounting via RADIUS. After installing IAS and configuring the RADIUS service, you will configure your RRAS server as a RADIUS client to your lab partner's RADIUS server. You will test the configuration by establishing a VPN connection with your partner's server, which will subsequently forward the authentication request back to your computer.

Installing Internet Authentication Service (IAS)

In this section, you will install IAS. You will need your 180-day evaluation *Microsoft Windows Server 2003 Enterprise Edition* CD, or the instructor will need to make the source files available on the classroom network.

1. Click Start, select Control Panel, and then click Add Or Remove Programs.

2. In the Add Or Remove Programs dialog box, click Add/Remove Windows Components.

3. In the Windows Components dialog box, select Networking Services to highlight it, and then click Details.

4. In the Networking Services dialog box, select the check box for Internet Authentication Services, click OK, and then click Next.

5. After IAS has finished installing, click Finish in the Completing The Windows Components Wizard dialog box.

6. Close Add Or Remove Programs.

Configuring the RADIUS Server

1. Click Start, select Administrative Tools, and then click Internet Authentication Service.

2. Right-click Internet Authentication Service (Local), and then click Properties, as shown below.

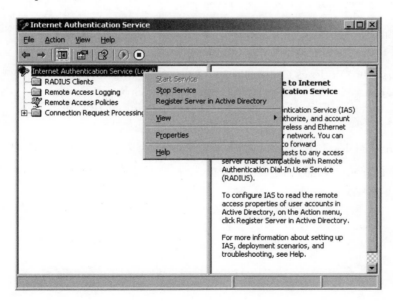

3. On the Internet Authentication Service (Local) Properties page, note the settings on the General tab, and then select the Ports tab.

QUESTION   What ports are used for RADIUS authentication and accounting?

4. Click OK.

5. Select Remote Access Logging, right-click Local File in the details pane, and then click Properties.

6. In the Local File Properties dialog box, review the selections, and then select all the check boxes in the Settings tab.

For more information on these settings, consult the article, "Logging User and Authentication Requests," in Windows Help.

7. Select the Log File tab, select the Database-Compatible option, select the Daily option, and then click OK.

8. Right-click RADIUS Clients, and then select New RADIUS Client.

9. In the New RADIUS Client dialog box, type **Computeryy** (where *yy* is the two-digit version of your lab partner's student number) in the Friendly Name box and in the Client Address (IP Or DNS) box, and then click Next.

10. In the Additional Information dialog box, ensure that RADIUS Standard is selected in the Client-Vendor drop-down list, type **R@d1u$** in the Shared Secret and Confirm Shared Secret boxes, select the Request Must Contain Message Authenticator Attribute option, and then click Finish.

NOTE   In a production environment, the shared secret password should be long and complex. An ideal password for RADIUS is 22 or more characters long and is created by a random password generation program.

11. Click Remote Access Policies, right-click Access By Windows Group, and then select Properties.

12. In the Access By Windows Group Properties dialog box, select the entry Windows-Group Matches "CONTOSO\VPN Access Group*y*" (where *y* is your lab partner's student number) in the Policy Conditions box, and then click Edit.

13. In the Groups dialog box, click Add.

14. In the Select Groups dialog box, select Locations, select Contoso.com, and then click OK.

15. In the Enter Object Names To Select box, type **VPN Access Groupx** (where *x* is your student number), and then click OK.

The reason for this step is that, although you will establish a VPN connection with your partner's server, your server will provide the authorization through the RADIUS policy. Note that members of either of the VPN access groups will be allowed to establish a connection as a result of this policy.

16. In the Access By Windows Group Properties dialog box, click OK.

17. Minimize the Internet Authentication Service console.

Configuring a RADIUS Client

In this section, you will configure your RRAS server to be a RADIUS client to your lab partner's RADIUS server.

> **IMPORTANT** Wait until your partner has completed the previous section before proceeding.

1. Switch to the Routing And Remote Access console.

2. Right-click Computer*xx* (Local) (where *xx* is the two-digit version of your student number), and then click Properties.

3. In the Computer*xx* (Local) Properties dialog box, select the Security tab.

4. Select the Authentication Provider drop-down list, select RADIUS Authentication, and then click Configure.

5. In the RADIUS Authentication dialog box, click Add.

6. In the Add RADIUS Server dialog box, type **Computeryy** (where *yy* is the two-digit version of your lab partner's student number) in the Server Name box.

7. Select Change, type **R@d1u$** in the New Secret and Confirm New Secret boxes, and then click OK.

8. Select the Always Use Message Authenticator check box, click OK, and then click OK to close the RADIUS Authentication dialog box.

9. Select the Accounting Provider drop-down list, select RADIUS Accounting, and then click Configure.

10. In the RADIUS Accounting dialog box, click Add.

11. In the Add RADIUS Server dialog box, type **Computeryy** in the Server Name box.

12. Select Change, type **R@d1u$** in the New Secret and Confirm New Secret boxes, click OK to close the Change Secret dialog box, click OK to close the Add RADIUS Server dialog box, and then click OK to close the RADIUS Accounting dialog box.

13. Click OK to close the Computer.*xx* (Local) Properties dialog box, click OK when prompted to restart RRAS to configure a new authentication provider, and then click OK when prompted to restart RRAS to configure a new accounting provider.

14. In the tree pane of the RRAS console, note that the Remote Access Policies and Remote Access Logging nodes are removed upon restart of the RRAS service.

    QUESTION   Why are the Remote Access Policies and Remote Access Logging nodes removed?

15. Minimize the Routing And Remote Access console.

Testing RADIUS Authentication

In this section, you will establish a VPN connection to your lab partner's server and then view the IAS log files to verify that authentication is working properly.

IMPORTANT   Wait until your lab partner has completed the previous section before proceeding.

1. Click Start, select Connect To, click Computer.*yy* (where *yy* is the two-digit version of your partner's student number), type **vpnuser.*x*** (where *x* is your student number) in the User Name box, type **P@ssw0rd** in the Password box, and then click Connect.

2. After you have established the VPN connection, select Start, select Run, type **%windir%\system32\logfiles** in the Open box, and then click OK.

3. Double-click the file named In*yymmdd*.log (where *yy* is the year, *mm* is the month, and *dd* is the day) to open it in Notepad.

4. Examine the entries in the log file and then close Notepad.

   If you do not see the log file in the directory, open the C:\Lab Manual\ Lab 07\IN040606.log sample file, and then proceed to step 4.

   QUESTION   In general, what information is recorded in the log file?

   TIP   IAS log files can be difficult to read and interpret. To facilitate reading of these log files, Windows 2003 ships with a tool called Iasparse.exe, which can be found in the \Support\Tools folder of the Microsoft Windows Server 2003 Enterprise Edition CD,

5. Disconnect the VPN session with your partner's computer.

EXERCISE 7-4: EXAMINING WIRELESS SETTINGS FOR 802.1X AUTHENTICATION

Estimated completion time: 20 minutes

Your branch office needs to implement a wireless network to enhance productivity. You have been asked to make detailed recommendations regarding the configuration of a wireless network to ensure a high degree of security. As preparation for writing up your recommendations, and even though you have yet to decide on the wireless access point (WAP) to purchase, you decide to explore in a test lab the configuration changes you would have to make to implement a wireless network that uses 802.1x authentication.

Configuring RADIUS for 802.1x Authentication

In this section, you will configure a remote access policy for 802.1x authentication.

1. Switch to the Internet Authentication Service console.

2. Right-click Radius Clients, and then click New Radius Client.

3. In the New Radius Client dialog box, type **802.1x - capable wireless access point** in the Friendly Name box.

4. In the Client address (IP or DNS) box, type **172.16.0.1** and then click Next.

NOTE The IP address that you enter is the one used by the WAP. That is, the WAP is a RADIUS client. The WAP must be capable of supporting 802.1x authentication. WAPs that are sold in the general consumer retail market generally cannot support 802.1x authentication.

5. In the Additional Information dialog box, ensure that RADIUS Standard is selected in the Client-Vendor drop-down list, type **R@d1u$** in the Shared Secret and Confirm Shared Secret boxes, select the Request Must Contain Message Authenticator Attribute check box, and then click Finish.

6. Right-click Remote Access Policies, click New Remote Access Policy, and then click Next in the Welcome To The Remote Access Policy Wizard page.

NOTE You can also set up a wireless policy, using the wizard, to create a policy for a typical scenario.

7. In the Policy Configuration Method dialog box, click the Set Up A Custom Policy option, type **802.1x Wireless Policy** in the Policy Name box, and then click Next.

8. In the Policy Conditions dialog box, click Add.

9. In the Select Attribute dialog box, select NAS-Port-Type, and then click Add.

10. In the NAS-Port-Type dialog box, select Wireless – IEEE 802.11 in the Available Types box, and then click Add to move it to the Selected Types box.

11. Repeat step 10 for Wireless – Other, and then click OK.

> **NOTE**   This sample remote access policy does not control access by Windows groups. In a production environment, it is better to specify individual user accounts or groups that are allowed access.

12. In the Policy Conditions dialog box, click Next.

13. In the Permissions dialog box, select the Grant Remote Access Permission option, and then click Next.

14. In the Profile dialog box, click Edit profile.

15. On the Edit Dial-In Profile page, select the Authentication tab.

16. Clear the check boxes for Microsoft Encrypted Authentication version 2 (MS-CHAP v2) and Microsoft Encrypted Authentication (MS-CHAP), and then click EAP Methods.

17. In the Select EAP Providers dialog box, click Add.

18. In the Add EAP dialog box, select Smart Card Or Other Certificate, click OK, and then click OK again to close the Select EAP Providers dialog box.

> **NOTE**   You could also select Protected Extensible Authentication Protocol (PEAP). This method is somewhat easier to implement because it is password based and does not require a public key infrastructure (PKI) and the use of both user and computer digital certificates on the wireless client workstation, as does Extensible Authentication Protocol-Transport Layer Security (EAP-TLS) (the method used when you select Smart Card Or Other Certificate). However, because authentication with EAP-TLS is certificate based rather than password based, EAP-TLS provides a stronger authentication method.

19. In the Edit Dial-in Profile dialog box, select the Advanced tab, and in the Attributes box, select Framed Protocol, select Remove, click OK, and then click No to close the Dial-In Setting dialog box that prompts you to consult the help files regarding multiple authentication methods.

20. In the Profile dialog box, click Next.

21. On the Completing The New Remote Access Policy Wizard page, click Finish.

> **QUESTION**   If the classroom had an 802.1x-capable WAP, what would you do next to complete the RADIUS configuration?

22. Minimize the Internet Authentication Service, and leave it open for Lab
Challenge 7-1, "Configuring Remote Access Policies."

Examining Wireless Group Policy Settings

In this section, you will examine wireless group policy settings that can be applied
to client computers with the appropriate wireless network adapters installed.

> **NOTE**   Normally, you would implement the wireless group policy before deploying
> the WAP and configuring the RADIUS server. The reason for this is to ensure that
> the wireless client computers are configured with a standard policy once you
> implement the wireless network.

1. Switch to Active Directory Users And Computers.

2. In the tree pane, navigate to and right-click the Employees*xx* OU
(where *xx* is the two-digit version of your student number), and then
click Properties.

3. On the Employees*x* Properties page, select the Group Policy tab, select
New, type **WirelessGroupPolicy***x* (where *x* is your student number) for
the name of the group policy, and then click Edit.

4. In the Group Policy Object Editor, under Computer Configuration,
expand Windows Settings, and then expand Security Settings.

5. Right-click Wireless Network (IEEE 802.11) Policies, and then click Create
Wireless Network Policy, as shown below.

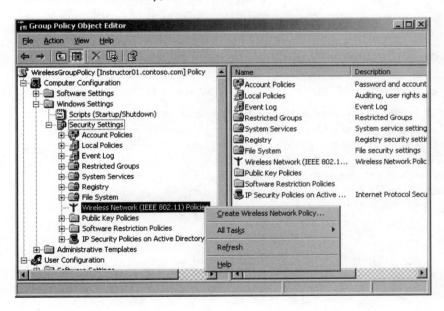

6. In the Welcome To The Wireless Network Policy Wizard dialog box, click Next.

7. In the Wireless Network Policy Name dialog box, type **802.1xWireless Policy** in the Name box, and then click Next.

8. In the Completing The Wireless Network Policy Wizard dialog box, ensure that the Edit Properties check box is selected, and then click Finish.

9. In the 802.1x Wireless Policy Properties dialog box, select the Networks To Access drop-down list, select Access Point (Infrastructure) Networks Only, and then select the Preferred Networks tab.

10. In the Preferred Networks tab, click Add.

11. In the New Preferred Settings dialog box, type **WAP-01** in the Network Name (SSID) box, ensure that the Data Encryption (WEP Enabled) and The Key Is Provided Automatically check boxes are selected, and then select the IEEE 802.1x tab.

    NOTE The service set identifier (SSID) is analogous to a network name. Generally, a WAP should be configured to not broadcast this name. When a WAP is configured not to broadcast the SSID, the wireless-enabled computers must be configured in advance with the SSID.

    The 802.1x protocol provides a delivery mechanism for WEP keys, so the check box that indicates the key is provided automatically must be selected.

    QUESTION What does WEP stand for?

12. In the 802.1x tab, ensure that the Enable Network Access Control Using IEEE 802.1x check box is selected and that Smart Card Or Other Certificate appears in the EAP Type drop-down list, and then click Settings.

13. In the Smart Card Or Other Certificate Properties dialog box, ensure that the settings for Use A Certificate On This Computer, Use Simple Certificate Selection (Recommended), and Validate Server Certificate are selected.

    NOTE Using these settings, Windows automatically tries to select the appropriate certificate for authentication and will verify that the certificate presented to the client is within a valid date range. Other settings on this dialog box enhance security somewhat, but at the cost of usability. For example, if you specify the name of a server in Connect To These Servers box, users will be prompted to verify the name when connecting to the wireless network.

14. In the Trusted Root Certificate Authorities frame, select Contoso CA, as shown below.

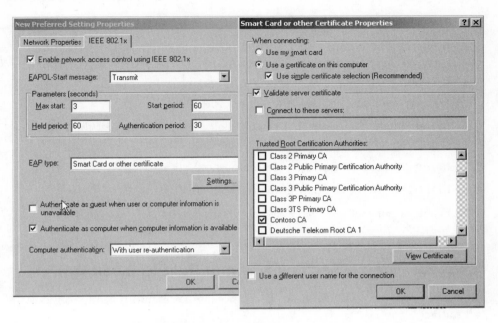

15. Click OK three times to close the 802.1x Wireless Policy Property dialog box.

16. Close the Group Policy Object Editor, and then close the Employees*x* Properties dialog box.

17. Close Active Directory Users And Computers.

EXERCISE 7-5: USING IPSEC

Estimated completion time: 30 minutes

Your branch office is responsible for the research and development of a new, cutting-edge anticancer drug. A number of other pharmaceutical companies are pursuing similar avenues of research, and the stakes are very high for the company that can be the first to patent this drug. Although you have taken special measures to harden the server where the research data is stored, management is concerned about industrial espionage. Specifically, they are concerned that the physical wiring plan might not provide sufficient security to prevent eavesdropping of network traffic. Management has asked you to ensure that only specific, designated workstations are allowed to communicate with this computer and that traffic between these workstations and the server is encrypted.

Adding the IP Security Policy Management Snap-In Console

1. Switch to the IPSec Tools console you created earlier.

2. From the File menu, select Add/Remove Snap-In, and then in the Add/Remove Snap-In dialog box, select Add.

3. In the Add Standalone Snap-In dialog box, select the IP Security Policy Management snap-in, and then click Add.

4. In the Select Computer Or Domain dialog box, ensure that the Local Computer option is selected, and then click Finish.

5. In the Add Standalone Snap-In dialog box, click Close.

6. In the Add/Remove Snap-in dialog box, click OK.

7. From the File menu, select Save.

Configuring an IPSec Policy with a Rule to Block Traffic

In this section, you will create an IPSec policy that includes a rule to block all traffic.

1. Right-click IP Security Policies On The Local Computer, and then select Create IP Security Policy.

   If you do not see the Create An IP Security Policy menu option, click IP Security Policies, and then repeat step 1.

2. In the Welcome To The IP Security Policy Wizard page, click Next.

3. In the IP Security Policy Name dialog box, type **High Security Research Computer** in the Name box, type **Allows only specific workstations to communicate using IPSec** in the Description box, and then click Next.

4. In the Requests For Secure Communication dialog box, clear the Activate The Default Response Rule check box, and then click Next.

5. In the Completing The IP Security Policy Wizard page, ensure that the check box for Edit Properties is selected, and then click Finish.

6. In the High Security Research Computer Properties dialog box, verify that the Use Add Wizard check box is selected, as shown below, and then click Add.

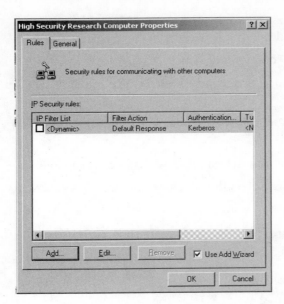

7. In the Welcome To the Create IP Security Rule Wizard dialog box, click Next.

8. In the Tunnel Endpoint dialog box, ensure that the This Rule Does Not Specify A Tunnel option is selected, and then click Next.

9. In the Network Type dialog box, ensure that the All Network Connections option is selected, and then click Next.

10. In the IP Filter List dialog box, select the All IP Traffic option, as shown below, and then click Next.

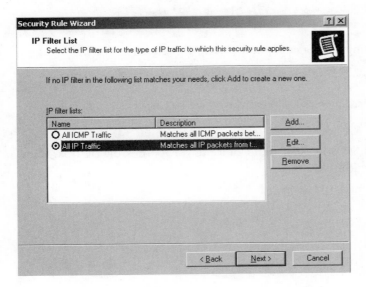

11. In the Filter Action dialog box, ensure that the Use Add Wizard check box is selected, and then click Add.

12. In the Welcome To The IP Security Filter Action Wizard page, click Next.

13. In the Filter Action Name dialog box, type **Block Traffic** in the Name box, and then click Next.

14. In the Filter Action General Options dialog box, select the Block option, and then click Next.

15. In the Completing The IP Security Action Filter Wizard page, click Finish.

16. In the Filter Action dialog box, select the Block Traffic option, as shown below, and then click Next.

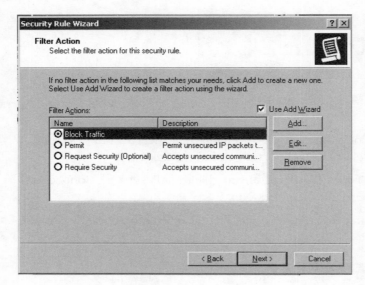

17. In the Completing The Security Rule Wizard page, click Finish.

18. In the New Rule Properties dialog box, click OK.

QUESTION   If this IPSec policy were to be activated (assigned) at this point, could this computer communicate with other computers?

Leave the High Security Research Computer Properties dialog box open for the next section.

Configuring an IPSec Rule to Require Security when Communicating with Specific Computers

In this section, you will add a rule to the IPSec policy that will allow specific workstations to communicate with the high security research computer.

1. In the High Security Research Computer Properties dialog box, ensure that the Use Add Wizard check box is selected, and then click Add.

2. In the Welcome To The Create IP Security Rule Wizard page, click Next.

3. In the Tunnel Endpoint dialog box, ensure that the This Rule Does Not Specify A Tunnel option is selected, and then click Next.

4. In the Network Type dialog box, ensure that the All Network Connections option is selected, and then click Next.

5. In the IP Filter List dialog box, click Add.

6. In the second IP Filter List dialog box, ensure that the Use Add Wizard check box is selected, type **Research Workstations** in the Name box, as shown below, and then click Add.

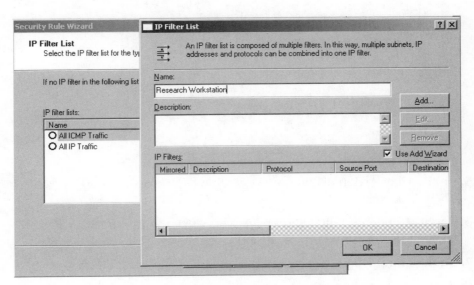

7. In the Welcome To The IP Filter Wizard page, click Next.

8. In the IP Filter Description And Mirrored Property dialog box, verify that the check box for Mirrored is selected, and then click Next.

9. In the IP Traffic Source page, ensure that My IP Address is displayed in the Source Address drop-down list, and then click Next.

10. In the IP Traffic Destination dialog box, select the Destination Address drop-down list, select A Specific IP Address, type *<**IP-address-of-your-lab-partner's-computer**>* in the IP Address box, and then click Next.

11. In the IP Protocol Type dialog box, ensure that Any is selected, and then click Next.

12. In the Completing The IP Filter Wizard page, click Finish.

13. In the IP Filter List dialog box, click OK.

14. In the IP Filter List dialog box, select the Research Workstations option, as shown below, and then click Next.

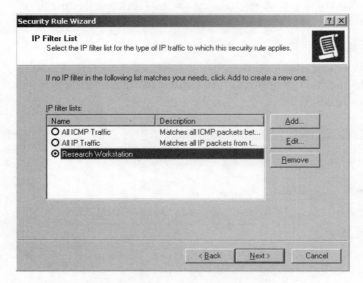

15. In the Filter Action dialog box, select the Require Security option, and then click Next.

16. In the Authentication Method page, verify that the Active Directory Default (Kerberos V5 Protocol) option is selected, and then click Next.

17. In the Completing The Security Rule Wizard page, click Finish.

   Leave the High Security Research Computer Properties dialog box open for the next section.

Permitting Unsecured Traffic when Communicating with Specific Computers

If you were to assign the IPSec policy you just created, all traffic would be blocked except for IPSec-negotiated traffic between your computer and your lab partner's computer. Because you are using Kerberos as the authentication method for the IPSec negotiation and because you need to contact the domain controller to perform Kerberos authentication, it is desirable to create a rule in the IPSec policy that permits traffic between your computer and the domain controller. In this section, you will create a rule that permits unsecured traffic between your computer and the domain controller. However, you will create the rule for the policy without using the IPSec wizards.

1. In the High Security Research Computer Properties dialog box that you left open from the previous section, clear the Use Add Wizard check box, and then click Add.

2. In the New Rule Properties dialog box, click Add.

3. In the IP Filter List dialog box, type Domain Controllers in the Name box, clear the Use Add Wizard check box, and click Add.

4. In the IP Filter Properties dialog box, on the Address tab, ensure that the Mirrored check box is selected, select the Destination Address drop-down list, and select A Specific IP Address.

5. In the Destination Address area, type.*x.y.z.200*, and then click OK.

   The IP address of the domain controller is $x.y.z.200$ (where x, y, and z are the first three numbers of your IP address).

6. In the IP Filter List dialog box, click OK.

7. In the New Rule Properties dialog box, on the IP Filter List tab, select the Domain Controllers option, and then select the Filter Action tab.

8. On the Filter Action tab, select the Permit option, and then click Close.

   The High Security Research Computer Properties dialog box now contains four IP Security rules, three of which are selected and active in the IPSec policy, as shown below. One of the selected rules blocks all traffic; the other rule allows traffic from a specific remote computer that can negotiate IPSec security. When a remote computer attempts to communicate with the computer where this IPSec policy is assigned, IPSec will look for a match to any of the rules defined within the policy. If it finds a match, it will perform the action specified in the rule. In this case, the computer will block traffic from all computers, except for the domain controller and your lab partner's computer. When communicating with the domain controller, your computer's IPSec policy will allow unsecured communication; when communicating with your lab partner's computer, your computer's IPSec policy will require secure communication.

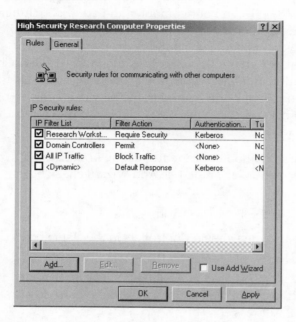

9. In the High Security Research Computer Properties dialog box, click OK.

Assigning and Testing IPSec Policies

In this section, one lab partner will assign the IPSec policy you created in the previous section to activate it. The other lab partner will assign the Client (Respond Only) IPSec policy. You will then verify that your two computers can communicate securely with each other.

IMPORTANT   Before beginning this section, you and your partner need to decide which computer will be assigned the custom High Security Research Computer IPSec policy and which computer will be assigned the default Client (Respond Only) IPSec policy. Perform step 1 on the computer that will be assigned the High Security Research Computer IPSec policy.

1. In the IP Sec Tools console, select IP Security Policies On Local Computer, right-click High Security Research Computer, and then click Assign.

IMPORTANT Perform step 2 on the computer that will be assigned the default Client (Respond Only) IPSec policy.

2. In the IP Sec Tools console, select IP Security Policies On Local Computer, right-click Client (Respond Only), and then click Assign.

IMPORTANT Perform the following steps on both computers.

3. Click Start, select Run, type **cmd** in the Open box, and then click OK.

4. At the command prompt, type **ping <*IP-address-of-partner's-computer*> -n 30**, and then press ENTER.

   It might take a few moments for you to establish secure communication with your lab partner's computer.

5. Switch to the IPSec Tools console, expand IP Security Monitor, expand Computer*xx* (where *xx* is the two-digit version of your student number), expand Main Mode, and then click Security Associations.

   QUESTION Do you see a security association with your partner's computer?

   If you cannot ping your lab partner's computer, you might need to restart the IPSec services. To stop and start the IPSec service on your computer, do the following:

   a. Click Start, select Run, type **cmd** in the Open box, and click OK.

   b. At the command prompt, type **net stop policyagent**, and press ENTER.

   c. At the command prompt, type **net start policyagent**, and press ENTER.

   d. Close the command prompt.

   If you are still cannot ping your lab partner's computer, review your IPSec settings.

   In step 6, you will ping another student computer in the classroom.

6. Switch to the command prompt, type **ping computer*zz* -n 10** (where *zz* is the number of another student computer in the classroom), and then press ENTER.

   QUESTION Was the ping successful? Why or why not?

IMPORTANT   You must unassign the IPSec policy to restore normal communication. Perform the next step on both computers.

7. In the IPSec Tools console, select IP Security Policies On Local Computer, right-click *<assigned IPSec policy on your computer>*, and then click Un-Assign.

8. If time permits, reverse roles and perform steps 1–7 again.

9. Close all open windows and log off.

LAB REVIEW QUESTIONS

Estimated completion time: 15 minutes

1. Which protocol, PPTP or L2TP, provides greater security? Explain your answer.

2. Which protocol, PPTP or L2TP, is more efficient for transmitting data? Provide reasons for your answer.

3. Why is it important to use strong passwords if you are using PPTP?

4. What are some of the advantages of using RADIUS authentication for VPN or dial-in access?

5. In the 802.1x configuration, you specify that the "keys are provided automatically." What "keys" are provided automatically, and what are some of the advantages of providing these keys automatically?

6. Can an IPSec policy contain multiple rules?

7. What are the three possible IPSec filter actions?

8. How many IPSec filter lists can be applied to an IPSec rule?

9. How can you protect the traffic between a dial-in server and a RADIUS server?

LAB CHALLENGE 7-1: CONFIGURING REMOTE ACCESS POLICIES

Estimated completion time: 20 minutes

You are an administrator responsible for configuring remote access polices for employees of your company.

A number of employees are sales personnel who often work out of the office. When the sales personnel come into the office, they sit at any available cubicle in a designated area. Because this area does not have enough network ports for the maximum number of sales personnel who can be there at any one given time, your company implemented a wireless network that uses 802.1x authentication. All sales personnel have laptop computers that they bring to the office and take to sales meetings outside the office.

Your company wireless access policy stipulates that only members of the SalesStaff group can access the wireless network. Access to the wireless network is allowed only between the hours of 7:00 A.M. and 6:00 P.M. on weekdays. A group called SalesManagers is a member of the SalesStaff group. Members of the SalesManager group have assigned offices and should not have access to the wireless network.

Your company remote access policy stipulates that PPTP VPN access is allowed at all times, but only to members of the SalesStaff group. The VPN connection must use the strongest authentication method possible and no less than 128-bit encryption. If the VPN connection is idle for more than five minutes, it must be disconnected by the server. A group named SalesTrainees is a member of the SalesStaff group. Members of this group should not have remote access permissions, either to establish a VPN connection or to use the wireless network.

For this lab challenge, in the Employees*x* OU (where x is your student number), create the appropriate groups and configure remote access policies on the RADIUS server that you configured in Exercises 7-3, "Using RADIUS Authentication," and 7-4, "Examining Wireless Settings for 802.1x Authentication." The remote access policies should implement the requirements described in this scenario.

TIP *You can use the remote access policies you created in earlier exercises.*

LAB 8
SECURING NETWORK APPLICATIONS

This lab contains the following exercises and activities:

- Exercise 8-1: Examining Web Browser Security Settings
- Exercise 8-2: Comparing Basic with Integrated Authentication
- Exercise 8-3: Securing Web Servers
- Exercise 8-4: Securing DNS
- Lab Review Questions
- Lab Challenge 8-1: Designing and Implementing a Secure DNS Infrastructure

After completing this lab, you will be able to

- Configure Web browser security settings.
- Configure basic and integrated authentication.
- Use Microsoft Network Monitor to analyze basic and integrated authentication.
- Enhance Web server security by identifying and disabling unnecessary services and components.
- Create an application pool to enhance Web site security.
- Configure primary and secondary forward lookup zones.
- Secure Domain Name System (DNS) zone transfer traffic.

Estimated completion time: 135 minutes

SCENARIO

You are a network administrator for Contoso Pharmaceuticals. Your manager has asked you to perform a security review of network applications that are used by clients and servers. Management is concerned about the adequacy of security settings for Microsoft Internet Explorer. Management also wants you to do the following:

- Evaluate the feasibility of using basic authentication for a Web site that is used by Contoso's business partners.

- Review the default configuration of Microsoft Internet Information Services (IIS) 6.0 and recommend ways to further harden the Web server to make it more secure and reliable.

- Recommend ways to provide greater security for Contoso's DNS infrastructure.

    NOTE   A number of exercises in this lab require that you work with a lab partner. Before beginning the lab, make sure your lab partner is ready to proceed.

EXERCISE 8-1: EXAMINING WEB BROWSER SECURITY SETTINGS

Estimated completion time: 15 minutes

In this exercise, you will review default security settings for Internet Explorer 6.0 to determine whether the security settings are adequate for connecting to hosts in the Internet and Trusted Sites zones.

Disabling Internet Explorer Enhanced Security Configuration for Administrator Groups

1. Log on to Contoso as Adminx (where x is your student number).

2. Click Start, select Control Panel, and then select Add Or Remove Programs.

3. In the Add Or Remove Programs dialog box, click Add/Remove Windows Components.

4. In the Windows Components Wizard page, click to highlight Internet Explorer Enhanced Security Configuration, and then click Details.

5. In the Subcomponents Of Internet Explorer Enhanced Security Configuration dialog box, clear the Administrator Groups check box, and then click OK.

6. In the Windows Components Wizard page, click Next, and then click Finish.

7. Close the Add or Remove Programs dialog box.

Creating a User Account to View Internet Explorer Security Configuration Settings

In this section, you will create a user account that will allow you to view the security settings in Internet Explorer. You must perform the steps in this section in order to successfully complete the steps in the subsequent sections of this exercise.

1. Click Start, select Administrative Tools, and select Active Directory Users And Computers.

2. In the tree pane of the Active Directory Users And Computers console, expand contoso.com, expand ALS, right-click the Employees*xx* OU (where *xx* is the two-digit version of your student number), select New, and then click User.

3. In the New Object – User dialog box, type **IEUser*x*** (where *x* is your student number) in both the Full Name and User Logon Name boxes, and then click Next.

4. In the Password and Confirm Password boxes, type **P@ssw0rd**, clear the User Must Change Password At Next Logon check box, click Next, and then click Finish.

   NOTE   Make sure that you clear the User Must Change Password At Next Logon option.

5. Close Active Directory Users And Computers and any other windows that are open on your computer.

Comparing Internet Explorer Enhanced Security Configuration Settings

1. Open Internet Explorer.

   A message appears, indicating that the Internet Explorer Enhanced Security Configuration is not enabled. Leave this message displayed in your browser.

2. On the taskbar, right-click the Internet Explorer icon, and then select Run As.

3. In the Run As dialog box, click the The Following User option, and then log on as Contoso\IEUser*x* (where *x* is your student number).

   When Internet Explorer opens, it attempts to connect to the Microsoft Web site. Click the stop button on the Internet Explorer toolbar to prevent this page from loading in the browser.

4. Right-click the taskbar, and then click Tile Windows Vertically.

5. In both instances of Internet Explorer, from the Tools menu, select Internet Options, and then select the Advanced tab.

6. Position the Internet Options dialog boxes so that they are side-by-side, as shown below.

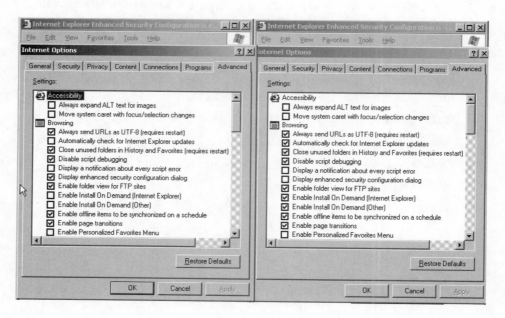

7. Scroll through the option settings in both Internet Options dialog boxes, note the differences, and then answer the following questions.

To view brief explanations of any of these settings, click the question mark in the upper-right hand corner of the dialog box, drag the mouse cursor to the option setting, and then click it.

QUESTION   What happens when Check For Server Certificate Revocation (Requires Restart) is enabled?

QUESTION   What is the effect of selecting the Enable Install On Demand (Internet Explorer) option?

8. In both Internet Options dialog boxes, select the Security tab, and then compare the respective security level settings for each of the Web content zones.

QUESTION   What is the difference in security level settings for the Internet and Trusted Sites zones between both instances of Internet Explorer?

9. In the instance of Internet Explorer that is enabled for Enhanced Security, select Local Intranet, and then click Custom Level; in the Settings dialog box, scroll to the bottom and locate the settings for User Authentication.

Note the settings.

QUESTION   What is the setting for User Authentication Logon?

10. Click Cancel.

11. In the same browser instance, in the Security tab, select Local Intranet, and then click Sites.

12. In the Local Intranet dialog box, select the Include All Local (Intranet) Sites Not Listed In Other Zones check box, and then click OK.

13. In the Security tab, ensure that Local Intranet is still selected, click Custom Level, and review the settings for User Authentication.

QUESTION   What is the setting for User Authentication Logon?

14. Click Cancel.

15. Click the Internet zone, and then click Custom Level.

Note the settings.

QUESTION   What is the setting for User Authentication Logon?

QUESTION   If the setting were changed to Automatic Logon With Current Username and Password, what would happen when a user connected to a site that required NTLM authentication?

16. Click Cancel.

17. Close both Internet Options dialog boxes, as well as both instances of Internet Explorer.

EXERCISE 8-2: COMPARING BASIC WITH INTEGRATED AUTHENTICATION

Estimated completion time: 30 minutes

In this exercise, you will use Network Monitor to compare the difference between basic authentication and integrated authentication when connecting to Web virtual directories that require authentication. You will first create two Web virtual directories. You will then configure the virtual directories to require that users authenticate using either integrated or basic authentication before they can gain access to it. Then you will use Network Monitor to analyze the authentication traffic when you connect to the virtual directories on your lab partner's computer.

Creating Virtual Directories for Basic and Integrated Authentication

1. Click Start, select Administrative Tools, and then select Internet Information Services (IIS) Manager.

2. In the Internet Information Services (IIS) Manager console, expand Web Sites, right-click Default Web Site, select New, and then click Virtual Directory.

3. In the Welcome To The Virtual Directory Creation Wizard page, click Next.

4. In the Virtual Directory Alias dialog box, type **Basic** in the Alias box, and then click Next.

5. In the Web Site Content Directory dialog box, click Browse.

6. In the Browse For Folder dialog box, expand Local Disk (C:), expand Inetpub, click Wwwroot, and then click Make New Folder.

7. In the folder name box, type **Basic** for the folder name, and then click OK.

   If you are not automatically given the opportunity to enter a new folder name for the New Folder you just created, right-click New Folder, select Rename, type **Basic** for the folder name, and then click OK.

8. In the Web Site Content Directory dialog box, ensure that the Path box contains C:\Inetpub\Wwwroot\Basic, and then click Next.

9. In the Virtual Directory Access Permissions dialog box, accept the default settings, and then click Next.

10. In the You Have Successfully Completed The Virtual Directory Creation Wizard page, click Finish.

11. In the Internet Information Services (IIS) Manager console, expand Web Sites, right-click Default Web Site, select New, and then click Virtual Directory.

12. In the Welcome To The Virtual Directory Creation Wizard page, click Next.

13. In the Virtual Directory Alias dialog box, type **Integrated** in the Alias box, and then click Next.

14. In the Web Site Content Directory dialog box, click Browse.

15. In the Browse For Folder dialog box, expand Local Disk (C:), expand Inetpub, click Wwwroot, and then click Make New Folder.

16. In the Folder Name box, type **Integrated** for the folder name, and then click OK.

   If you are not automatically given the opportunity to enter a new folder name for the folder you just created, right-click New Folder, select Rename, type **Integrated** for the folder name, and then click OK.

17. In the Web Site Content Directory dialog box, ensure that the Path box contains C:\Inetpub\Wwwroot\Integrated, and then click Next.

18. In the Virtual Directory Access Permissions dialog box, accept the default settings, and then click Next.

19. In the You Have Successfully Completed The Virtual Directory Creation Wizard page, click Finish.

20. Leave the Internet Information Services (IIS) Manager console open.

Configuring Virtual Directories for Basic and Integrated Authentication

In this section, you will create HTML files for use in the virtual directories you have just created. You will then configure the directories to require either basic or integrated authentication.

1. Click Start, select Run, type **notepad** in the Open box, and then click OK.

2. In Notepad, type the following HTML code (where *xx* is the two-digit version of your student number):

   <html>

   <title>

   Basic Authentication Virtual Directory for Computer*xx*

   </title>

   <body>

   Virtual directory on Computerxx to examine Basic Authentication.

   </body>

   </html>

3. From the File menu, select Save As; from the Save In drop-down list, navigate to C:\Inetpub\Wwwroot\Basic; type **"default.htm"** (with the quotation marks) in the File Name box; and then click Save.

   The reason you need to include the quotation marks around the filename when you save it is to ensure that the file is saved with an .htm, rather than .txt, extension.

4. With Notepad still open, replace all instances of the word "Basic" with the word "Integrated."

5. From the File menu, select Save As; from the Save In drop-down list box, navigate to C:\Inetpub\Wwwroot\Integrated; type **"default.htm"** (with the quotation marks) in the File Name box; and then click Save.

6. Close Notepad.

7. From the Internet Information Services (IIS) Manager console, right-click the Basic virtual directory and then select Properties, as shown below.

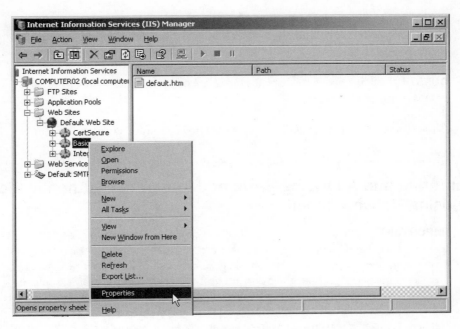

8. In the Basic Properties page, select the Directory Security tab.

9. In the Authentication And Access Control area, select Edit.

10. In the Authentication Methods dialog box, clear the Enable Anonymous Access check box, clear the Integrated Windows Authentication check box, and then select the Basic Authentication (Password Is Sent In Clear Text) check box.

11. Read the warning that appears in the IIS Manager dialog box, and then click Yes.

    QUESTION   Why does the warning not apply to Hypertext Transfer Protocol Secure (HTTPS) connections?

12. In the Authenticated Access area, in the Default Domain box, type **contoso.com**, click OK, and then click OK again to close the Basic Properties dialog box.

13. Right-click the Integrated virtual directory, and then click Properties.

14. In the Integrated Properties dialog box, select the Directory Security tab.

15. In the Authentication And Access Control area, click Edit.

16. In the Authentication Methods page, clear the Enable Anonymous Access check box, click OK, and then click OK again to close the Integrated Properties dialog box.

QUESTION   What authentication methods are selected by default when you create a virtual directory?

17. Close the Internet Information Services (IIS) Manager console.

Capturing and Analyzing Basic and Integrated Authentication by Using Network Monitor

IMPORTANT   Wait until your lab partner has completed the previous section before proceeding. To make it easier to interpret the resulting network capture traffic, only one student at a time should perform steps 1–7. As an alternative to creating a capture of actual basic and integrated authentication traffic, you can use the Network Monitor capture file named WebAuthentication.cap, which is found in the C:\Lab Manual\Lab 08 folder. To use this file, open it from the File menu of Network Monitor. If you choose to use the capture file, proceed to step 8 below.

1. Click Start, select Administrative Tools, and then click Network Monitor.

2. Open Internet Explorer.

3. Switch to Network Monitor, and then from the Capture menu, select Start.

4. Switch to Internet Explorer, type **computer*yy*/basic** (where *yy* is the two-digit version of your partner's student number) in the Address box, and then press Enter.

5. In the Connect To Computer*yy* dialog box, type **admin*x*** (where *x* is your student number) in the User Name box, type your password in the Password box, and then click OK.

6. In the Address box, type **computer*yy*/integrated** (where *yy* is the two-digit version of your partner's student number), and then press Enter.

Note that you are not prompted for authentication credentials when you connect to a virtual directory that requires integrated authentication. The reason for this is the Internet Explorer security setting, which allows the browser to use the current username and password of the logged-on user when connecting to Intranet (Local) sites for the Admin*x* account.

7. Switch to Network Monitor, and then select Stop And View from the Capture menu.

   IMPORTANT   *The second lab partner can now proceed with steps 1–7.*

8. From the Display menu, select Filter.

9. In the Display Filter dialog box, double-click Protocol == Any.

10. In the Expression page, in the Protocol tab, click Disable All.

11. In the Disabled Protocols window on the right side, select HTTP, and then click Enable so that HTTP is listed as the only protocol in the Enabled Protocols window (as shown below); click OK to close the Expression dialog box; and then click OK to close the Display Filter dialog box.

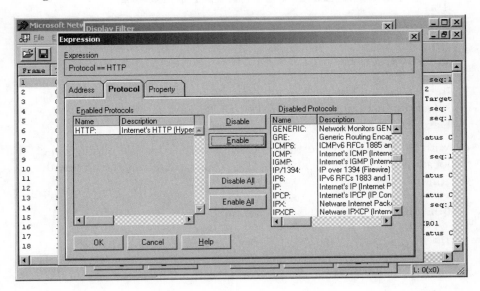

12. In the Microsoft Network Monitor capture summary screen, double-click the first frame that displays Status Code – 401 in the Description column, expand HTTP in the middle pane (as shown below), and then examine the details of the HTTP payload.

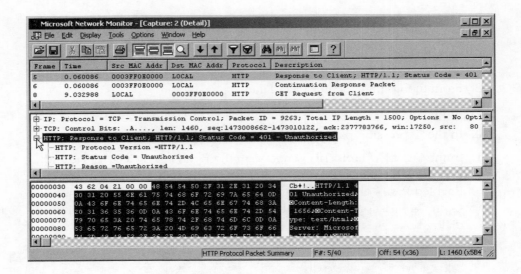

QUESTION What is listed as the authentication method?

13. In the top pane, immediately below the frame you examined in step 12, select the first frame that displays GET Request From Client in the Description column.

14. With HTTP: GET Request From Client expanded in the middle pane, locate the header field labeled HTTP: Authorization and examine the contents of the field.

   QUESTION What does this field contain?

   TIP If the classroom has a connection to the Internet, go to *http://www.wc.cc.va.us/dtod/base64/* and decode the content of this field by copying and pasting the alphanumeric string following the word "Basic."

15. In the top pane, immediately below the frame you examined in step 14, select the first frame that displays Status Code = 200.

   QUESTION What does a status code of 200 indicate?

16. In the top pane, immediately below the frame you examined in step 15, select the frame that displays Status Code – 401 in the Description

column; in the middle pane, ensure that HTTP: Response To Client is expanded; and then locate the two fields that are labeled HTTP: WWW-Authenticate.

QUESTION   *What authentication methods are listed in the HTTP payload?*

17. In the top pane, below the frame you examined in step 16, select the frame that displays Status Code – 301 in the Description column; in the middle pane, ensure that HTTP: Response To Client is expanded; and then locate the HTTP: WWW-Authenticate header field.

    This field represents a Type 2 NTML response. It contains the challenge that the Web server sends to the client browser as well as the agreed-upon options in response to previous NTML authentication traffic from the client.

18. Toward the bottom of the capture, locate the frame that displays Status Code = 200 in the Description column.

19. Immediately above the preceding frame, examine the details of the frames that display GET Request From Client and Continuation Response Packet in the Details column.

    NOTE   *These frames contain the response to the NTLM challenge to prove to the Web server that the client browser knows the password. To respond to the challenge, the client browser performs a number of operations on the entered password to generate keys that are used to encrypt the challenge. The encrypted challenge is concatenated with other information, encoded, and sent back to the server. The server decrypts the challenge and allows access if the correct credentials have been entered on the Web browser client.*

20. Close Network Monitor, and if prompted, do not save the capture or unsaved entries in the address database.

21. Close all open windows.

EXERCISE 8-3: SECURING WEB SERVERS

Estimated completion time: 25 minutes

In this exercise, you will examine the default configuration of IIS 6.0 running on Microsoft Windows Server 2003. You will first examine the services that can potentially be disabled on a computer running Windows Server 2003 that is configured as a dedicated Web server. You will then examine the Web services that are enabled in a default installation of IIS 6.0. Finally, you will configure an application pool to isolate a virtual Web site from other virtual Web sites running on the same server.

Reducing Attack Surface by Disabling Unnecessary Services

1. Click Start, select Administrative Tools, and then click Services.

2. In the details pane, double-click Application Management.

   Note the startup type and the description of the service.

   QUESTION   Why would it be a good idea to disable this service on a dedicated Web server?

3. In the Application Management Properties (Local Computer) dialog box, select the Start Up Type drop-down list.

   QUESTION   What are the three possible Start Up types?

4. Leave the Start Up type set to Manual, and then in the Application Management Properties (Local Computer) dialog box, select the Dependencies tab.

   QUESTION   Are there any service dependencies?

5. In the Application Management Properties (Local Computer) dialog box, click Cancel.

6. In the details pane of the Services console, double-click Distributed File System, note its startup type, and then read the description of the service.

   QUESTION   Why would it be a good idea to disable this service on a dedicated Web server?

7. In the Distributed File System Properties (Local Computer) dialog box, click Cancel.

8. In the Services console, examine the properties of the following services:

   ❑ Background Intelligent Transfer Service

   ❑ Distributed Link Tracking Client

   ❑ Distributed Link Tracking Server

   ❑ Error Reporting Service

   ❑ Netmeeting Remote Desktop Sharing

   ❑ Print Spooler

   ❑ Remote Desktop Help Sessions Manager

   ❑ Telnet

   ❑ Terminal Services

   ❑ Upload Managers

   NOTE You can disable any of these services on a dedicated Web server, conditional upon a number of factors. For example, you might want to use Terminal Services to perform remote administration, so you would not disable this service. This list is not comprehensive. You might want to disable additional services on a dedicated Web server.

9. Close the Services console.

Reducing Attack Surface by Prohibiting Unnecessary Web Service Extensions

1. Click Start, select Administrative Tools, and then click Internet Information Services (IIS) Manager.

2. Expand Computer*xx* (Local Computer) (where *xx* is the two-digit version of your student number), and then click Web Service Extensions.

3. In the details pane, note the Web service extensions and whether they are prohibited or allowed.

   QUESTION Are any Web service extensions allowed? Why or why not?

4. In the Web Service Extensions details frame, click the Open Help link, and then read the corresponding article on enabling and disabling dynamic content.

   QUESTION What is the default configuration of IIS 6.0 for delivering dynamic content?

5. Close the Microsoft Management Console help application.

Creating and Implementing Application Pools to Enhance Reliability, Performance, and Security of Web Sites

In this section, you will configure an application pool that will be used to isolate the processes used for a Web application from the process used by other Web applications that reside in other virtual Web sites or virtual directories. After creating an application pool, you will create an additional Web site that coexists with the default Web site on your computer. You will configure the new Web site to use the newly created application pool.

1. In the Internet Information Services (IIS) Manager console, right-click Application Pools, select New, and then click Application Pool.

2. In the Add New Application Pool dialog box, type **Web Service AppPool** in the Application Pool ID box, and then click OK.

3. Right-click the Web Service AppPool object, and then click Properties.

4. In the Web Service AppPool Properties dialog box, select the Recycle Worker Process (Number Of Requests) check box, and then set the value to 60,000 requests.

5. In the Web Service AppPool Properties dialog box, select the Recycle Worker Processes (At The Following Times) check box, and then click Add.

6. In the Select Time dialog box, select 6:00, as shown below, and then click OK.

    Note that this dialog box presents a 24-hour clock so that 6:00 A.M. is represented as 6:00 and 6:00 P.M. is represented as 18:00.

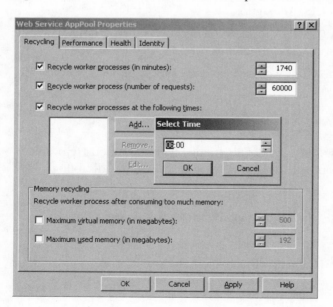

7. Select the Performance tab, and then in the Web Garden area, select 3 in the Maximum Number Of Worker Processes spin box.

QUESTION   What is a Web Garden?

8. Select the Health tab, and then review the default settings.

QUESTION   What is a primary purpose of the settings in this tab?

9. Select the Identity tab, and then select the Predefined drop-down list box.

QUESTION   What are the three predefined accounts?

10. Verify that Network Service is selected in the Predefined drop-down list box, and then click OK.

The Network Service account is a special account that has the fewest user rights required to run a Web application.

11. In the Internet Information Services (IIS) Manager console, right-click Web Sites, select New, and then click Web Site.

12. In the Welcome To The Web Site Creation Wizard page, click Next.

13. In the Web Site Description dialog box, type **Web Service**, and then click Next.

14. In the IP Address And Port Settings dialog box, type **8000** in the TCP Port This Web Site Should Use (Default: 80) box, and then click Next.

NOTE   Changing the default port will allow this new Web site to coexist with the default Web site on the same server. To allow multiple Web sites to coexist on the same server, you could also add additional IP addresses to the server for use by individual Web sites or use host headers to distinguish between Web sites that are sharing the same IP address.

15. In the Web Site Home Directory dialog box, click Browse.

16. In the Browse For Folder dialog box, expand Local Disk (C:), select Inetpub, click Make New Folder, type **webservice** as the name of the folder, and then click OK.

17. In the Web Site Home Directory dialog box, ensure that the entered path is C:\Inetpub\Webservice, ensure that the Allow Anonymous Access To This Web Site check box is selected, and then click Next.

18. In the Web Site Access Permissions dialog box, review the default settings, click Next, and then click Finish.

19. In the Internet Information Service (IIS) Manager console, right-click the Web Service Web site object, and then click Properties.

20. In the Enable Logging area, click Properties.

QUESTION Where is the log file for this Web site stored?

21. In the Logging Properties dialog box, click Cancel.

22. In the Web Service Properties dialog box, select the Home Directory tab.

23. In the Home Directory dialog box, in the Application Settings area, select the Application Pool drop-down list box, select Web Service AppPool, and then click OK.

24. Click Start, select Run, type **notepad c:\inetpub\wwwroot\default.htm** and then click OK.

25. In Notepad, replace Home Page with Web Service Home Page.

26. From the File menu, select Save As.

27. In the Save In drop-down list box, navigate to C:\Inetpub\Webservice, and then click Save.

28. Close Notepad.

IMPORTANT Wait until your lab partner has completed the previous steps before proceeding.

29. Open Internet Explorer, type **http://computer*yy*:8000** in the Address box (where *yy* is the two-digit version of your lab partner's student number), and then press Enter. You should see your partner's default.htm file for the Web Services Web site.

QUESTION If this Web server hosted a .Net Web service application and the application failed, what would happen to other Web sites located on the same computer?

30. Close all open windows.

EXERCISE 8-4: SECURING DNS

Estimated completion time: 25 minutes

In this exercise, you will examine the default settings for the Windows 2003 DNS service. You will then create and configure a primary forward lookup zone and configure it to allow zone transfers to your lab partner's computer. Then you will configure a secondary zone to copy DNS records from your lab partner's primary DNS zone.

Examining Default DNS Server Settings

1. Click Start, select Administrative Tools, and then click DNS.

2. In the Dnsmgmt console, right-click Computer*xx* (where *xx* is the two-digit version of your student number), and then click Properties.

3. In the Computer*xx* Properties dialog box, select the Root Hints tab.

   The Root Hints tab lists the DNS servers that are authoritative for the root or "." zone. By default, your DNS server is configured with the root hints of DNS servers that comprise the starting point for DNS queries when your DNS server attempts to resolve a DNS host name to an IP address (also known as a forward lookup) or to resolve an IP address to a DNS hostname (also known as a reverse lookup).

   QUESTION   What addresses are listed in the Root Hints tab?

4. Select the Advanced tab.

   Notice that the setting for Secure Cache Against Pollution is enabled by default. This setting prevents the DNS server from updating its cache with records that it did not ask for in a query to a particular DNS server. For example, if the DNS server queries a remote DNS server for the IP address of www.tailspintoys.com, and the remote DNS server responds with the record for www.tailspintoys.com and also with a record for www.wingtiptoys.com, it will not update its cache with the record for www.wingtiptoys.com.

5. Click Cancel.

6. From the Help menu, select Help Topics.

7. In the help console, select the Search tab, type **"how dns query works" recursion** (including the quotation marks) in the Type In The Words To Search For box, and then click List Topics.

   Including the quotation marks will limit the number of articles returned in the search result.

8. Double-click the How DNS Query Works search result title, read the article, and then answer the following questions.

   QUESTION   What is recursion?

   QUESTION   If you disabled recursion on the DNS server, what DNS queries would the DNS server respond to?

9. Close the help application.

Creating and Configuring a Primary Forward Lookup Zone

In this section, you and your lab partner will each create a different forward lookup zone to resolve DNS queries. A forward lookup zone comprises the DNS records that resolve host names to IP addresses. The records are stored either as a text file or in the Active Directory directory service, depending on whether you are creating a standard zone or an Active Directory integrated zone.

The lab partner with the lower student number will create a forward lookup zone for the tailspintoys.com DNS domain. The lab partner with the higher student number will create a forward lookup zone for the wingtiptoys.com DNS domain.

1. Click Start, select Control Panel, select Network Connections, right-click Local Area Connection, and then click Properties.

2. In the Local Area Connection Properties dialog box, select Internet Protocol (TCP/IP), and then click Properties.

3. In the Internet Protocol (TCP/IP) Properties dialog box, note your IP address in the IP Address box, and in the Alternate DNS Server box, type **<*your-computer's-IP-address*>**, click OK, and then click OK again.

4. Switch to the Dnsmgmt console, right-click Forward Lookup Zones, and then click New Zone.

5. In the Welcome To The New Zone Wizard page, click Next.

6. In the Zone Type page, ensure that the Primary Zone option is selected, as shown below, and then click Next.

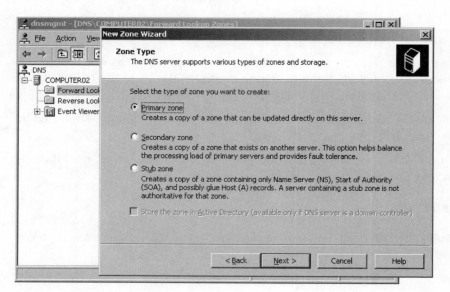

7. In the Zone Name box, type **_yourprimarydomain_.com** (where _yourprimarydomain_ is either tailspintoys if you have the lower student number or wingtiptoys if you have the higher student number), and then click Next.

Make sure you enter the complete name—either tailspintoys.com or wingtiptoys.com.

8. In the Zone File dialog box, ensure that Create A New File With This File Name is selected, and then click Next.

9. In the Dynamic Update dialog box, accept the default setting of Do Not Allow Dynamic Updates, and then click Next.

10. In the Completing The New Zone Wizard page, click Finish.

11. In the Dnsmgmt console, under Forward Lookup Zones, select _yourprimarydomain_.com.

QUESTION In the details pane, how many resource records do you see? What are the record types for the records that you see?

12. Right-click _yourprimarydomain_.com, and then click New Host (A).

13. In the New Host dialog box, type **NS1** in the Name (Uses Parent Domain If Blank) box, type **_<your-computer's-IP-address>_** in the IP Address box, click Add Host, and then click OK.

The dialog box is shown below.

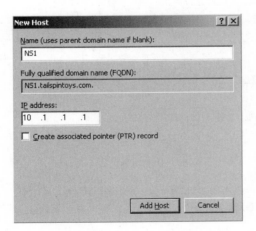

14. In the New Host dialog box, type **NS2** in the Name (Uses Parent Domain If Blank) box, type **_<your-lab-partner's-IP-address>_** in the IP Address box, click Add Host, click OK, and then click Done.

15. Right-click *yourprimarydomain*.com, and then click Properties.

16. In the *yourprimarydomain*.com Properties page, select the Name Servers tab.

17. In the Name Servers box, ensure that the computer*xx*.contoso.com (where *xx* is your student number) name server record is selected, click Remove, and then click Add.

18. In the New Resource Record dialog box, click Browse.

19. In the Browse dialog box, in the Records box, double-click Computer*xx*, double-click Forward Lookup Zones, double-click *yourprimarydomain*.com, click NS1, and then click OK.

The dialog box is shown below.

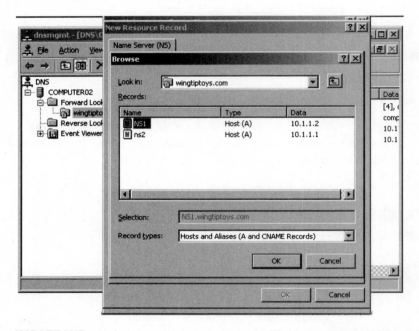

IMPORTANT Make sure you do not skip step 20. You must add NS2 as the second name server in the Name Servers tab.

20. Click OK to return the Name Servers tab of the *yourprimarydomain*.com Properties dialog box, and then click Add.

21. In the New Resource Record page, click Browse.

22. In the Browse dialog box, in the Records box, double-click Computer.*xx*, double-click Forward Lookup Zones, double-click *yourprimarydomain*.com, click NS2, and then click OK.

23. Click OK to close the New Resource Record page.

   The Name Servers tab should display two name server records, as shown below.

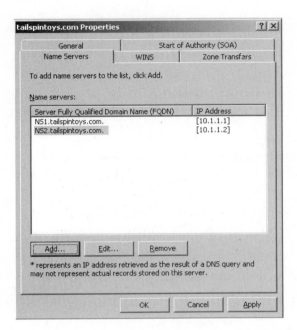

24. In the *yourprimarydomain*.com Properties dialog box, select the Zone Transfers tab.

   QUESTION   What are the default settings in the Zone Transfers tab?

25. Click Notify.

   QUESTION   What are the default notification settings?

26. Click Cancel, and then click OK to close the *yourprimarydomain*.com Properties dialog box.

Creating and Configuring a Secondary Forward Lookup Zone

In this section, you will configure a secondary forward lookup zone that will contain a read-only copy of your lab partner's primary forward lookup zone resource records.

IMPORTANT   Wait until your lab partner has completed the previous section before proceeding.

1. In the Dnsmgmt console, right-click Forward Lookup Zones, and then click New Zone.

2. In the Welcome To The New Zone Wizard page, click Next.

3. In the Zone Type page, select the Secondary Zone option, and then click Next.

4. In the Zone Name box, type *yourpartner'sprimarydomain.com* (where *yourpartner'sprimarydomain*.com is either wingtiptoys.com or tailspintoys.com), and then click Next.

5. In the Master DNS Servers page, enter *<your-lab-partner's-IP-address>* in the IP Address box, click Add, and then click Next.

6. In the Completing The New Zone Wizard page, click Finish.

7. Under Forward Lookup Zones, click the secondary zone you just created.

NOTE   You might initially see an error message indicating that the zone information was not transferred. Wait a few moments, and then press F5 to refresh the display. If you still cannot perform a zone transfer, review your configuration and your lab partner's configuration.

QUESTION   What computers are authorized to receive a read-only copy of the entire zone file?

8. Close all open windows and log off.

LAB REVIEW QUESTIONS

Estimated completion time: 15 minutes

1. In addition to configuring Web server permissions to authorize access, what other permissions should you configure?

2. Why is NTLM authentication more secure than basic authentication?

3. What aspect of the CIA (confidentiality, integrity, and availability) triad can Web application pools enhance?

4. One of the default settings for the Internet zone is to prompt for a user name and password. Why is this an appropriate setting for the Internet zone?

5. Why should you restrict zone transfers to only a predetermined and authorized list of DNS servers?

6. Creating multiple secondary DNS servers to hold read-only copies of the primary zone enhances what aspect of the CIA (confidentiality, integrity, and availability) triad?

7. In addition to restricting zone transfers to a predetermined list of DNS servers, what other steps should you take to protect zone data?

8. Enabling the setting to protect against DNS cache pollution enhances what aspect of the CIA (confidentiality, integrity, and availability) triad?

9. If you use basic authentication, what should you do to protect the confidentiality of authentication credentials?

LAB CHALLENGE 8-1: DESIGNING AND IMPLEMENTING A SECURE DNS INFRASTRUCTURE

Estimated completion time: 25 minutes

Part 1: Designing a Secure DNS Infrastructure

You are the network administrator for Contoso Pharmaceuticals. Currently, the demilitarized zone (DMZ) contains two DNS servers, ns1.contoso.com and ns2.contoso.com, that host a primary and a secondary zone for the contoso.com domain namespace. The zones contain records for the externally accessible Web and mail servers. These two DNS servers also provide Internet name resolution for a Web proxy server that provides access to Internet Web sites for internal client browsers. They do not contain records for any internal hosts. The DNS name for the internal network and Active Directory is contoso.local. The DNS servers that are authoritative for the contoso.local namespace are accessible only by DNS clients on the internal network.

Recently, these two DNS servers in the DMZ were flooded with a huge number of recursive queries from a number of DNS servers that had been compromised by a hacker. During the attack, the Web proxy server could not resolve Internet host names and customers could not resolve the host name–to-IP address mappings of the Web and mail servers.

As a result of the attack, you have been asked to redesign the DNS infrastructure in the DMZ to provide greater security. Management's primary concern is that your DNS design protect against future DNS denial of service (DoS) attacks and eliminate any single points of failure, but they are also concerned about protecting the integrity and confidentiality of the DNS data, where appropriate. Management has informed you that you can purchase additional hardware and software if necessary. Also, Contoso's Internet service provider (ISP) has offered to help you however they can.

For the first part of this lab challenge, you will design the DNS infrastructure based on your responses to the following questions. If required by your instructor, write up a formal proposal based on your responses to these questions and be prepared to hand it in.

1. Should you separate DNS server roles? If so, what roles would you separate and why?

2. If you answered yes to question 1, will you need to install additional DNS servers?

3. How can your ISP help you enhance the fault tolerance of the contoso.com zone?

4. How can your ISP help you enhance the performance of DNS queries from internal DNS resolvers?

5. Based on your responses to the previous questions, how would you configure inbound and outbound access rules for DNS traffic on your firewall?

TIP   DNS uses User Datagram Protocol (UDP) port 53 for queries and Transmission Control Protocol (TCP) port 53 for zone transfers.

Part 2: Securing a DNS Server Against DoS Attacks

You are responsible for a DNS server that hosts the primary zone file for the contoso.com namespace. The DNS server is currently configured to allow zone transfers to another internal DNS server, which you manage. Your ISP has agreed to host a secondary zone file for contoso.com on its DNS server. The server name is ns1.fabrikam.com, and its IP address is 172.16.32.1. You need to configure the DNS server to allow zone transfers to ns1.fabrikam.com. Also, you need to configure the server to provide a maximum degree of protection against any DNS query flood attacks.

For this part of the lab challenge, make the necessary configuration changes to your DNS server.

LAB 9
SECURING INTERNET MESSAGING

This lab contains the following exercises and activities:

■ Exercise 9-1: Examining SMTP Relay Settings

■ Exercise 9-2: Configuring DNS Mail Exchanger (MX) Records

■ Exercise 9-3: Examining Default POP3 Security

■ Exercise 9-4: Using Secure Password Authentication (SPA)

■ Lab Review Questions

■ Lab Challenge 9-1: Digitally Signing and Encrypting E-mail

After completing this lab, you will be able to

■ Configure the SMTP service to prevent unauthorized relaying of SMTP messages.

■ Configure Domain Name System (DNS) Mail Exchanger (MX) resource records.

■ Configure delivery priorities on MX records.

■ Configure the Post Office Protocol 3 (POP3) service on a Microsoft Windows Server 2003 server.

■ Configure Microsoft Outlook Express to connect to a POP3 server.

■ Configure Outlook Express to use Secure Password Authentication (SPA).

■ Use Microsoft Network Monitor to capture and analyze POP3 and SMTP traffic.

■ Use Network Monitor to identify weaknesses and strengths of authentication mechanisms used for POP3.

■ Configure digital signing and encryption of e-mail messages.

Estimated completion time: 115 minutes

SCENARIO

You are a network administrator for a branch office of Contoso Pharmaceuticals. One of your responsibilities is to manage the security of inbound and outbound e-mail. A primary role of the branch office is to research and develop new drugs and to manage clinical trials of those drugs. The outside researchers who are conducting these trials have been given accounts so that they can send and receive e-mail using the company's internal Microsoft Exchange Server. Because of the large losses that could result to the company if information about these new drugs were to fall into the hands of unscrupulous competitors, e-mail must be secure.

In this lab, you will examine and configure the SMTP relay settings to ensure that anonymous users cannot use your SMTP service to relay messages to other destinations. You will then configure DNS MX records to ensure that Internet hosts can locate the SMTP servers that handle inbound SMTP mail. Finally, you will configure a POP3 server and client to provide progressively higher levels of security.

EXERCISE 9-1: EXAMINING SMTP RELAY SETTINGS

Estimated completion time: 25 minutes

Recently, a salesperson contacted you and said that he couldn't send mail to one of his customers at fabrikam.com. After further investigation, you discover that the mail administrator at fabrikam.com has configured Fabrikam's SMTP server to drop all e-mail from IP addresses that appear on a blacklist of known open relays. You are convinced that your IP address has been mistakenly included in this blacklist. However, before contacting the owners of the blacklist, you first want to verify that your SMTP server is configured correctly. To perform this test, you will open a Telnet session to the SMTP service on your computer to test the relay settings. You will then examine the default relay settings on the SMTP service and reconfigure these settings to test their effect.

Using Telnet to Test Default SMTP Relay Settings

1. Log on to Contoso as Admin*x* (where *x* is your student number).

2. Click Start, click Run, type **cmd** in the Open box, and then click OK.

3. At the command prompt, type **telnet** and then press ENTER.

   Note that when using the Telnet console, you cannot backspace to correct typographical errors. If you make a mistake typing a command, press ENTER and then type the command again.

4. At the Telnet prompt, type **set localecho** and then press ENTER.

   This command causes Telnet to display characters as you type them.

5. Type **open computer*xx* 25** (where *xx* is the two-digit version of your student number), and then press ENTER.

   This command causes Telnet to open a connection to Transmission Control Protocol (TCP) port 25, the port used for SMTP, on your computer. The SMTP service responds with a message indicating it is ready. Note that the response includes the default domain for e-mail, in this case computer*xx*.contoso.com.

6. Type **ehlo** and then press ENTER.

   This command causes the SMTP service to respond with a list of the Enhanced SMTP (ESMTP) options it supports. It also identifies the sender service to the receiver service.

7. Type **mail from: admin*x*@computer*xx*.contoso.com** and then press ENTER.

   This command identifies the sender.

   QUESTION   Have you authenticated with the SMTP service by issuing this command?

8. Type **rcpt to: mailadmin@fabrikam.com** and then press ENTER.

   QUESTION   What message did you receive in response to this command?

9. Type **rcpt to: user*x*@computer*xx*.contoso.com** and then press ENTER.

   QUESTION   What message did you receive in response to this command?

   QUESTION   Why are you able to send mail to the target e-mail address?

10. Type **quit**, press ENTER twice, and then leave the Telnet window open.

Examining and Configuring SMTP Relay Settings

1. Click Start, select Administrative Tools, and then click Internet Information Services (IIS) Manager.

2. In the Internet Information Services (IIS) Manager console, expand Computer*xx* (Local Computer) (where *xx* is the two-digit version of your student number), right-click Default SMTP Virtual Server, as shown below, and then select Properties.

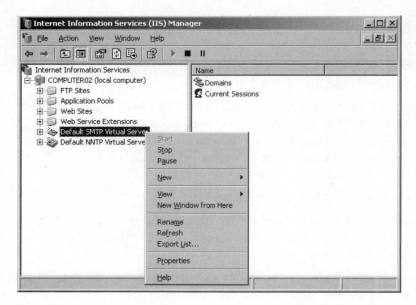

3. In the Default SMTP Virtual Server Properties dialog box, select the Access tab, and then click Relay, as shown below.

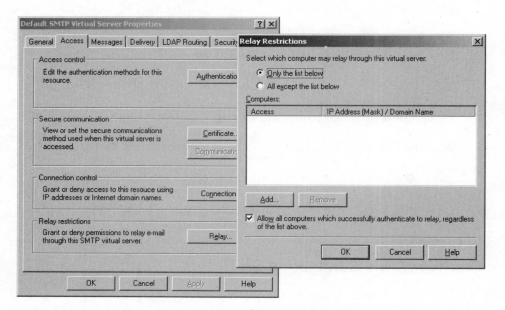

QUESTION   In what circumstances is relaying permitted?

4. In the Relay Restrictions dialog box, select the All Except The List Below option, click OK, and then click OK to close the Default SMTP Virtual Server Properties dialog box.

5. Switch to the Telnet prompt.

6. Type **open computer*xx* 25** (where *xx* is the two-digit version of your student number), and then press ENTER.

7. Type **ehlo** and then press ENTER.

8. Type **mail from: adminx@computer*xx*.contoso.com** and then press ENTER.

9. Type **rcpt to: mailadmin@fabrikam.com** and then press ENTER.

    QUESTION   What response code did you receive?

    QUESTION   Why are you able to send e-mail to mailadmin@fabrikam.com?

10. Type **quit** and press ENTER twice, type **quit** and press ENTER to close the Telnet window, and then close the command prompt.

    NOTE   The next steps will restore the SMTP service to the default settings for relaying.

11. Switch to the Internet Information Services (IIS) Manager console, right-click Default SMTP Virtual Server, and then click Properties.

12. On the Default SMTP Virtual Server Properties page, select the Access tab, and then click Relay.

13. In the Relay Restrictions dialog box, select the Only The List Below option, and then click OK twice.

14. Leave the Internet Information Services (IIS) Manager console open.

EXERCISE 9-2: CONFIGURING DNS MAIL EXCHANGER (MX) RECORDS

Estimated completion time: 20 minutes

Your office recently installed the SMTP service on a server running Windows Server 2003. This SMTP service will be used in conjunction with the Microsoft ISA Server 2000 Message Screener component to reduce spam coming into your network. Once messages have been processed, they will be forwarded to an internal Exchange Server. You need to configure DNS resource records to allow Internet hosts to deliver mail to this server and to another SMTP server located in a subsidiary office.

    IMPORTANT   Before you can complete this exercise, you and your lab partner must have previously completed Lab 8, Exercise 8-4, "Securing DNS."

Adding a Primary MX Record

1. Click Start, select Administrative Tools, and then click DNS.

2. In the Dnsmgmt console, click Forward Lookup Zones.

3. In the details pane, right-click the forward lookup zone that displays Standard Primary in the Type column, as shown below, and then select New Host (A).

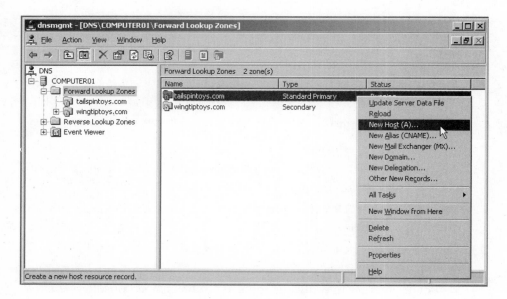

4. In the New Host dialog box, type **smtp** in the Name (Uses Parent Domain Name If Blank) box, type **<*your-computer's-IP-address*>** in the IP Address box, click Add Host, and then click OK.

5. In the New Host dialog box, type **pop3** in the Name (Uses Parent Domain If Blank) box, type **<*your-computer's-IP-address*>** in the IP Address box, click Add Host, click OK, and then click Done.

6. In the details pane, right-click the forward lookup zone that displays Standard Primary in the Type column, and then click New Mail Exchanger (MX).

7. In the New Resource Record dialog box, click Browse.

   NOTE   In the next step, you will add an MX record for one of the host records you created above.

8. In the Browse dialog box, double-click Computer*xx* (where *xx* is the two-digit version of your student number), double-click Forward Lookup Zones, double-click the forward lookup zone that displays Standard Primary in the Type column, click the SMTP host record, and then click OK.

9. Click OK to close the New Resource Record dialog box.

10. Double-click the forward lookup zone that displays Standard Primary in the Type column.

11. In the details pane, right-click the MX record you created and then select Properties, as shown below.

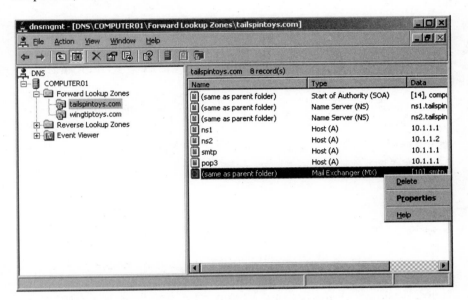

12. In the Mail Exchanger (MX) dialog box, click the question mark in the upper right corner, drag the cursor to the Mail Server Priority box, and then click the mouse to bring up an explanation of the field.

QUESTION If more than one MX record is present, how will mail be delivered to the domain?

13. Click to clear the explanation, and then click Cancel.

NOTE Wait until your lab partner has completed this section before proceeding to the next section.

Adding a Secondary MX Record

In this section, you will add a secondary MX record to your DNS zone. The steps are intended to illustrate the concept of secondary records. The SMTP service on your computer is not configured to support the proper delivery of e-mail using secondary MX records.

1. Double-click the forward lookup zone that displays Secondary in the Type column and verify the presence of the MX record in the zone.

   NOTE   If you do not see the MX record, right-click the forward lookup zone in the tree pane, and then click Refresh.

2. In the tree pane, click Forward Lookup Zones, right-click the forward lookup zone that displays Standard Primary in the Type column, and then click New Mail Exchanger (MX).

3. In the New Resource Record dialog box, type **20** in the Mail Server Priority box.

   IMPORTANT   Make sure that you change the Mail Server Priority to 20; otherwise, parts of the lab might fail.

4. Click Browse.

   NOTE   In the next step, you will add an MX record that points to your lab partner's SMTP server.

5. In the Browse dialog box, double-click Computer*xx* (where *xx* is the two-digit version of your student number), double-click Forward Lookup Zones, double-click the forward lookup zone that displays Secondary in the Type column, click the SMTP host record, and then click OK.

6. Click OK.

7. Close the DNS Management console.

EXERCISE 9-3: EXAMINING DEFAULT POP3 SECURITY

Estimated completion time: 30 minutes

Currently, employees of your office use Outlook Web Access (OWA) over Hypertext Transfer Protocol Secure (HTTPS) to access their mailboxes on an Exchange Server. However, several employees have asked if they can use Outlook Express to connect to the mail server when they are offsite. You have been asked to investigate the security implications of using POP3 clients in a default configuration to connect to mailboxes on the Exchange server.

Configuring POP3 Domains and Mailboxes

NOTE Although both students can perform the following steps in this section, only one student's POP3 server will be used in subsequent sections to analyze POP3 and SMTP traffic. If you and your lab partner prefer, these steps can be performed by one partner while the other lab partner watches.

1. Click Start, select Administrative Tools, and then click POP3 Service.

    The POP3 Service is not installed by default and was added to your computer as part of the classroom setup.

2. In the POP3 Service console, right-click Computer*xx* (where *xx* is the two-digit version of your student number), and then click Properties.

3. In the Computer*xx* Properties dialog box, ensure that Active Directory Integrated is displayed in the Authentication Method drop-down list box, as shown below, and then click OK.

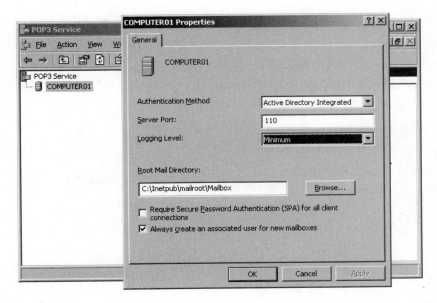

4. In the tree pane of the POP3 Service console, right-click Computer*xx*, select New, click Domain, type **contoso.com** in the New Domain dialog box, as shown below, and then click OK.

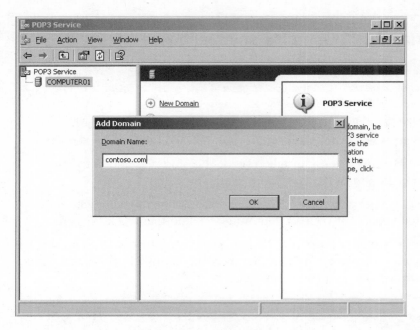

5. In the tree pane of the POP3 Service console, right-click Contoso.com, select New, and then click Mailbox.

6. In the Add Mailbox dialog box, clear the Create Associated User For This Mailbox check box, as shown below.

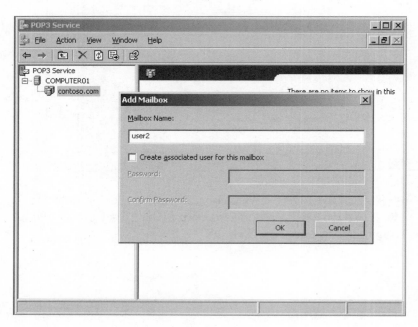

7. In the Mailbox Name box, type **user***y* (where *y* is your lab partner's student number), and then click OK.

   QUESTION What is the format of the account name used for clear text authentication?

8. Click OK to clear the mailbox creation success message.

9. Repeat steps 5–8 to create a mailbox for User*x* (where *x* is your student number).

10. Minimize the POP3 Service console.

Examining Changes to SMTP Domains

1. Switch to the Internet Information Services (IIS) Manager console.

2. Expand Default SMTP Virtual Server, and then click Domains.

   Both computer*xx*.contoso.com and contoso.com should be listed as local domains. If you do not see these domains, right-click the Domains node in the tree pane of the console, and then click refresh.

   QUESTION Why is it necessary for contoso.com to be listed here in addition to computer*xx*.contoso.com?

3. Minimize the Internet Information Services (IIS) Management console.

Configuring Outlook Express for POP3 Mail

In this section, you will configure Outlook Express to connect to your mailbox on the POP3 server.

   NOTE For this section, only one POP3 server should be used. Before performing the following steps, you and your lab partner need to determine which POP3 server you will use. In the space below, record the computer name of the POP3 server.

POP3 Server Computer Name:

1. Click Start, select All Programs, and then click Outlook Express.

2. Wait a few seconds for the Internet Connection Wizard page to appear, then type **user***x* (where *x* is your student number) in the Display Name box, and then click Next.

3. In the E-Mail Address box, type **userx@contoso.com** and then click Next.

4. In the Incoming Mail (POP3, IMAP, Or HTTP) Server box, type **Computerzz** (where *zz* is the two-digit number of the computer that will serve as the POP3 server for you and your lab partner).

5. In the Outgoing Mail (SMTP) Server box, type **Computerzz**, and then click Next.

6. On the Internet Mail Logon page, type **userx@contoso.com** in the Account Name box.

7. Clear the Remember Password check box, as shown below, and then click Next.

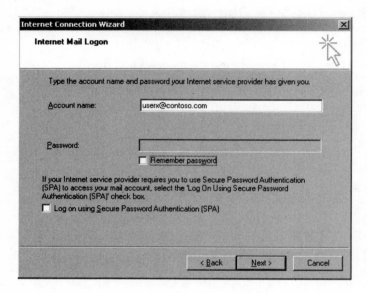

8. On the Congratulations page, click Finish.

9. On the Outlook Express toolbar, click Create Mail.

10. In the New Message dialog box, in the To box, type **userx@contoso.com; usery@contoso.com** (where *x* is your student number, and *y* is your lab partner's student number).

11. In the Subject box, type **POP3 Test**.

12. In the message box, type **This is a test message**.

13. Click Send, and then press CTRL+M.

    By pressing CTRL+M, you accelerate the delivery of the message.

14. In the Logon dialog box, verify that user*x*@contoso.com appears in the User Name box, type **P@ssw0rd** in the Password box, and then click OK.

15. Click Inbox.

You should see e-mail messages in your Inbox from yourself and your lab partner.

16. Close Outlook Express.

Capturing POP3 and SMTP Traffic

NOTE Both lab partners can capture traffic at the same time. However, only the student who connects to his or her lab partner's computer to send and receive mail should perform the steps necessary to compose and send the e-mail. If you are the lab partner who is composing the e-mail message for this section, make sure you synchronize your steps with your lab partner. To simplify this activity, you might want one lab partner to capture the network data and the other lab partner to send and receive the e-mail.

1. Click Start, select Administrative Tools, and then click Network Monitor.

If you see a message prompting you to choose a network interface, choose the Local Area Connection, not the Virtual Private Network interface.

2. Click Start, select All Programs, and then click Outlook Express.

IMPORTANT Do not enter your password to log on to the POP3 server.

3. Switch to Network Monitor, and from the Capture menu, select Start.

4. Switch to the Outlook Express Logon dialog box, enter your password, and then click OK.

5. On the Outlook Express toolbar, click Create Mail.

6. Compose a brief test e-mail addressed to your lab partner and to yourself, and then click Send.

NOTE Wait until your lab partner has completed this step before continuing.

7. Press CTRL+M to download the message to the Inbox.

8. Switch to Network Monitor, and from the Capture menu, click Stop And View.

Analyzing POP3 and SMTP Traffic

In this section, you will analyze the POP3 and SMTP traffic you captured previously. To make the analysis of the traffic easier, you will use Network Monitor to create display filters that will allow you to examine POP3 and SMTP traffic in isolation from all other traffic. You will first create a display filter for POP3 traffic and then examine the traffic. Then, you will create a display filter for SMTP traffic and examine that traffic. If you have difficulty with these steps, you can find a number of sample capture and display filter files in the C:\Lab Manual\Lab 09 folder.

1. In the Microsoft Network Monitor capture summary screen, from the Display menu, click Filter.

2. Double-click the Protocol == Any expression.

3. In the Expression dialog box, select the Property tab.

4. In the Protocol:Property window, expand the TCP object, and then select Destination Port.

5. In the Relation window, select ==, select the Decimal option, type **110** in the Value box, as shown below, and then click OK.

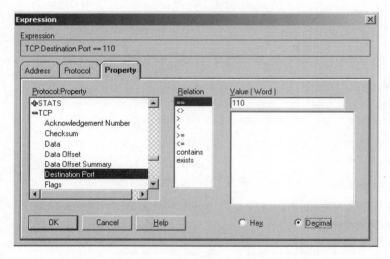

6. In the Display Filter dialog box, click the Expression button in the Add area on the right-hand side.

7. In the Protocol:Property window, select Source Port, ensure that the value for the port is 110 and that the Decimal option is selected, and then click OK.

8. In the Display Filter dialog box, select the ANY <--> ANY expression, and then click Line in the Delete area on the right-hand side.

9. In the Display Filter dialog box, click the AND operator, click the Change Operator button to change the operator from AND to OR, as shown below, and then click Save.

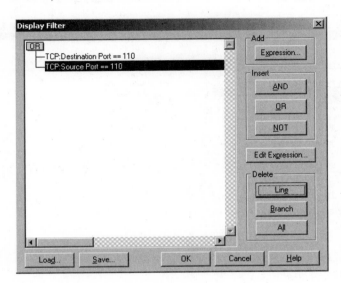

10. In the Save Display Filter dialog box, select the Save In drop-down list, navigate to C:\Lab Manual\Lab 09\Labwork, type **pop3** in the File Name box, click Save, and then click OK in the Display Filter dialog box.

    NOTE Make sure you do not accidentally overwrite the Pop3.df sample file that is included in the C:\Lab Manual\Lab 09 folder.

11. Press F4 to toggle to the zoom pane, as shown below.

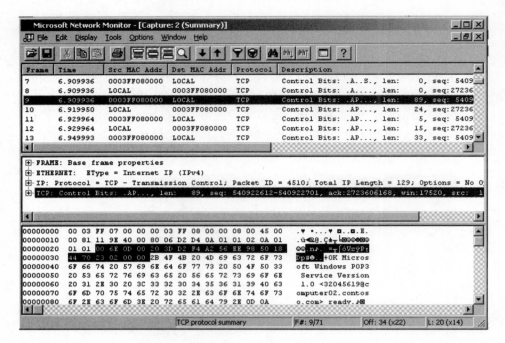

12. Click the top frame in the Summary window, and then press the Down arrow to review the contents of subsequent frames in the Detail and Hex windows.

QUESTION   Do any of the frames contain potentially sensitive information? If so, what information do they contain?

13. In the Microsoft Network Monitor capture summary screen, from the Display menu, click Filter.

14. Click the TCP:Destination Port==110 expression, and then click Edit Expression.

15. In the Value box, delete 110 and replace it with 25, and then click OK.

16. Click the TCP:Source Port==110 expression, and then click Edit Expression.

17. In the Value box, delete 110 and replace it with 25, and then click OK.

18. In the Display Filter dialog box, click Save.

19. In the Save Display Filter dialog box, ensure that C:\Lab Manual\ Lab 09\Labwork is selected in the Save In drop-down list, type **SMTP** in the File Name box, click Save, and then click OK.

20. Click the top frame in the Summary window, and then press the Down arrow to review the contents of subsequent frames in the Detail and Hex windows.

> **QUESTION** *Do any of the frames contain potentially sensitive information that is viewable in clear text? If so, what information do they contain?*

21. Close the capture summary window and leave Network Monitor open.

EXERCISE 9-4: USING SECURE PASSWORD AUTHENTICATION (SPA)

Estimated completion time: 20 minutes

Management is concerned about some of the security weaknesses of POP3, and they want you to investigate SPA as a means to enhance security for POP3 users. In this exercise, you will configure the POP3 server to require SPA and configure Outlook Express to use SPA. You will then capture a POP3 session to see the effect of this configuration change.

Configuring the POP3 Server to Require Secure Password Authentication (SPA)

1. Switch to the POP3 Service console.

2. Right-click Computer*xx* (where *xx* is the two-digit version of your student number), and then click Properties.

3. In the Computer*xx* Properties dialog box, select the Require Secure Password Authentication (SPA) For All Client Connections check box.

4. Click Apply.

5. Click Yes when prompted to restart the POP3 service.

6. Click OK.

7. Minimize the POP3 Service console.

Configuring Outlook Express POP3 Account Settings to Use SPA

1. Switch to Outlook Express.

2. From the Tools menu, select Accounts.

3. In the Internet Accounts dialog box, ensure that the Mail tab is selected and that the default mail account is selected, and then click Properties.

4. In the Computer*zz* Properties dialog box (where *zz* is the two-digit number of the computer that serves as the POP3 server for you and your lab partner), select the Servers tab.

5. In the Account Name box, delete the text string "@contoso.com" so that only **User***x* (where *x* is your student number) is displayed in the box.

6. Click the Log On Using Secure Password Authentication check box, and then click OK.

7. In the Internet Accounts dialog box, click Close.

8. Leave Outlook Express open for the next section.

Capturing and Analyzing SPA Traffic

NOTE   Both lab partners can capture traffic at the same time. However, only the student who connects to his or her lab partner's computer to send and receive mail should perform the steps necessary to compose and send the e-mail. If you are the lab partner who is composing the e-mail message for this section, make sure you synchronize your steps with your lab partner. To simplify this activity, you want one lab partner to capture the network data and the other lab partner to send and receive the e-mail message.

1. Switch to Network Monitor.

2. From the Capture menu, select Start, and then click No when prompted to save the previous capture.

3. Switch to Outlook Express, and then press CTRL+M.

4. In the Log On dialog box, type **user***x* in the Username box, type **contoso** in the Domain box, enter your password, and then click OK.

5. Compose and send an e-mail message to your lab partner.

6. Wait until your lab partner has sent the e-mail, and then press CTRL+M to download the message.

7. Switch to Network Monitor, and from the Capture menu, select Stop And View.

8. Press F8 to open the Display Filter.

9. In the Display Filter dialog box, click Load.

10. In the Load Display Filter dialog box, select POP3.DF from the C:\Lab Manual\Lab 09\Labwork folder, select Open, and then click OK.

If you had trouble creating the POP3 display filter, you can load the sample Pop3.df file from the C:\Lab Manual\Lab 09 folder.

11. Press F4 to toggle the zoom pane.

12. On the toolbar, click the Find icon (the large binoculars).

13. In the Find Frame Expression dialog box, ensure that the Property tab is selected.

14. In the Protocol:Property window, select TCP:Data.

15. In the Relation window, select Contains, and select the ASCII option.

16. In the Value (Array Of Bytes) box, type **AUTH**, as shown below, and then click OK.

Make sure you use uppercase letters for the search value.

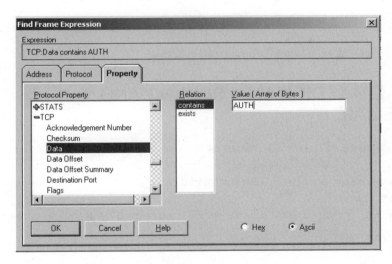

17. Click the Find Next and Find Previous icons and review the data.

QUESTION   What authentication mechanism does SPA use?

18. Review the remaining POP3 frames in the capture.

   QUESTION   Do any of the frames contain potentially sensitive information that is viewable in clear text? Hint: To find any clear text information, you can create a find expression for one of the text strings you used in your e-mail message.

19. Close all open windows and log off.

LAB REVIEW QUESTIONS

1. How can preventing unauthorized SMTP relaying reduce social engineering attacks?

2. How can preventing unauthorized SMTP relaying reduce denial of service (DoS) attacks?

3. Why is it desirable to have multiple DNS MX resource records?

4. You have configured Outlook Express to connect to a POP3 server. When you send an e-mail from a POP3 client, what protocol does Outlook Express use?

5. When you configure a POP3 client to use SPA, is the confidentiality and integrity of the message protected?

6. What can you do to ensure the confidentiality of an SMTP e-mail message?

7. What assurances does a digital signature provide?

LAB CHALLENGE 9-1: DIGITALLY SIGNING AND ENCRYPTING E-MAIL

Estimated completion time: 20 minutes

Much of the e-mail exchanged among employees of Contoso Pharmaceuticals contains highly sensitive and proprietary information. After reviewing your report on the security vulnerabilities of POP3 e-mail, management has decided that POP3 e-mail can be used by employees only if the messages are encrypted in transit between the sender and recipient.

Working with your lab partner, make the appropriate configuration changes to send and receive encrypted e-mail when using a POP3 client. When you have exchanged encrypted and digitally signed messages with your lab partner, open a message that is both encrypted and digitally signed and take a screen shot of the message. Then save the screen shot to C:\Lab Manual\Lab 09\Labwork\ *YourLastName*-LC91.bmp (where *YourLastName* is your last name).

The following instructions show you how to save a screen shot.

1. Open the message and size the window the message appears in so that it does not take up too much space.

2. Make sure the message window is in the foreground, and then press ALT+PRINTSCR to copy the screen shot to the clipboard.

3. Click Start, select Run, type **pbrush** in the Open box, and click OK.

   The Paint program opens.

4. In Paint, press CTRL+V to copy the screen shot from the clipboard.

5. In Paint, from the File menu, select Save As.

6. In the Save As dialog box, click the Save In drop-down list, and navigate to C:\Lab Manual\Lab 09\Labwork.

7. In the File Name box, type the name of the file, and then click Save.

   Your screen shot should look something like the figure below. Note the icons on the right-hand side indicating an encrypted and signed message.

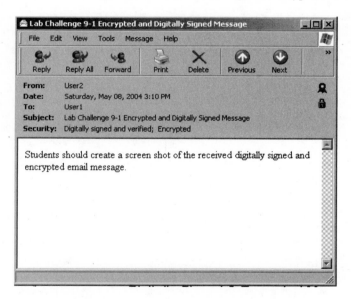

Your instructor might require you to submit the screen shot for evaluation. If this is the case, your instructor will provide additional instructions for submitting the file.

When you have finished taking the screen shot of the encrypted and digitally signed message, answer the questions below.

> **TIP**   To perform this lab challenge, you will have to log on as Contoso\Userx (where x is your student number) and configure Outlook Express to connect to the POP3 server used for the previous exercises. Note that when you log on to the POP3 service using Outlook Express, you will not see any of the e-mails you sent previously. These e-mails have been downloaded from the POP3 service and stored in a file accessible to the Adminx account used throughout the lab.

1. What do you need before you can send a digitally signed e-mail?

2. You are sending an encrypted e-mail. What is used to encrypt the e-mail: the recipient's public key, the recipient's private key, your public key, or your private key?

3. What is a digital ID in Outlook Express?

LAB 10
SECURING YOUR PERIMETER NETWORK

This lab contains the following exercises and activities:

■ Exercise 10-1: Using Netstat to View Open Ports

■ Exercise 10-2: Viewing Open Ports on Remote Computers

■ Exercise 10-3: Creating Packet Filters by Using Routing and Remote Access Services

■ Exercise 10-4: Creating Packet Filters by Using IPSec

■ Lab Review Questions

■ Lab Challenge 10-1: Creating Packet Filters for PPTP

After completing this lab, you will be able to

■ Use Netstat to view the port state on the local computer.

■ Use Netstat to record the port state to a text file according to a configured interval.

■ Use a scanning tool to examine open ports on a remote computer.

■ Configure packet filters by using Routing and Remote Access Services (RRAS).

■ Configure packet filters by using Internet Protocol Security (IPSec).

■ Create packet filters for a dedicated RRAS and Remote Authentication Dial-In User Service (RADIUS) server.

Estimated completion time: 130 minutes

SCENARIO

You are a network administrator for Contoso Pharmaceuticals. You are responsible for the security of computers that are located in the perimeter network (demilitarized zone, or DMZ). Although these computers are behind a firewall that implements strict inbound and outbound access rules, you want to harden them even more. You are particularly concerned about a Domain Name System (DNS) server that is configured to perform zone transfers to a remote host. You want to protect this computer by configuring packet filtering rules on the computer itself to implement a defense-in-depth strategy. With Microsoft Windows Server 2003, you have a number of options available to you to create packet filters. For example, you can use RRAS or IPSec to create packet filter rules.

As part of your research into providing more security for the DNS server, you want to determine whether it is preferable to implement packet filters by using RRAS or by using IPSec. However, before you can configure packet filtering on your server, you need to examine the Transmission Control Protocol (TCP) and User Datagram Protocol (UDP) ports that are currently open on the computer to establish a baseline. You will start by viewing the port status, using Netstat and a port scanning tool. You will then create packet filters by using RRAS. Finally, you will create packet filters by using IPSec.

EXERCISE 10-1: USING NETSTAT TO VIEW OPEN PORTS

Estimated completion time: 15 minutes

In this exercise, you will explore Netstat by evaluating what ports need to be blocked either by removing services or by packet filtering.

1. Log on to Contoso as Admin*x* (where *x* is your student number).

2. Click Start, select Run, type **cmd** in the Open box, and then click OK.

3. At the command prompt, type **netstat /?** and then review the available switches for the Netstat command.

4. Type **netstat —es** and then press ENTER.

   QUESTION   What does the output of the command display?

5. Type **netstat —na** and then press ENTER.

   The output of the command shows the protocol used (TCP or UDP), the TCP or UDP port number, the local and foreign (remote) address, and the connection state for TCP connections (Listen, Establish, Time_Wait, and so on). The port number is the TCP or UDP port number and is indicated by the number immediately to the right of the IP address. For example, UDP 0.0.0.0:53 indicates that UDP port 53 is in use, which is the port used for DNS query requests.

QUESTION   List the open TCP ports that have a value below 1024.

QUESTION   List the open UDP ports that have a value below 1024.

6.   Type **netstat –a** and then press ENTER.

QUESTION   What is the difference in the output of this Netstat command compared with the output of the Netstat command in step 5?

7.   Type **netstat –no** and then press ENTER.

QUESTION   What is the difference in the output of this Netstat command compared with the output of the Netstat command in steps 5 and 6?

8.   Type **netstat –o 5 > "c:\lab manual\lab 10\labwork\netstat.log"** (including the quotation marks), press ENTER, and then leave the command prompt open.

This command causes Netstat to output information every five seconds and write the output to a text file called netstat.log. When you redirect the output to a text file, you do not see the output of the Netstat command on the screen; you see a flashing cursor on the screen immediately below the command, indicating that Netstat is currently running in the command console window.

9.   Open Microsoft Internet Explorer and connect to http://computer*yy* (where *yy* is the two-digit version of your lab partner's student number).

10.   Click Start, select Run, type **cmd** in the Open box, and then click OK.

11.   Type **ftp computer*yy*** and then press ENTER.

12.   When prompted for the ftp username, type **ftp** and then press ENTER.

13.   When prompted for the password, type **admin*x*@contoso.com**, and then press ENTER.

14.   At the ftp prompt, type **ls** and then press ENTER.

15.   Type **quit** and then press ENTER.

16.   Click Start, select Run, type **\\computer*yy*** in the Open box, and then click OK.

17. Switch to the command prompt where you issued the Netstat command, and then press CTRL+C.

18. Click Start, select Run, type **notepad "c:\lab manual\lab 10\labwork\netstat.log"** in the Open box, and then click OK.

   QUESTION   What information is listed in the Netstat.log file?

19. Close all open windows.

EXERCISE 10-2: VIEWING OPEN PORTS ON REMOTE COMPUTERS

Estimated completion time: 10 minutes

   NOTE   You must have completed Lab 8, "Securing Network Communications," before beginning this exercise.

In this exercise, you will use a port scanner tool to test for open ports on your lab partner's computer. You and your lab partner will then reconfigure your DNS server to disallow zone transfer traffic. After reconfiguring your DNS server, you will then run the port scanning tool again to determine if the port responsible for DNS zone transfers (TCP port 53) shows up in the results of the port scan.

   IMPORTANT   You should never perform a port scan of a remote computer unless you have prior permission from the owner of the computer. Port scans can sometimes be interpreted as denial of service (DoS) attacks or as a prelude to an attack on vulnerable ports. If you perform an unauthorized port scan, you might violate your company's security policy. If you perform a port scan of hosts on the Internet, you might also violate your agreement with your Internet service provider (ISP).

1. Open Windows Explorer, navigate to C:\Lab Manual\Lab10, and then double-click Scanner.exe.

2. In the IP area of the SuperScan 3.00 window, in the Start and Stop boxes, type the IP address of your lab partner's computer.

3. In the Scan Type area, select the All Ports From option, and then in the All Ports From boxes, type **1** and **2000**, as shown below.

   NOTE   To reduce the time required for scanning, you will test for responses on the first 2000 ports only, which include the well-known ports 1–1024.

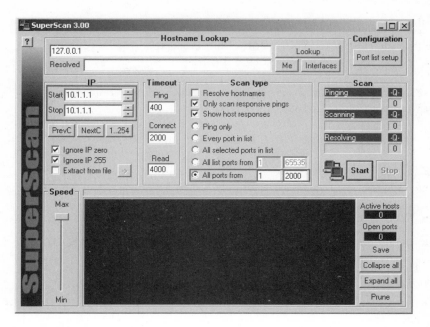

4. Click Start.

5. When the scan is complete, click Expand All, as shown below.

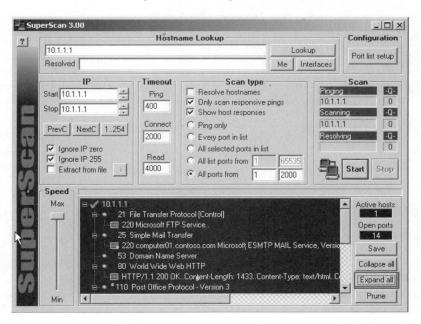

6. Examine the output of the port scan.

Note that the output of this version of SuperSscan shows only open TCP ports. It does not scan for open UDP ports.

QUESTION   In the output of the port scan, locate the Domain Name Server entry. What port number is listed for this entry?

7. Click Start, select Administrative Tools, and then click DNS.

NOTE   In the following steps, you will configure your DNS forward lookup zone to disallow zone transfer requests from any host. Zone transfers use TCP port 53.

8. In the Dnsmgmt console, click Forward Lookup Zones.

9. In the details pane, right-click the forward lookup zone that displays Standard Primary in the Type column, and then click Properties.

10. Select the Zone Transfers tab.

11. Clear the Allow Zone Transfers check box, as shown below, and then click OK.

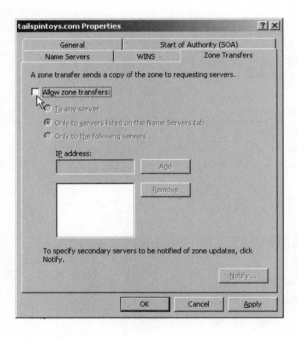

NOTE   Wait until your lab partner has completed the previous steps before proceeding with the next step.

12. In the details pane, right-click the forward lookup zone that displays Secondary in the Type column, and then select Reload From Master.

    You should receive a Zone Not Loaded By DNS Server error message, indicating that the zone transfer failed.

13. Close the Dnsmgmt console.

14. Switch to SuperScan 3.00.

15. In the SuperScan 3.00 window, click Start.

16. When the scan has finished, click Expand All.

17. Examine the output of the scan.

    Notice that the Domain Name Server port (TCP port 53) is still listed in the scan results of your partner's computer. The DNS server is still listening on this port and the computer will still accept TCP connection requests from any host to this port, even though the DNS server is configured not to allow DNS zone transfers to occur.

18. Leave the SuperScan window open for the next exercise.

EXERCISE 10-3: CREATING PACKET FILTERS BY USING ROUTING AND REMOTE ACCESS SERVICES

Estimated completion time: 20 minutes
In this exercise, you will use RRAS packet filters to drop ICMP Echo Requests and DNS Zone Transfer traffic from remote hosts.

Creating Inbound Filters to Block ICMP Echo Requests and DNS Zone Transfer Requests

1. Click Start, select Administrative Tools, and then click Routing And Remote Access.

2. In the Routing And Remote Access console, expand Computer*xx* (Local Computer) (where *xx* is the two-digit version of your student number), expand IP Routing, select General, right-click Local Area Connection, as shown below, and then click Properties.

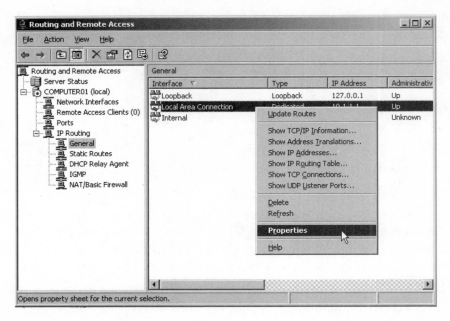

3. In the Local Area Connection Properties dialog box, click Inbound Filters, as shown below.

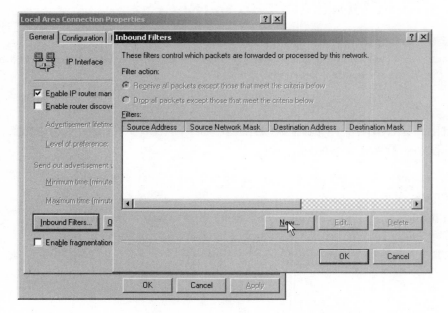

4. In the Inbound Filters dialog box, ensure that the Receive All Packets Except Those That Meet The Criteria Below option is selected, and click New.

5. In the Add IP Filter dialog box, select the Protocol drop-down list box, and then select ICMP.

6. In the ICMP Type box, type **8**, as shown below, and then click OK.

ICMP Echo Requests are used by the Ping command to determine whether a computer is available on the network. If a remote computer drops ICMP Echo Request traffic, the Ping command will return a Request Timed Out message. ICMP Echo Request packets are identified as type 8. Because a source or destination network is not specified, the filter will apply to any source or destination address.

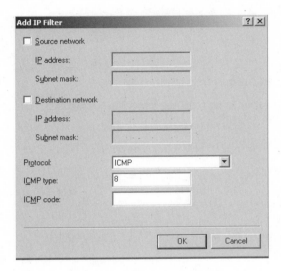

7. On the Inbound Filters page, click New.

8. In the Add IP Filter dialog box, select the Protocol drop-down list box, and then select TCP.

9. In the Destination Port box, type **53**, and then click OK.

With this configuration, your computer will drop all packets with a destination port of TCP 53 from any host.

10. In the Inbound Filters dialog box, click OK.

11. In the Local Area Connection Properties dialog box, click Apply to enforce the filter configuration while leaving the dialog box open.

Testing Inbound Filters

IMPORTANT   *Wait until your lab partner has completed the previous section before proceeding.*

1. Click Start, select Run, type **cmd** in the Open box, and then click OK.

2. In the command prompt, type **ping computer*yy*** (where *yy* is the two-digit version of your lab partner's student number), and then press ENTER.

   QUESTION   *What Ping response message did you receive?*

3. Switch to SuperScan 3.00.

4. In the SuperScan 3.00 window, in the Scan Type area, clear the Only Scan Responsive Pings check box, and then click Start.

   If you do not perform step 4, SuperScan will not perform a port scan of your lab partner's computer.

5. Wait until the scan is finished, and then click Expand All.

   QUESTION   *What does the red X in the Scan Results window indicate?*

   QUESTION   *Why do you not see an open port for the DNS server (53)?*

6. Switch to the Routing And Remote Access console, and then click Inbound Filters.

   Notice that the only options available for packet filtering are exclusive. You can either allow all traffic except that specified by the configured filters or you can drop all traffic except that specified by the configured filters. Given these exclusive options, RRAS does not provide a very granular level of control over packet filter rules, as would be the case with a true firewall product. For example, it is not possible to deny traffic with a destination port of TCP 53 from all hosts and then create an exception to that rule that would allow traffic with a destination port of TCP 53 from a specific host.

   IMPORTANT   *Make sure you perform the following steps to remove the RRAS packet filters.*

7. In the Inbound Filters dialog box, select the first filter in the list, click Delete, and then click Delete again to remove the remaining filter.

8. Click OK, and then, in the Local Area Connection Properties dialog box, click OK again.

   Wait until your lab partner has completed the previous steps before proceeding.

9. Switch to the command prompt, and then ping your lab partner's computer.

   NOTE The response to the Ping command indicates that the filters have been successfully removed.

10. Close the command prompt, the Routing And Remote Access console, and any remaining open windows except SuperScan 3.0.

EXERCISE 10-4: CREATING PACKET FILTERS BY USING IPSEC

Estimated completion time: 45 minutes

In addition to providing the ability to authenticate and encrypt TCP/IP traffic, IPSec can be used to allow or deny traffic based on a number of criteria, such as the source and destination IP address or the source and destination TCP and UDP ports. In this section, you will examine how you can leverage IPSec policy rules to provide a more granular level of control for packet filtering than RRAS does.

Creating an IPSec Policy Rule to Block Traffic from Any Host

1. On the desktop, double-click the IP Sec Tools console you created in Lab 7, "Securing Communications."

2. In the IP Sec Tools console, right-click IP Security Policies On The Local Computer, and then click Create IP Security Policy.

3. On the Welcome To The IP Security Policy Wizard page, click Next.

4. On the IP Security Policy page, in the Name box, type **Selectively Allow DNS and Block All ICMP Traffic** and then click Next.

5. On the Request For Secure Communication page, clear the Activate The Default Response Rule check box, and then click Next.

6. On the Completing The IP Security Policy Wizard page, click Finish.

7. In the Selectively Allow DNS And Block All ICMP Properties dialog box, ensure that the Use Add Wizard Option check box is cleared, and then click Add.

8. In the IP Filter List tab of the New Rule Properties dialog box, click Add.

9. In the IP Filter List dialog box, type **Block DNS and ICMP Traffic**, clear the Use Add Wizard check box, as shown below, and then click Add.

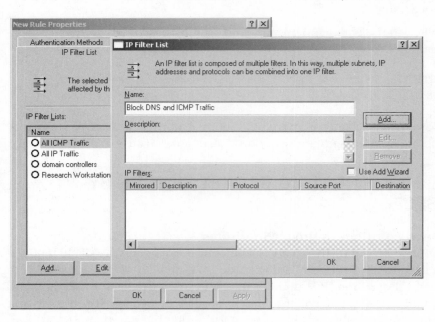

10. In the IP Filter Properties dialog box, in the Addresses tab, select the Source Address drop-down list box, and then select Any IP Address.

11. In the IP Filter Properties dialog box, from the Addresses tab, select the Destination Address drop-down list box, and then select My IP Address, as shown below.

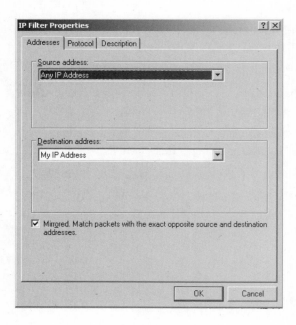

12. Select the Protocol tab.

13. In the Protocol tab of the IP Filter Properties dialog box, in the Select A Protocol Type drop-down list, select TCP.

14. In the Protocol tab of the IP Filter dialog box, in the Set The IP Protocol Port section, select the To This Port option button, type **53**, as shown below, and then click OK.

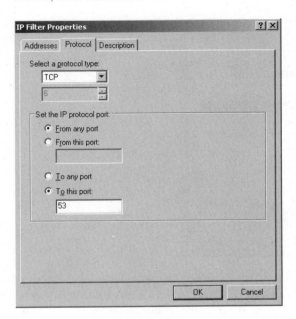

15. In the IP Filter List dialog box, click Add.

16. In the IP Filter dialog box, select the Source Address drop-down list from the Addresses tab, and then select Any IP Address.

17. In the IP Filter dialog box, select the Destination Address drop-down list from the Addresses tab, and then select My IP Address.

18. Clear the Mirrored Match Packets With The Exact Opposite Source And Destination Addresses check box.

This step is necessary to allow the computer to be able to ping other hosts.

19. Select the Protocol tab.

20. In the Protocol tab of the IP Filter Properties dialog box, in the Select A Protocol Type drop-down list, select ICMP, and then click OK.

21. In the IP Filter List dialog box, click OK to confirm your entries.

22. In the IP Filter List tab of the New Rule Properties page, select the Block DNS And ICMP Traffic option, as shown below, and then select the Filter Action tab.

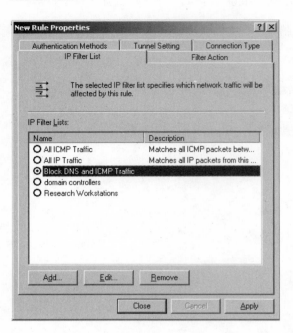

You might already have a Block Traffic option button that you created in Lab 7, "Securing Communications." The presence of this filter action will not affect this lab exercise. If you successfully completed Lab 7, you can optionally proceed to step 26 and select the Block Traffic option, rather than creating a redundant filter action in steps 23–25. Otherwise, perform steps 23–25 to create the filter action.

23. In the Filter Action tab, clear the Use Add Wizard check box, and then click Add.

24. On the New Filter Action Properties page, in the Security Methods tab, select the Block option, and then select the General tab.

25. In the General tab of the New Filter Action Properties dialog box, type **Block** for the name of the filter action, and then click OK.

26. In the Filter Action tab of the New Rule Properties page, select the Block option, as shown below, and then click Close.

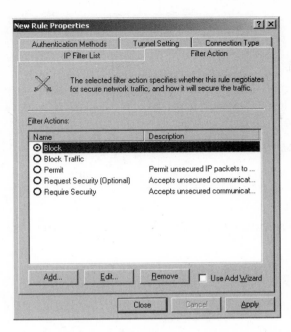

27. In the Selectively Allow DNS And Block All ICMP Traffic Properties dialog box, click OK.

28. In the IPSec Tools console, select IP Security Policies On The Local Computer; in the Name column, right-click Selectively Allow DNS And Block All ICMP Traffic Properties; and then click Assign.

   NOTE   Wait until your lab partner has completed the previous steps before proceeding.

29. Click Start, select Run, type **cmd** in the Open box, and then click OK.

30. At the command prompt, type **ping computeryy** (where *yy* is the two-digit version of your lab partner's student number), and then press ENTER.

   QUESTION   What ping response message did you receive?

31. Switch to SuperScan 3.00.

32. In the SuperScan 3.00 window, click Start.

33. Wait until the scan is finished, and then review the scan result output. Minimize Super Scan 3.0.

   QUESTION   Why isn't there an open port for the DNS server (53)?

Adding an IPSec Policy Rule to Allow Traffic from a Specific Host

1. In the IPSec Tools console, select IP Security Policies On The Local Computer; in the Name column, right-click Selectively Allow DNS And Block All ICMP Traffic; and then click Properties.

2. In the Selectively Allow DNS And ICMP Properties dialog box, ensure that the Use Add Wizard check box is cleared, and then click Add.

3. In the IP Filter List tab on the New Rule Properties dialog box, click Add.

4. In the IP Filter List dialog box, type **Allow Dns From Lab Partner** in the Name box, verify that the Use Add Wizard check box is cleared, and then click Add.

5. In the IP Filter Properties dialog box, select the Source Address drop-down list, and then select A Specific IP Address.

6. In the IP Address box, type your lab partner's IP address.

7. Click the Destination Address drop-down list, and then select My IP Address, as shown below.

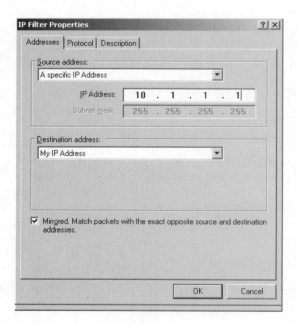

8. Select the Protocol tab.

9. In the Protocol tab on the IP Filter Properties dialog box, in the Select A Protocol Type drop-down list, select TCP.

10. In the Protocol tab on the IP Filter Properties dialog box, in the Set The IP Protocol Port section, select the To This Port option button, type **53**, and then click OK.

11. In the IP Filter List dialog box, click OK to confirm your entry.

12. In the IP Filter List tab on the New Rule Properties dialog box, select the Allow DNS From Lab Partner option, as shown below, and then click the Filter Action tab.

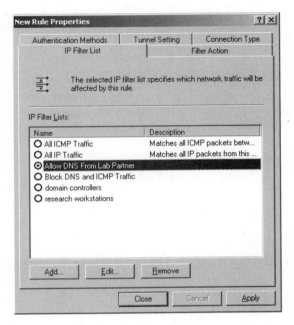

13. In the Filter Action tab on the New Rule Properties dialog box, select the Permit option button, and then click Apply.

14. Click OK, and then click OK to close the Selectively Allow DNS And Block All ICMP Properties dialog box.

    The next steps will ensure that the changes to the IPSec policy are applied immediately.

15. Switch to the command prompt.

16. At the command prompt, type **net stop policyagent** and then press ENTER.

17. At the command prompt, type **net start policyagent** and then
press ENTER.

NOTE   Wait until your lab partner has completed the previous steps before
proceeding.

18. At the command prompt, type **ping computeryy** (where *yy* is the two-
digit version of your lab partner's student number), and then press ENTER.

QUESTION   What ping response message did you receive?

19. Switch to SuperScan 3.00.

20. In the SuperScan 3.00 window, click Start.

21. Wait until the scan is finished, and then review the scan result output.

In the scan results, you should see an open port for the DNS server (53).
If you do not see this port in the output of the scan results, review your
configuration, paying special attention to the filter action for the Allow
DNS From The Lab Partner IP Filter List rule. You might also need to
restart the Policyagent service.

QUESTION   Why do you see an open port for the DNS server (53)?

22. Minimize SuperScan 3.00

Adding an IPSec Filter to Allow Traffic from a Specific Subnet

In this section, you will add a rule that will allow your computer to send and
receive ICMP traffic to and from hosts that belong to a specific subnet.

1. Switch to the command prompt.

2. At the command prompt, type **ping instructor01** and then press ENTER.

QUESTION   Why do you receive a Request Timed Out response, even though your
IPSec policy allows outbound ICMP traffic?

3. Switch to the IPSec Tools console.

4. In the IPSec Tools console, select IP Security Policies On The Local
Computer; in the Name column, right-click Selectively Allow DNS And
Block All ICMP Traffic; and then click Properties.

5. In the Selectively Allow DNS And Block All ICMP Properties dialog box,
ensure that the Use Add Wizard check box is cleared, and then click Add.

6. In the IP Filter List tab on the New Rule Properties dialog box, click Add.

7. In the IP Filter List dialog box, type **Allow ICMP From Classroom Subnet** in the Name box, ensure that the Use Add Wizard check box is cleared, and then click Add.

8. Click the Source Address drop-down list, select A Specific IP Subnet, type **x.y.z.0** (where *x.y.z* are the first three numbers of your IP address) in the IP Address box, and then type 255.255.255.0 in the Subnet Mask box.

9. Click the Destination Address drop-down list, select A Specific IP Subnet, type **x.y.z.0** (where *x.y.z* are the first three numbers of your IP address) in the IP Address box, and then type 255.255.255.0 in the Subnet Mask box, as shown below.

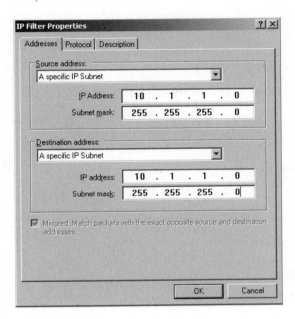

10. Select the Protocol tab.

11. Select the Select A Protocol Type drop-down list, select ICMP, and then click OK.

12. In the IP Filter List dialog box, click OK.

13. In the New Rule Property dialog box, select the Allow ICMP From Classroom Subnet option, and then select the Filter Action tab.

14. In the Filter Action tab, select the Permit option.

15. Click Close.

16. In the Selectively Allow DNS And Block All ICMP Traffic Properties dialog box, click OK.

17. In the IPSec Tools console, right-click the Selectively Allow DNS And Block All ICMP policy, and then select Rename.

18. Rename the policy to **Selectively Allow DNS And ICMP Traffic**.

19. Switch to the command prompt.

20. At the command prompt, type **ping instructor01** and then press ENTER.

    You receive a positive response to your ping from instructor01.

    IMPORTANT   Make sure you perform the following steps to restore your computer to its original state.

21. In the IPSec Tools console, right-click the Selectively Allow DNS And Block All ICMP policy, and then select Unassign.

22. Switch to the command prompt.

23. At the command prompt, type **net stop policyagent** and then press ENTER.

24. At the command prompt, type **net start policyagent** and then press ENTER.

25. Close all open windows and log off.

LAB REVIEW QUESTIONS

Estimated completion time: 10 minutes

1. Can you use the Netstat command to view the listening ports on a remote computer?

2. In the output of the Netstat –a command, what does the LISTENING state indicate?

3. Why is it a good idea to perform port scans of internal company computers on a regular basis?

4. Why is it a good idea to create packet filters for outbound as well as inbound traffic?

5. What advantage does packet filtering in IPSec have over packet filtering in RRAS?

6. When you create an IPSec IP filter, what effect does selecting the Mirrored option have?

LAB CHALLENGE 10-1: CREATING PACKET FILTERS FOR PPTP

Estimated completion time: 30 minutes

> **NOTE**   You must have completed Lab 7, "Securing Communications," before beginning this lab challenge.

Before beginning this lab challenge, you might need to reconfigure the computer that will act as the PPTP client to use PPTP, rather than Layer Two Tunneling Protocol (L2TP), to connect to the RRAS server. See Lab 7, "Securing Communications," for details on reconfiguring your client to use PPTP. Also, this lab challenge requires that you determine what ports are used for RADIUS accounting and authentication. To determine what ports are used for RADIUS accounting and authentication, you can use Network Monitor to capture traffic related to RADIUS authentication. Alternatively, you can load the C:\Lab Manual\Lab 10\Pptp-radius.cap file in Network Monitor to determine this information. It would also be helpful to consult the Microsoft Windows Help files before doing this lab challenge.

You recently installed a dedicated RRAS and Internet Authentication Service (IAS) server in your perimeter network. Employees will use this server to establish virtual private network (VPN) tunnels to the corporate network using Point-to-Point Tunneling Protocol (PPTP). This server also uses RADIUS to perform a centralized authentication function for other VPN servers. Because this is a dedicated server, you want to ensure that only essential outbound or inbound traffic related to PPTP and RADIUS is allowed on the Internet-facing network interface of this computer.

For this lab challenge, work with your lab partner to configure one of your servers with the appropriate packet filters to drop all inbound and outbound traffic except for traffic related to PPTP and RADIUS. Record the packet filter configuration you create in the Lab10Worksheet.doc, which you can find in the C:\lab manual\Lab 10 folder. When you have completed the worksheet, save it as C:\Lab Manual\Lab 10\Labwork*YourLastName*-Lab10-PPTP-filters.doc (where *YourLastName* is your last name). If your instructor requires you to submit the file for evaluation, he or she will provide additional instructions for submitting it. If time permits, remove the packet filters on the RRAS server and re-create the RRAS configuration on the other computer.

IMPORTANT   Because you are creating RRAS packet filters on a computer with only one network interface adapter, you might experience delays in accessing the properties of the network interface adapter in RRAS after you have implemented the filters. You might have to wait a short time to open up the property pages after implementing the filters.

After completing this lab challenge, remember to remove the packet filters to restore your computer to its original configuration.

LAB 11
MAINTAINING OPERATIONAL SECURITY

This lab contains the following exercises and activities:

- Exercise 11-1: Enhancing Physical Security
- Exercise 11-2: Using the System Key Utility
- Exercise 11-3: Ensuring the Proper Disposal of Data
- Exercise 11-4: Using Cipher.exe to Permanently Delete Data
- Exercise 11-5: Enhancing Data Availability
- Exercise 11-6: Backing Up and Restoring Data Using the Incremental Backup Type
- Lab Review Questions
- Lab Challenge 11-1: Backing Up Critical Files

After completing this lab, you will be able to

- Plan for the physical security of servers.
- Use the System Key utility to enhance the protection of computers running Microsoft Windows Server 2003.
- Plan for the proper disposal of data.
- Use Cipher.exe to dispose of data remaining in unallocated hard drive space.
- Plan for data recovery.
- Back up and restore data using the Windows 2003 Backup utility.

Estimated completion time: 150 minutes

SCENARIO

You are a security administrator for Contoso Pharmaceuticals, and you have a wide range of responsibilities. You make recommendations to management for securing the physical infrastructure of the network. You also make recommendations for the safe disposal of sensitive data. Finally, you are responsible for the efficient and reliable backup of a number of critical servers.

EXERCISE 11-1: ENHANCING PHYSICAL SECURITY

Estimated completion time: 30 minutes

In this exercise, you and your lab partner will work together to create a list of recommendations for enhancing the physical security of domain controllers in Contoso's branch offices, based on the scenario below. A number of questions follow the scenario to help you create your list of recommendations.

Compile your recommendations in a text file that you create using Notepad or Wordpad. After you have finished compiling a list of recommendations, your instructor will lead the class in a discussion of the exercise. Your instructor might require you to submit the text file containing your recommendations for evaluation. If so, the instructor will give you specific instructions for naming and submitting the file.

Scenario

You are a network administrator at the headquarters for Contoso Pharmaceuticals. Because of the sensitivity of the data stored at headquarters, the company has made a significant investment in security measures. For example, physical access to domain controllers and other critical servers is severely restricted. However, domain controllers for the contoso.com domain and a number of child domains are located in geographically remote branch offices. There is a wide disparity in the security environments of these branch offices. For example, some offices are located in single-story buildings that lack 24-hour onsite security personnel. Other offices are located in multistory buildings that have 24-hour onsite security personnel and where after-hour elevator access is restricted to authorized personnel only. In some instances, the domain controllers and other servers are located in the office of the branch office network administrator. The figure below shows the typical arrangement of a dual-purpose room that serves as the network administrator's office and as the file server room.

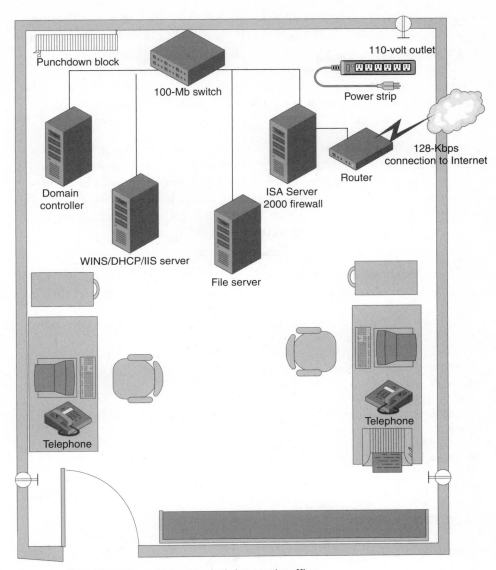

Branch office network administrator's office

You are concerned about the lack of physical security of the domain controllers and other servers in some of these offices. Because of the size of the Active Directory directory service, the design of Active Directory and the speed of the WAN links, it is not practical to remove the domain controllers from these remote offices. Doing so would result in excessively long logon times, resulting in a loss of productivity. Furthermore, having domain controllers at the branch offices increases fault tolerance and the availability of Active Directory.

You have brought your concerns to management. They agree that the physical security of the domain controllers needs to be enhanced throughout the company and are willing to provide a budget for the improvements. However, before a budget is approved, management wants to see a list of recommendations that will be incorporated into a revised security policy that will outline the minimum standards for physically securing domain controllers at all offices. Management has asked you to provide this list of recommendations.

Because the recommendations need to cover the minimum requirements for physically securing all domain controllers, they need to take into account local conditions. In your preliminary research, you have learned that in all locations the lease agreements allow you to make physical changes to the offices, including reconfiguring office space, adding new wiring, and changing ventilation ducts. However, providing 24-hour onsite security personnel is not possible or economical at all locations.

The following list of questions will help you compile your list of recommendations. You should, however, go beyond the provided questions to create your final list.

QUESTION   If 24-hour onsite security is not possible in all locations, what other measures can you use to provide constant monitoring?

QUESTION   In cases where the network administrator shares office space with the servers, what changes should you make?

QUESTION   What measures can you take to restrict physical access to rooms where the servers are located?

QUESTION   Is the plenum space a concern? If so, how would you deal with it?

QUESTION   Should you log access to the server room? If so, how would you do this?

QUESTION   Who should have access to the server room?

QUESTION   Would any changes to the heating or air conditioning system be required?

QUESTION   If it is necessary to build or modify a server room, what consideration should you give to the power requirements?

QUESTION   What recommendations would you make for a fire suppressant system?

QUESTION   How would you deal with risks that some fire suppressant systems create, in particular those fire suppressant systems that extinguish the fire by removing oxygen from the environment?

QUESTION   Why should you include in your plan an emergency shutdown procedure for computers in your server room in the event of a fire?

EXERCISE 11-2: USING THE SYSTEM KEY UTILITY

Estimated completion time: 10 minutes

You are a network administrator for Contoso Pharmaceuticals. While management is positive about your plan for enhancing the physical security of the domain controllers and member servers, they are concerned that these tight security measures might be compromised. In particular, they would like have some way of increasing the security of the accounts databases if an unauthorized individual gains physical access to the computers. In this exercise, you will use the System Key utility (Syskey) to provide stronger encryption of your server's Security Accounts Management (SAM) database.

Updating Syskey to Use a Password for Startup

1. Log on to Contoso as Admin*x* (where *x* is your student number).

2. Click Start, select Run, type **syskey** in the Open box, and then click OK.

3. In the Securing The Windows Account Database dialog box, read the description, ensure that the Encryption Enabled option is selected, and then click Update.

4. In the Startup Key dialog box, select Password Startup, as shown below; type **P@ssw0rd** in the Password and Confirm Password boxes; and then click OK.

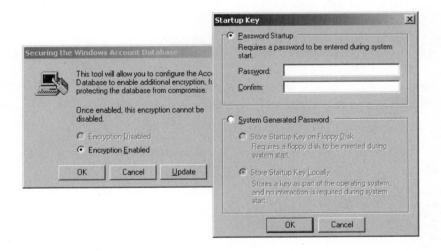

QUESTION   What option in the Startup Key dialog box provides the greatest security?

5. Click OK to acknowledge the success message.

6. Close all open windows.

7. Press CTRL+ALT+DEL, and then click Shutdown.

8. In the Shutdown Windows dialog box, select the What Do You Want The Computer To Do drop-down list, and then select Restart.

9. Select the Option drop-down list box, as shown below, and then select Security Issue from the list of shutdown categories.

10. In the Comment box, type **Planned restart to update Syskey configuration to require a startup password** and then click OK.

   Wait while Microsoft Windows restarts.

11. In the Startup Password dialog box, type **P@ssw0rd** in the Password box, as shown below, and then click OK.

12. Log on to Contoso as Adminx (where *x* is your student number).

13. Click Start, select Run, type **eventvwr** in the Open box, and then click OK.

14. In Event Viewer, select the System log, and then double-click the most recent event that displays 1074 in the Event column, as shown below.

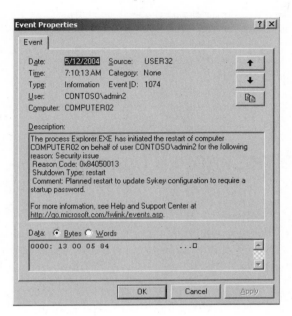

15. Close Event Viewer.

QUESTION   How can the System Event Shutdown tracker improve an organization's change management processes, especially when administrators have shown an unwillingness to follow proper procedures for manually documenting changes to computer systems?

Restoring Default Syskey Settings

1. Click Start, select Run, type **syskey** in the Open box, and then click OK.

2. In the Securing The Windows Account Database, click Update.

3. In the Startup Key dialog box, select System Generated Password, select Store Startup Key Locally, and then click OK.

4. In the Windows Startup Password dialog box, type **P@ssw0rd** in the Password box; click OK; and then click OK to acknowledge the success message.

5. Close all open windows and restart the computer.

While the computer is restarting, answer the following questions.

QUESTION   Why is the default Syskey setting less secure than the other options?

QUESTION   In order to crack an accounts database that has been secured by Syskey, it is necessary to acquire a copy of the Security Accounts Management (SAM) database and the system files from the target computer. What countermeasures can you take to prevent or detect possible unauthorized copying of these files?

6. When the computer restarts, log on to Contoso as Admin*x* (where *x* is your student number).

EXERCISE 11-3: ENSURING THE PROPER DISPOSAL OF DATA

Estimated completion time: 20 minutes

In this exercise, you and your lab partner will work together to create a list of recommendations for properly disposing of data stored on hard drives and backup tapes. A number of questions follow the scenario to help you create your list of recommendations.

You should compile these recommendations in a text file that you create using Notepad or Wordpad. After you have finished compiling your list of recommendations, your instructor will lead the class in a discussion of the exercise. Your instructor might require you to submit the text file containing your recommendations for evaluation. If so, the instructor will give you specific instructions for naming and submitting the file.

Scenario

You are a network administrator for Contoso Pharmaceuticals. Your company is about to upgrade a number of servers, workstations, and backup tape devices. The company wants to donate the used hardware to a local school. Also, because your new backup devices are not compatible with the backup tapes you are currently using, the company wants to donate the spare backup tapes to the local school as well. However, the company has informed the school that, if security considerations warrant it, some of the donated computers will not include hard drives.

You have been asked to make recommendations regarding the disposal of this equipment. Some of the hard drives and backup tapes contain highly sensitive and proprietary information.

QUESTION   Will formatting the hard drives prevent recovery of sensitive data?

QUESTION   What measures should you take to ensure that data cannot be recovered from the donated hard drives?

QUESTION   Some of the server hard drives contain highly sensitive information. Would you recommend that these hard drives be donated?

QUESTION   What should you do to ensure that data cannot be recovered from the backup tapes?

QUESTION   Would you include the backup tapes in the donated items?

QUESTION   There are a number of utilities designed to thoroughly erase data. Should you recommend specific utilities?

EXERCISE 11-4: USING CIPHER.EXE TO PERMANENTLY DELETE DATA

Estimated completion time: 10 minutes

Many employees of Contoso Pharmaceuticals use laptop computers. Because of the sensitive nature of the data that might be on these laptop computers, company policy dictates that all sensitive or proprietary data on laptop computers must be encrypted with Encrypting File System (EFS). Your manager has expressed concern about the process that EFS uses to encrypt data. Specifically, she is concerned that when EFS encrypts data, it makes a temporary copy of the file in case there is a failure during the encryption process. When the encryption process is complete, the temporary file is deleted. However, the deleted file is still present as "deallocated" data on the hard drive, and the data is still recoverable until it has been overwritten.

Your manager wants you to show her how to use the Cipher.exe command to permanently remove the deallocated data on laptop volumes. Because she intends to create guidelines on the use of the Cipher command, she would like some indication of when it is appropriate to run this command. To reinforce the fact that removing data using the Cipher command is a disk-intensive activity and should therefore be run at times when it will not affect user productivity, you will use System Monitor to examine disk activity while the Cipher command runs.

1. Click Start, select Run, type **cmd** in the Open box, and then click OK.

2. At the command prompt, type **cipher /?** and press ENTER; note the syntax for the /w switch; and then read the description for the /w switch.

   QUESTION   The description states that the /w switch removes unused data from the entire volume. What is the purpose of the /w switch syntax allowing you to specify a directory, for example, cipher /w:C:\Test?

3. Click Start, select Run, type **perfmon** in the Open box, and then click OK.

4. In the Performance console, select System Monitor, and then click the Add icon on the toolbar, as shown below.

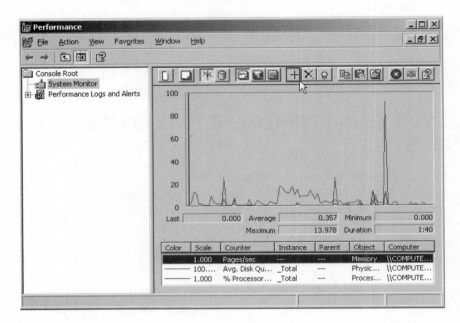

5. In the Add Counters dialog box, select the Performance Object drop-down list, and then select Physical Disk.

6. In the Select Counters From List box, select %Disk Write Time, and then click Add, as shown below.

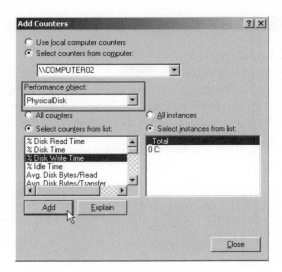

7. In the Select Counters From List box, select Disc Writes/Sec, click Add, and then click Close.

8. Switch to the command prompt.

9. At the command prompt, type **cipher /w:c:** and then press ENTER.

10. While the Cipher command is running, switch to the Performance console.

11. In the Performance console, select the Physical Disk: %Disk Write Time counter you added in step 7, press CTRL+H to highlight the real-time performance activity in the graph, and observe the activity. Then, using the up and down arrows, look at their values.

   QUESTION   Do the counters indicate intensive disk activity?

   Depending on the size and speed of your hard drives, this command could take a few minutes to run. After observing the effect of the Cipher command on system performance, you might want to take a short break or use the time to do some of the review questions at the end of the lab.

12. Switch to the command prompt, and then wait for the command to finish.

   QUESTION   What three write operations did the Cipher /w command perform?

13. Close the command prompt and the Performance console.

EXERCISE 11-5: ENHANCING DATA AVAILABILITY

Estimated completion time: 20 minutes

In this exercise, you and your lab partner will work together to create a list of recommendations for ensuring that your backup and recovery times for a critical server meet the minimum requirements as specified by management. A number of questions follow the scenario to help you create your list of recommendations.

You should compile your recommendations in a text file that you create using Notepad or Wordpad. After you have finished compiling your list of recommendations, your instructor will lead the class in a discussion of the exercise. Your instructor might require you to submit the text file containing your recommendations for evaluation. If so, the instructor will give you specific instructions for naming and submitting the file.

Scenario

A server used by Contoso Pharmaceuticals contains a large amount of critical data stored in a Microsoft Windows SQL 2000 database that is used extensively to support daily operations of the company. The amount of critical data on the server is close to 50 GB in size, and it is located on a redundant array of independent disks (RAID) 5 volume. The transaction logs for the database are located on a mirrored volume of the same computer. You recently bought a new backup device that is, according to the manufacturer, capable of a native data throughput of around 30 Mbps. The backup device is connected to a dedicated backup computer. This computer is located on the same 100-Mbps Ethernet segment as the server that contains the critical data.

Management has stated that, in the event of a catastrophic failure to the server that contains the critical data, the data must be restored and available to users within an hour. A maximum of two hours worth of data loss is tolerable.

You test backups and restores of 50 GB of data and find that backup and restore times are far longer than the required minimums. What should you recommend as a solution to ensure that backups can be restored within the minimum time specified by management?

> **QUESTION**   The tape device supports a very high-rate native throughput rate. It should easily be able to restore 50 GB in an hour, even with the Verify option enabled. What are the likely bottlenecks?

QUESTION   What kinds of backups should you perform: full, differential, incremental, or a combination of these? How often should you perform them?

QUESTION   If you bought backup software that had specific plug-ins for SQL 2000 databases, what effect would it have on the rate of backups and restores?

QUESTION   Assuming that catastrophic failure means the complete destruction of the computer— for example, if there were a fire in the server room—would you be able to build a computer, load an operating system, install SQL, and restore the data within an hour? If not, what solution can you recommend?

EXERCISE 11-6: BACKING UP AND RESTORING DATA USING THE INCREMENTAL BACKUP TYPE

Estimated completion time: 25 minutes

To gain an understanding of different backup types, you will perform a full backup of test data, and then you will modify some of the data and perform an incremental backup.

Performing Normal and Incremental Backups

1. Open Windows Explorer and browse to C:\Lab Manual\Lab 11\Backup.

   This folder contains text files copied from the *Microsoft Windows 2003 Installation* CD.

2. From the View menu, select Details, and then note the file attributes in the Attribute column.

   QUESTION   What attribute type is listed in the Attributes column for each file?

3. Click Start, select All Programs, select Accessories, select System Tools, and then click Backup.

4. On the Welcome To The Backup Or Restore Wizard page, clear the Always Start In Wizard Mode check box, as shown below, and then click the Advanced Mode link.

5. In the Backup Utility console, select the Backup tab.

6. In the folder tree, expand the C drive, browse to C:\Lab Manual\Lab 11\, and then select the Backup folder.

7. In the Backup Media Or File Name box, click Browse, and then click Cancel when prompted to insert a floppy disk into the A drive.

8. On the Save As page, select the Save In drop-down list and browse to C:\Lab Manual\lab 11, type **Lab11Backup** in the File Name box, and then click Save.

The graphic below shows the results of the backup configuration.

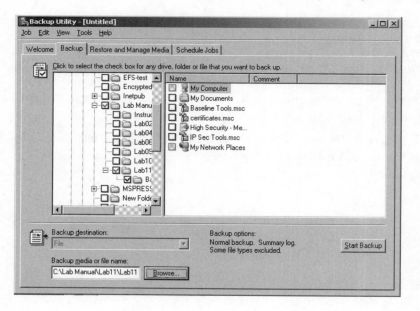

9. Click Start Backup.

10. In the Backup Job Information dialog box, click Start Backup.

The Backup Progress dialog box opens. After a few minutes, the status bar indicates the backup job is complete.

11. To view the report, click Report.

12. Examine the details of the report, and then close the Notepad window.

13. In the Backup Progress dialog box, click Close.

14. Switch to Windows Explorer, and then view the attributes of the files in the C:\Lab Manual\Lab 11\Backup folder.

QUESTION How have the file attributes changed? What does this indicate?

15. Double-click one of the files to open it in Notepad, press ENTER to make a change to the file, save the file, close Notepad, and then view the file attribute.

QUESTION Did the file attribute on the file change?

16. Switch to the Backup Utility console.

17. In the Backup tab, in the folder tree, expand the C drive, browse to C:\Lab Manual\Lab 11\, and then click the Backup folder.

18. In the Backup Media Or File Name box, ensure that the C:\Lab Manual\Lab 11\Lab11Backup.bkf file is selected, and then click Start Backup.

19. In the Backup Job Information dialog box, ensure that the Append This Backup To The Media option is selected, and then click Advanced.

20. Select the Backup Type drop-down list; select Incremental, as shown below; and then click OK.

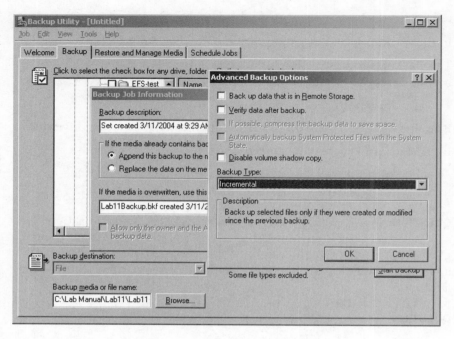

21. In the Backup Job Information dialog box, click Start Backup.

22. When the backup is complete, examine the summary in the Backup Progress dialog box, and then click Close.

23. Switch to Windows Explorer and view the attribute on the file you modified in step 15.

    QUESTION   Did the file attribute on the file change?

    QUESTION   If you had performed a differential backup, would the file attribute have changed?

24. Double-click a different file from the one you modified in step 15, press ENTER to make a change to the file, save the file, close Notepad, and then view the file attribute.

25. Switch to the Backup Utility console.

26. In the Backup tab, in the folder tree, expand the C drive, browse to C:\Lab Manual\Lab 11\, and then click the Backup folder.

27. In the Backup Media Or File Name box, ensure that the C:\Lab Manual\ Lab 11\Lab11Backup.bkf file is selected, and then click Start Backup.

28. In the Backup Job Information dialog box, ensure that the Append This Backup To The Media option is selected, and then click Advanced.

29. Select the Backup Type drop-down list, select Incremental, and then click OK.

30. In the Backup Job Information dialog box, click Start Backup.

31. When the backup is complete, examine the summary in the Backup Progress dialog box, and then click Close.

32. Switch to Windows Explorer and view the attribute on the file you modified in step 24.

You can view the information in the Date Modified column to identify which files you modified.

Restoring Data from a Normal and Incremental Backup

In this section, you will delete the files you backed up and then restore them from the normal and incremental backups. You will first restore the normal backup and then restore the incremental backups in the order that you performed them.

1. In Windows Explorer, browse to C:\Lab Manual\Lab 11\, right-click the Backup folder, and then select Delete.

2. Click Yes to confirm the deletion and send the folder the Recycle Bin.

3. Switch to the Backup Utility console.

4. Select the Restore And Manage Media tab.

5. Fully expand the first backup set, and then click the C:\Lab Manual\ Lab 11\Backup folder, as shown below.

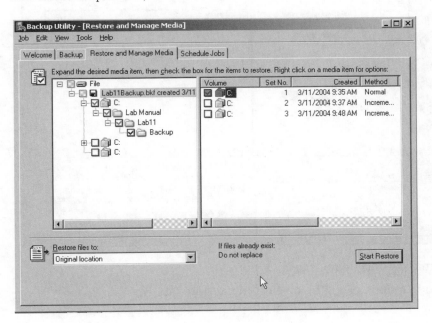

6. Click Start Restore.

7. Click Advanced in the Confirm Restore dialog box, review the settings, and then click OK.

8. Click OK in the Confirm Restore dialog box.

The Restore Progress dialog box appears.

9. When the restore process is complete, click Report to review the details of the restore process, and then close Notepad.

You will have to scroll down to see the information on the number of files that are restored.

10. Close the Restore Progress dialog box.

11. Switch to Windows Explorer, and then browse to C:\Lab Manual\ Lab 11\Backup to confirm the success of the restore process.

Note that the information in the Date Modified column indicates that all the files were last modified at the same time.

12. Switch to the Backup Utility console, fully expand the second backup set, and then click the C:\Lab Manual\Lab 11\Backup folder, as shown below.

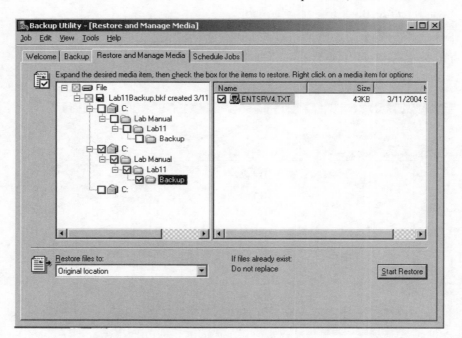

13. From the Tools menu, select Options.

14. In the Options dialog box, select the Restore tab.

15. Select the option to Replace The File On The Disk Only If The File On Disk Is Older, and then click OK.

16. In the Backup Utility console, click Start Restore, and then click OK in the Confirm Restore dialog box.

17. When the restore process is complete, close the Restore Progress dialog box.

18. Fully expand the third backup set, and then click the C:\Lab Manual\ Lab 11\Backup folder.

19. Click Start Restore, and then click OK in the Confirm Restore dialog box.

20. When the restore process is complete, click Report to review the details of the restore jobs, and then close Notepad.

21. Close the Restore Progress dialog box.

22. Switch to Windows Explorer, and then view the files in the C:\ Lab Manual\Lab 11\Backup folder.

    You should see that both of the files you modified have been restored. Note that if you had performed a normal backup followed by differential backups, instead of incremental backups, you would have had to perform only two restore operations: first you would restore the normal backup, and then you would restore the last differential backup. When considering backup types, you should always consider the tradeoffs implicit in the choice of the backup type. The backup type you choose will determine the amount of time it takes to restore the data.

23. Close all open windows and log off.

LAB REVIEW QUESTIONS

Estimated completion time: 15 minutes

1. You are considering buying a UPS for a server room located in a branch office in Tampa, Florida. Why would it be a good idea to collect data on lightning activity in this, or any other region, before purchasing the UPS?

2. Although tools now exist that can run brute-force attacks on Syskey-protected accounts databases, why is it still a good idea to enable Syskey?

3. When you delete a file from a hard drive, what actually changes on the hard drive itself?

4. How does the Cipher.exe /w command remove unallocated data?

5. You are considering a backup solution for a number of critical servers on your network. List three or four factors you should consider before deciding on a solution.

6. Describe the difference between a differential and an incremental backup type.

7. Which backup type takes longer to restore: incremental or differential?

LAB CHALLENGE 11-1: BACKING UP CRITICAL FILES

Estimated completion time: 20 minutes

You have recently been made responsible for maintaining and securing a Windows Server 2003 member server. This server has a particularly important role on your network because it issues computer and user digital certificates, both through autoenrollment and Web enrollment. Upon performing a review of the server, you discover that some of the data on the server is regularly backed up, but the registry, system files, boot files, Internet Information Services (IIS) metabase, and certificate services database are not backed up on a regularly scheduled basis. You decide to create a backup job that will back up these critical files on a weekly basis. You schedule the backup to run at 10:00 P.M. every Saturday evening. You want to create this backup job with the least amount of administrative effort.

After you complete this challenge, take a screen shot of the Backup tab showing the backup selections and a screen shot of the Schedule Job dialog box showing the weekly job. Save these screen shots as Backup.bmp and Schedule.bmp in the C:\Lab Manual\Lab 11\Labwork folder. If your instructor requires you to submit the screen shots for evaluation, you will be given further instructions.

> **TIP** To take a screen shot, make sure the window element of interest is in the foreground, and then press ALT+PRINTSCREEN to copy the screen shot into the buffer. Open the Paint program, and then press CTRL+V to paste the screen shot into Paint. Finally, save the .bmp file in Paint with the appropriate name.

LAB 12
MAINTAINING ORGANIZATIONAL SECURITY

This lab contains the following exercises and activities:

■ Exercise 12-1: Creating an Acceptable E-Mail Use Policy

■ Exercise 12-2: Enforcing a Software Restriction Policy

■ Exercise 12-3: Using Windows File Protection to Enhance System Stability

■ Exercise 12-4: Enforcing an Internet Acceptable Use Policy

■ Exercise 12-5: Using Windows Tools to Document System Information

■ Lab Review Questions

■ Lab Challenge 12-1: Enforcing Security Policies By Using Group Policy

After completing this lab, you will be able to

■ Understand the elements of a security policy.

■ Create an acceptable use policy.

■ Use Windows File Protection (WFP) to ensure that critical system files are not accidentally or maliciously removed or corrupted.

■ Enforce security policies that prohibit specific software from running on computers.

■ Use group policies to enforce acceptable use policies.

■ Use tools, such as Msinfo32.exe, to document systems.

Estimated completion time: 145 minutes

SCENARIO

You are a network administrator at Contoso Pharmaceuticals. Among your many responsibilities, you participate in the Computer Security Steering Committee as a representative of the IT group. The steering committee is responsible for formulating computer security and acceptable use policies. You are often asked to demonstrate to the committee whether security or acceptable use policies can be enforced through a technological solution, rather than merely through user education and awareness and through the threat of sanctions for noncompliance. Also, you are responsible for ensuring that computer systems are properly documented throughout the company.

EXERCISE 12-1: CREATING AN ACCEPTABLE E-MAIL USE POLICY

Estimated completion time: 35 minutes

In this exercise, you will work with your lab partner to create an acceptable e-mail use policy.

Scenario

Recently, Contoso Pharmaceuticals lost a wrongful dismissal suit against a former employee who was terminated because he violated the acceptable e-mail use policy. The current e-mail policy has a blanket prohibition against using company e-mail for personal reasons. The employee used company e-mail to run a home business. However, when the case went to trial, it was determined that use of company e-mail for personal reasons was commonplace throughout the company. Furthermore, it was also found that the e-mail policy was never enforced, except in this one instance. The judge, therefore, would not allow violation of the policy as just cause for dismissal. The company was found liable for court costs and an extensive severance payment.

You have been asked to be on a committee that will recommend a new e-mail acceptable use policy. One of the first things the committee determined is that the current e-mail acceptable use policy is far too restrictive and, consequently, unenforceable. The committee will write the new policy from scratch, and you have been asked to submit a first draft of the policy.

Instructions

To complete the lab exercise, you will work with your lab partner to create an acceptable e-mail use policy. To help you create the policy, you can use the template that is in the C:\Lab Manual\Lab 12 folder. The template file contains practical guidelines for completing the various sections of the policy. The C:\Lab Manual\ Lab 12 folder also contains the Site Security Handbook (Request for Comments, or RFC, 2196), which might help you construct the policy. The handbook is located in the C:\Lab Manual\Lab 12\Rfc2196.txt file.

Using WordPad and the _Email_Policy_template.doc file located in the C:\ Lab Manual\Lab12 directory, create the e-mail policy. Save it as C:\Lab Manual\ Lab 12\Labwork\ *YourLastName*_EMail_Policy.doc (where *YourLastName* is your last name). Your instructor might require you to submit the file for evaluation. If so, your instructor will provide additional instructions for submitting it for evaluation.

EXERCISE 12-2: ENFORCING A SOFTWARE RESTRICTION POLICY

Estimated completion time: 20 minutes

As a result of lawsuits that have imposed extremely punitive penalties on companies that stored copyright-protected MP3 files, Contoso Pharmaceuticals has formed a committee to reexamine its acceptable use policy. As a member of the committee, you have been asked to determine whether it is possible to use group policy or some other mechanism to enforce a new acceptable use policy to restrict the use of specific software, such as software that is used for peer-to-peer file sharing.

In this exercise, you will examine the feasibility of using software restriction policies to enforce the company's proposed acceptable use policy.

1. Log on to Contoso as Admin*x* (where *x* is your student number).

2. Click Start, select Run, type **gpedit.msc** in the Open box, and then click OK.

3. In the Group Policy Object Editor console, in the tree pane, browse to \Computer Configuration\Windows Settings\Security Settings, right-click Software Restriction Policies, and then select New Software Restriction Policies, as shown below.

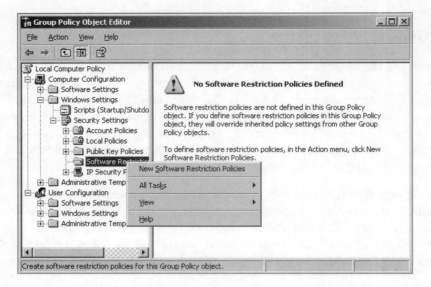

4. In the tree pane, select Security Levels, and in the details pane, double-click Disallowed.

   Note the description.

5. Click Cancel.

6. In the tree pane, select Additional Rules.

7. In the details pane, note the four default rules, and then answer the following questions.

   QUESTION   *What kind of path do these four rules use?*

   QUESTION   *Is it possible to use wildcards for the path rules?*

8. In the tree pane, right-click Additional Rules, and then click New Hash Rule.

9. In the New Hash Rule dialog box, click Browse.

10. In the Open dialog box, select the Look In drop-down list, browse to C:\Program Files\Windows Media Player, select Wmplayer.exe, and then click Open.

11. In the New Hash Rule dialog box, ensure that Disallowed is selected in the Security Level drop-down list, and then click OK.

12. In the Group Policy Object Editor console, in the tree pane, select Software Restriction Policies, and then double-click Enforcement in the details pane.

13. In the Enforcement Properties dialog box, select the All Users Except Local Administrators option, as shown below, and then click OK.

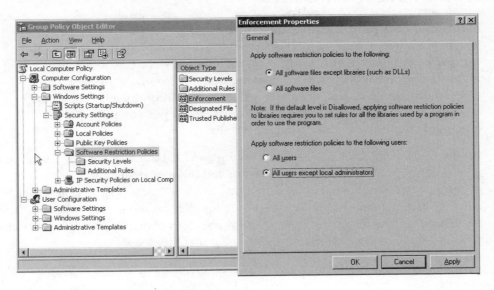

14. Close the Group Policy Object Editor console.

15. Click Start, select Shut Down, select Restart in the What Do You Want Your Computer To Do drop-down list, type **restart to apply software restriction policy** in the Comment box, and then click OK.

Software restriction policies represent a rare instance when it is necessary to restart the computer in order for the policy to be applied.

16. After the computer restarts, log on to Contoso as User*x*.

17. Click Start, select Run, type **wmplayer.exe** in the Open box, and then click OK.

QUESTION   What message did you receive?

18. Log off, and then log on to Contoso as Admin*x*.

19. Click Start, select Run, type **wmplayer.exe** in the Open box, and then click OK.

The Welcome To The Windows Media Player 9 Series page opens.

20. Close the Welcome To The Windows Media Player 9 Series page.

EXERCISE 12-3: USING WINDOWS FILE PROTECTION TO ENHANCE SYSTEM STABILITY

Estimated completion time: 20 minutes

Recently, an e-mail virus hoax has started to spread rapidly throughout your company. The hoax is spread by well-meaning individuals who are forwarding what they believe is an e-mail from an authoritative source informing them how to detect and remove a virus from infected systems. Unfortunately, the e-mail message instructs people to locate and delete an important and legitimate executable file used by the operating system.

Even though your company has a security policy that informs employees never to take action regarding viruses unless instructed by management or the IT department, management is concerned that in some instances the policy will be ignored. Management has therefore posted an alert on the intranet Web site and has issued memos informing users of the hoax, instructing them about appropriate actions they should take if they receive the e-mail hoax.

Your manager has asked you how the computers running Microsoft Windows XP in your office are protected from the hoax. You demonstrate to her a feature known as Windows File Protection (WPF), which was introduced with Microsoft Windows 2000.

Examining Windows File Protection Settings

In this section, you will examine the policy settings for WFP.

1. Click Start, select Run, type **gpedit.msc** in the Open box, and then click OK.

2. In the tree pane of the Group Policy Object Editor console, browse to \Computer Configuration\Administrative Templates, expand System, and then click Windows File Protection, as shown below.

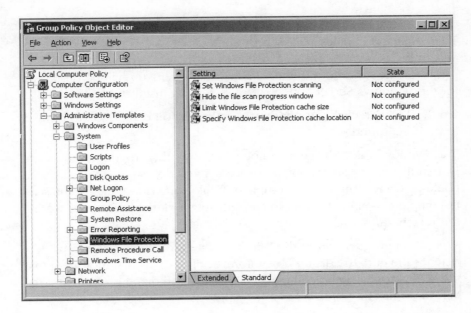

3. In the details pane, double-click Set Windows File Protection Scanning Properties, select the Explain tab, and then read the description.

4. When you are finished reading the description, click Next Setting, and then read the description.

5. Read the descriptions of the remaining Windows File Protection settings, and then answer the following questions.

QUESTION   By default, when does Windows perform file scans?

QUESTION   What is the default maximum size of the file cache?

QUESTION   What is the default location of the folder holding the protected files?

6. Click Cancel to close the open Windows File Protection setting dialog box, and then close the Group Policy Object Editor without making any changes.

7. Click Start, select Run, type **cmd** in the Open box, and then click OK.

8. At the command prompt, type **sfc /?** and press ENTER, and then examine the available switches.

9. At the command prompt, type **sfc /scannow** and then press ENTER.

   The command initiates WFP, which immediately scans protected files to ensure their integrity and replaces any missing or corrupted files. If a protected file is not found in the \Dllcache folder, you will be prompted for the Windows Server 2003 Enterprise Edition installation CD.

10. On the Taskbar, click the Windows File Protection dialog box to bring it to the foreground.

    The Windows File Protection dialog box shows the progress of the scan. Depending on the speed of your processor and disk subsystems, the scan could take a few minutes to complete. While you are waiting for the scan to complete, you might want to take advantage of the time by answering the review questions or taking a short break.

11. When the progress bar in the Windows File Protection dialog box reaches the end, the dialog box automatically disappears, indicating that the WFP scan has been completed. Close the command prompt after the WFP scan has finished.

Verifying WFP Operation

In this section, you will ensure that the standard background file change protection that WFP provides is working properly. To perform this test, you will rename Calc.exe and ensure that Windows places a new copy of the file in the folder.

1. Open Windows Explorer, and then browse to C:\Windows\System32.

2. In the C:\Windows\System32 folder, right-click Calc.exe, select Rename, type **Calc.old**, press ENTER, and then click Yes when prompted to change the extension.

3. Wait a few moments, and then press F5 to refresh the folder display.

4. Locate Calc.exe in the folder.

   Note that the size and creation date are identical to the Calc.old file.

5. Close Windows Explorer.

6. Click Start, select Run, type **eventvwr** in the Open box, and then press ENTER.

7. In the Event Viewer console, select the System log.

8. In the details pane, double-click the events that display Windows File Protection in the Source column.

   QUESTION   What WFP events are listed in the System log?

9. Close Event Viewer.

EXERCISE 12-4: ENFORCING AN INTERNET ACCEPTABLE USE POLICY

Estimated completion time: 25 minutes

Contoso Pharmaceutical's acceptable use policy stipulates that employees must not modify their Microsoft Internet Explorer browser settings. However, a number of employees have ignored the policy and have added unapproved Web sites to the Trusted Security Zone and have changed the proxy server settings so that external HTTP requests go directly through the configured default gateway rather than through the Web proxy server. As a result of these unapproved changes, a number of Trojan horse programs have been introduced on the network. A sexual harassment complaint has also been directed against an employee who was viewing inappropriate Web sites during work hours.

Your manager has asked you to enforce the relevant section of the acceptable use policy through pilot group policy settings defined on an Active Directory organizational unit (OU). If these settings meet the requirements of enforcing the acceptable use policy, they will be incorporated into an appropriate domain-level group policy.

Creating a Group Policy Object to Restrict Changes to Internet Explorer Settings

In this section, you will create a Group Policy object that restricts employees from making changes to key Internet Explorer settings.

1. Click Start, select Administrative Tools, and then click Active Directory Users And Computers.

2. In the Active Directory Users And Computers console, expand Contoso.com, expand ALS, right-click the Employees*xx* OU (where *xx* is your student number), and then click Properties.

3. On the Employees*xx* Property page, select the Group Policy tab.

4. In the Group Policy tab, click New, type **IE restrictions** for the name of the group policy, press ENTER, and then click Edit.

5. In the Group Policy Object Editor, expand User Settings, expand Windows Settings, expand Internet Explorer Maintenance, and then click Connection, as shown below.

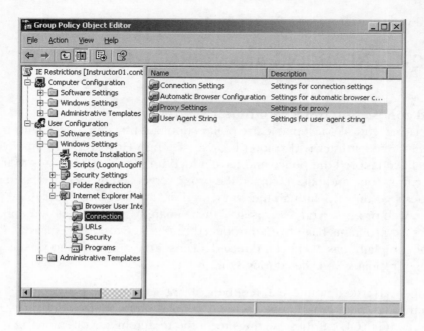

6. In the details pane, double-click Proxy Settings.

7. In the Proxy Settings dialog box, select the Enable Proxy Settings check box, type **instructor01** in the Address Of Proxy box, type **8080** in the Port box, as shown below, and then click OK.

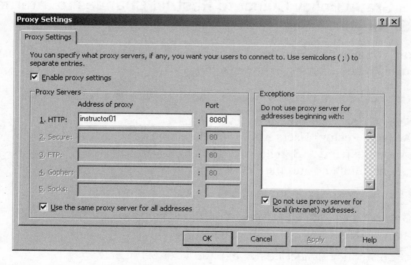

8. In the Group Policy Object Editor, under User Configuration, expand Administrative Templates, expand Windows Components, and then click Internet Explorer, as shown below.

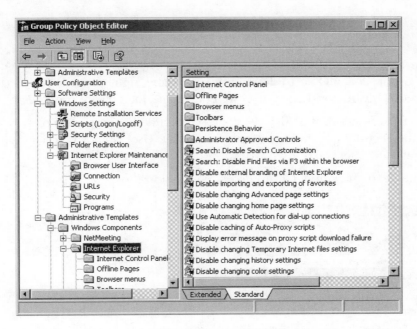

9. In the details pane, double-click Disable Changing Proxy Settings.

10. On the Disable Changing Proxy Settings Property page, click the Enabled option, and then click OK.

In steps 11–13 below, you will configure group policy settings that apply to the computer, rather than the user object. Because the computer object does not exist in the Employees*xx* OU, the policy settings will have no effect; they are intended as a demonstration of the possible computer settings you could use to enforce restrictions on Internet Explorer. In Lab Challenge 12-1, "Enforcing Security Policies Using Group Policy," you will configure additional group policy settings that apply to user objects and that have a similar effect on the settings that apply to computer objects that you configure.

11. In the Group Policy Object Editor, expand Computer Configuration, expand Administrative Templates, expand Windows Components, and then click Internet Explorer.

12. In the details pane, double-click Security Zones: Do Not Allow Users To Change Policies; in the Security Zones: Do Not Allow Users To Change Policies Properties dialog box, select the Enabled option; and then click OK.

13. In the details pane, double-click Security Zones: Do Not Allow Users To Add/Delete Sites; in the Security Zones: Do Not Allow Users To Add/Delete Sites Properties dialog box, select the Enabled option; and then click OK.

NOTE In the following steps, you will examine the group policy permissions to ensure that the IE Restrictions group policy will apply to all users within the Employeesxx OU.

14. In the Group Policy Object Editor, in the tree pane, right-click the IE Restrictions [Instructor01.contoso.com] Policy, and then click Properties.

15. On the IE Restrictions [Instructor01.contoso.com] Policy Properties page, select the Security tab, and then in the Group Or User Names box, click Authenticated Users, as shown below.

Note the Read and Apply Group Policy permissions.

16. In the Group Or User Names box, click Admin*x* (where *x* is your student number).

Even though the Admin*x* account is a member of Authenticated Users, the group policy will not be applied to this account because the account object is located in a different OU and the group policy is applied only to the Employees*xx* OU.

17. Close the IE Restrictions [Instructor01.contoso.com] Policy Properties page, close the Group Policy Object Editor, close the Employees*xx* Property page, and then close Active Directory Users And Computers.

Verifying Group Policy Settings to Restrict Changes to Internet Explorer

In this section, you will verify the group policy settings that you created in the previous section. First, you will execute a command to apply the group policy immediately. Then you will use the Runas command to test the group policy.

1. Log off as Contoso\Adminx and log on as Contoso\Userx (where x is your student number).

2. Open Internet Explorer.

3. From the Tools menu, select Internet Options.

4. On the Internet Options page, select the Connections tab, and then select LAN Settings.

5. In the Local Area Network (LAN) Settings dialog box, note that the Proxy Server settings are grayed out and you cannot change them.

6. Close the Local Area Network (LAN) Settings dialog box, and then select the Security tab.

   Note that you can still modify these settings because the group policy was applied to the computer configuration, rather than the user configuration. Your computer object is in a different OU, and the group policy was not applied to it.

7. Close Internet Explorer and log off.

8. Log on as Contoso\Adminx.

9. Open Internet Explorer and repeat steps 3–6.

   Note that the Adminx account can change the Proxy Server settings in Internet Explorer.

10. Close Internet Explorer.

EXERCISE: 12-5: USING WINDOWS TOOLS TO DOCUMENT SYSTEM INFORMATION

Estimated completion time: 20 minutes

Contoso Pharmaceuticals has recently established a small branch office. The branch office has a new and relatively inexperienced network administrator. You have been asked to visit the office and lend some assistance. When you arrive at the office, you discover that no documentation exists for the client and server computer configurations in the office. Contoso has standardized on third-party software for performing software and hardware inventory. However, licenses for this inventory software have not yet been purchased for use in the branch office. You want to show the new administrator some of the ways to document software, hardware, and configuration information using the tools available in Windows 2003 and Windows XP.

Using MSInfo32.exe to Document System Information

In this section, you will look at the information produced by the MSinfo32.exe utility and then save the information to a text file.

1. Click Start, select Run, type **msinfo32.exe** in the Open box, and then press ENTER.

   The System Information utility opens, showing system summary information as the initial view.

2. In the tree view of the System Information console, expand some of the categories and spend a few minutes familiarizing yourself with the information the utility provides.

3. In the tree view of the System Information console, click System Summary, and from the File menu, select Export.

4. In the Export As dialog box, select the Save In drop-down list and then select C:\Lab Manual\Lab 12\Labwork; in the File Name box, type **computer*xx*_msinfo** (where *xx* is the two-digit version of your student number); and then click Save.

5. Open Windows Explorer, browse to C:\Lab Manual\Lab 12\Labwork, and then double-click the Computer*xx*_Msinfo.txt file you created in step 4.

   Note that the text file contains the same information you viewed in step 2 above. You might also note that the format of the file does not lend itself well to exporting to a spreadsheet or database for analysis.

6. Close Notepad and leave the System Information Console open for the next section.

Using the File Signature Verification Utility to Document Protected Files

1. From the Tools menu of the System Information console, select File Signature Verification Utility.

2. In the File Signature Verification dialog box, click Start.

   The utility begins the process of verifying the integrity of critical system files. This process takes a few minutes.

3. Click OK when the dialog box appears, informing you that the files have been scanned and verified.

4. In the File System Verification dialog box, click Advanced.

5. In the Advanced File Signature Verification Settings dialog box, select the Logging tab.

6. In the Logging tab, click View Log.

   Notepad opens the Sigverif.txt log file.

7. From the Edit menu, select Find.

8. In the Find box, type **calc.exe**, and then click Find Next.

   Note that Calc.exe is listed as a protected file.

9. Close all open windows.

Using Systeminfo.exe to Document System Summary Information

1. Click Start, select Run, type **cmd** in the Open box, and then press ENTER.

2. At the command prompt, type **systeminfo > "C:\Lab Manual\ Lab 12\Labwork\computer.xx_systeminfo.txt"** (where *xx* is the two-digit version of your student number), and then press ENTER.

   Make sure you include the quotation marks around the file path in the command.

   The command causes the output to be sent to a text file, rather than being displayed on the screen.

3. When the command has finished executing, click Start, select Run, type **C:\Lab Manual\Lab 12\Labwork\computer.xx_systeminfo.txt** in the Open box, and then click OK.

4. Review the information contained in the text file.

QUESTION *Does the output of Systeminfo.txt provide information on hotfixes that have been applied?*

5. Close all open windows.

Using Netdiag to Document Network Configuration

Although Netdiag is intended to be used primarily as a troubleshooting tool, it is also useful for documenting network and computer configuration settings.

1. Click Start, and then click Help And Support.

2. Under the Support Tasks heading, click the Tools link.

3. In the Tools column, select Help And Support Center Tools, and then select Network Diagnostics, as shown below.

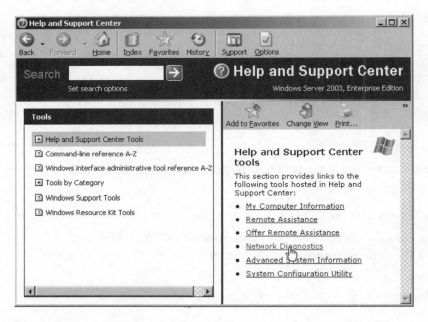

4. On the Network Diagnostics page, select Set Scanning Options.

5. Under Options, select the Verbose check box.

6. Click Scan Your System.

After a few moments, the results of the tests appear.

NOTE Note that a number of categories in the report have a "+" sign beside them. This means that the category can be expanded to see more detail. If you want to save the report to a file and want the detailed information to be present in the saved file, you must expand the categories that you are interested in before saving the report to a file.

7. Expand the categories for which you would like to see detailed information saved to a file.

8. Click Save To File.

9. In the dialog box that appears, note the two locations where the file has been saved, and then click OK.

10. On the taskbar, click the Desktop icon, and then double-click the Netdiag file you just created.

QUESTION What is the relationship between the information you see in the output of Netdiag and the information you see in the file?

11. Close all open windows and log off.

LAB REVIEW QUESTIONS

1. Why is it often undesirable to create overly broad and rigid acceptable use policies?

2. Why is it desirable to enforce policies through software, where technologically possible?

3. You want to install some legacy third-party software on a computer running Windows XP. However, you have been told that this software overwrites some system files with its own versions of the files. Will you be able to install the software? Why or why not?

4. Why is it a good idea to restrict the ability to add Web sites to the Trusted and Intranet Security zones?

5. Tools such as Msinfo32.exe and Systeminfo.exe are very good tools for documenting system configurations in a small environment, but they have a number of limitations that make them inappropriate for storing and analyzing information for a large number of systems. In a large environment, you would probably want to use other tools to inventory hardware, software, and system configuration. What limitations make

Msinfo32.exe and Systeminfo.exe inappropriate for storing and analyzing information for a large number of systems? What capabilities would you want in tools that can collect hardware and software configuration information for a large number of computer systems?

6. One of your company policies states that employees should not disable the settings in Microsoft Outlook Express that strip dangerous attachments from e-mails. What is the best way to enforce that policy?

LAB CHALLENGE 12-1: ENFORCING SECURITY POLICIES BY USING GROUP POLICY

Estimated completion time: 25 minutes

For this lab challenge, you will modify the IE Restrictions group policy you created in Exercise 12-4, "Enforcing an Internet Acceptable Use Policy." In Exercise 12-4 you discovered that, because of the location of the computer objects in Active Directory, the group policy you created that selectively restricted changes to security zones is not applied to users' computers. In this lab challenge, you will make the IE Restrictions policy even more restrictive and create a group policy configuration for users that will restrict the users' ability to change security zone settings.

Scenario

You are a network administrator for Contoso Pharmaceuticals. You have authority in the Active Directory directory service to manage an organizational unit for your branch office. You have been asked to create a group policy that will prevent users from changing Internet Explorer configurations. Specifically, the group policy must prevent users from changing the following settings:

- Privacy settings
- Trusted Zone settings
- Advanced Page settings
- Connection settings
- Proxy Server settings
- Automatic Configuration settings
- History settings
- Home Page settings

One of the challenges in creating the group policy is that computer objects for employee computers are in a different OU from the employee account objects. You do not have administrative control over this OU and cannot change the group policy for that OU. At least one or more of the listed policy settings must be implemented under computer configuration within the group policy. You discussed the issue with your manager, who told you that, where appropriate, you can use group policy to remove the pages from Internet Options in Internet Explorer so that users will not be able to view these settings at all. In fact, she says it is preferable to prevent users from seeing the Internet Options pages that control these configurations.

After you complete this challenge, log on as Contoso\User.x and take a screen shot of the Internet Options General tab. Save the screen shot as Ieoptions.bmp in the C:\Lab Manual\Lab 12\Labwork folder. If your instructor requires you to submit the screen shot for evaluation, he or she will provide further instructions.

> **TIP**   To take a screen shot, make sure the window element of interest is in the foreground, and then press ALT+PRINT SCREEN to copy the screen shot into the clipboard. Open the Paint program, and then press CTRL+V to paste the screen shot into Paint. Finally, save the .bmp file in Paint with the appropriate name.

LAB 13
DETECTING AND RESPONDING TO INCIDENTS

- Exercise 13-1: Configuring and Examining Default Audit Policy Settings

- Exercise 13-2: Configuring Auditing of Security Log Access

- Exercise 13-3: Auditing Logon Events to Detect Intrusion Attempts

- Exercise 13-4: Auditing File System Events

- Exercise 13-5: Examining ISA Server Web Proxy Logs

- Exercise 13-6: Collecting Initial Evidence After a Security Incident

- Lab Review Questions

- Lab Challenge 13-1: Configuring Audit Policies for High Security Servers and Workstations

After completing this lab, you will be able to

- Configure a computer to default baseline audit settings.

- Configure auditing to track attempts to access the Security log.

- Configure auditing to track successful and failed attempts to log on to a computer.

- Configure auditing to track attempts to access files.

- Configure auditing to track attempts to delete files.

- Configure auditing to track attempts to access or modify registry settings and printers.

- Analyze Security logs for suspicious events that indicate attempts to compromise systems.

- Analyze Microsoft Internet Security and Acceleration (ISA) Server Web Proxy logs for unusual or suspicious traffic.

- Distinguish between successful and unsuccessful attempts to compromise systems.

- Collect volatile system data in response to a computer security incident.

- Collect evidence from a computer, using command-line tools that use a small footprint in memory.

- Understand general principles regarding best practices for collecting evidence that might need to be admissible in a court of law.

Estimated completion time: 155 minutes

SCENARIO

You are a network administrator for Contoso Pharmaceuticals. You are responsible for ensuring that computers under your control are configured to log events that might indicate successful or unsuccessful attempts to compromise security. You are also responsible for reviewing firewall logs for suspicious activity that might warrant further investigation and action. As a member of the computer security incident response team (CSIRT), you are also responsible for performing the initial investigation of systems that might have been compromised.

EXERCISE 13-1: CONFIGURING AND EXAMINING DEFAULT AUDIT POLICY SETTINGS

Estimated completion time: 15 minutes

In this exercise, you will configure and examine the default audit policy settings to determine if they are sufficient to detect intrusion attempts. First, in order to ensure a standard default configuration, you will use the Security Configuration And Analysis tool and the Setup Security template to ensure that your computer is configured with the default audit settings. Then, you will examine the default audit settings and review the current contents of the Security log.

> **NOTE**   To complete this section, you must have previously created a Microsoft Management Console (MMC) named Baseline Tools, as outlined in steps 1–11 of Lab 2, Exercise 2-1, "Creating and Applying Security Templates."

1. Log on to Contoso as Admin*x* (where *x* is your student number).

2. On the desktop, double-click the Baseline Tools MMC console that you created in Lab 2, Exercise 2-1, "Creating and Applying Security Templates."

3. In the Baseline Tools console, right-click Security Configuration And Analysis, and then select Import Template.

If the option to import a template is grayed, you will first have to click Open Database and then select or create a database file named Computer*xx*.sdb (where *xx* is the two-digit version of your student number) before you can perform step 3.

4. In the Import Template dialog box, select the Clear This Database Before Importing check box, select the Setup Security.inf file, and then click Open.

5. Right-click Security Configuration And Analysis, and then click Configure Computer Now.

6. In the Configure System dialog box, click OK to accept the default log path and start the configuration.

Security Configuration And Analysis displays the Configuring Computer Security message box, which shows the progress of the configuration process, indicating which areas of the system are being configured.

7. Wait until the template has been applied, then right-click Security Configuration And Analysis, and then select Analyze Computer Now.

8. In the Perform Analysis dialog box, click OK to accept the default log path and start the analysis.

Security Configuration And Analysis displays an Analyzing System Security message box, which shows the progress of the configuration process, indicating which areas of the system are being analyzed.

9. When the analysis is complete, in the Baseline Tools console, browse to Security Configuration And Analysis\Local Policies, select Audit Policies, and examine the default audit settings in the details pane.

QUESTION   What audit settings are enabled on the computer?

10. In the details pane, right-click Audit Logon Events, select Help, and then read the description.

QUESTION   What audit settings are necessary to record a logon event on both the workstation and a domain controller when a domain account is used to log on to the domain from the workstation?

11. Close the MMC that displays the help file, close the Baseline Tools console, and then click Yes when prompted to save the console settings.

12. Click Start, select Run, type **eventvwr** in the Open box, and then click OK.

13. In Event Viewer, select the Security log, and then double-click the topmost security event.

14. On the Event Properties page, briefly examine the entry, and then click the down arrow to examine the next entry.

15. Repeat step 13 to examine the next 10–15 items, and then click Cancel in the Event Properties dialog box when you have finished examining entries.

    This will help you to become more familiar with the content of the Security logs.

16. In the tree pane, right-click the Security log, select Properties, examine the settings, and then answer the following questions.

    QUESTION   What is the default maximum size of the Security log?

    QUESTION   What will happen if the size of the entries in the Security log reaches the maximum threshold for the size of the log file?

17. In the Security Properties dialog box, click Cancel.

18. In the tree pane, right-click the Security log, and then select Clear All Events.

19. In the Event Viewer dialog box, click No when prompted to save the Event log.

20. Close all open windows and log off.

EXERCISE 13-2: CONFIGURING AUDITING OF SECURITY LOG ACCESS

Estimated completion time: 15 minutes
You understand the importance of the Security log for detecting possible attacks. You also understand that the Security log is a prime target of attackers trying to cover their tracks, so you want to configure audit policy settings to detect any unauthorized attempts to gain access to the Security log. In this exercise, you will first attempt to access the Security log in the security context of a nonadministrative account. You will then examine the contents of the Security log in the security context of an administrative account to determine the effectiveness and scope of the default audit policy settings. Finally, you will configure audit policy settings so that the Security log will record failed attempts to access the Security log itself.

1. Log on as Contoso\User*x* (where *x* is your student number).

2. Click Start, select Run, type **eventvwr** in the Open box, and then click OK.

   Event Viewer opens.

3. Right-click the System log, and then click Properties.

   QUESTION   *Can you determine the size of the log files from the Event Viewer interface while logged as Userx?*

4. Click Cancel to close the System Properties dialog box.

5. In Event Viewer, select the Security log.

   A message box appears, indicating access is denied.

6. Click OK to clear the warning message, and then select the other logs in Event Viewer.

   QUESTION   *Why can you view other logs, but not the Security log?*

7. Close Event Viewer.

8. Click Start, select Run, type **runas /user:Contoso\admin*x* eventvwr** in the Open box, and then click OK.

9. In the command prompt, type the password for the Contoso\Admin*x* account, and then press ENTER.

   Event Viewer opens in the context of an administrative account.

10. In Event Viewer, select the Security log, double-click the topmost entry, and then examine the entry.

11. On the Event Properties page, click the down arrow until you reach the bottom of the log file, and then answer the following questions.

    When you reach the bottom of the log file, an Event Viewer dialog box appears, prompting you to proceed to the beginning of the log file. Select No.

    QUESTION   *What three event categories do you see?*

    QUESTION   *Do you see an event that indicates the Security log was cleared?*

    QUESTION   *Do you see any events indicating the use of the alternative Run As credentials?*

    QUESTION   *Do you see any events indicating that a user with nonadministrative credentials attempted to access the Security log?*

12. Click Start, select Run, type **runas /user:Contoso\adminx "mmc secpol.msc"** (with the quotation marks) in the Open box, click OK, type your correct password at the command prompt, and then press ENTER.

13. In the Local Security Settings console, browse to Security Settings\Local Policies, and then select Audit Policy.

14. In the details pane, right-click Audit Privilege Use, select Help, and then read the description of the Audit Privilege Use policy setting.

    QUESTION   What kinds of events will cause an audit record to be generated in the Security log if you enable the Audit Privilege Use policy setting?

15. Close the Microsoft Management Console help window.

16. In the details pane, double-click Audit Privilege Use.

    NOTE   In the following steps, you will configure the Audit Privilege Use settings to generate audit records when a user tries to perform an action that she does not have the user right to perform. If this setting is enabled, an audit log will be generated when a nonadministrative account is used in an attempt to read the Security log. You can also generate an audit event for the same action by using the Audit Object Access setting. The Audit Object Access setting will be covered in the next exercise.

17. On the Audit Privilege Use Properties page, select the Failure check box, and then click OK.

    QUESTION   You could also enable the Success setting. What is a disadvantage of enabling both Success and Failure?

18. Close the Local Security Settings console.

19. Click Start, select Run, type **eventvwr** in the Open box, and then click OK to open a second instance of Event Viewer.

    A second instance of Event Viewer opens in the security context of the User.x account.

20. Select the Security log, and then click OK to clear the warning message.

21. Close the second instance of Event Viewer.

22. Switch to the first instance of Event Viewer, right-click the Security node, and then click Refresh.

    QUESTION   What event indicates a failed attempt to access the Security log?

23. Leave Event Viewer open for the next exercise.

EXERCISE 13-3: AUDITING LOGON EVENTS TO DETECT INTRUSION ATTEMPTS

Estimated completion time: 5 minutes

You want to ensure that the Security logs record events that will help you detect attempts to log on to computers by using stolen or false credentials.

1. Click Start, select Run, type **runas /user:Contoso\adminx "mmc secpol.msc"** (with the quotation marks) in the Open box, click OK, type **badpassword** at the command prompt, and then press ENTER.

   A message very briefly appears in the command prompt window, and then the command prompt window abruptly closes because you used an incorrect password. If you have a fast computer, the command prompt might close so quickly and abruptly that you do not see the message. If you want to see the message, you can launch the Run As command from within a command prompt, rather than the Run dialog box.

2. Switch to Event Viewer, right-click the Security log, and then select Refresh.

   QUESTION   Does the Security log record the failed logon attempt?

   QUESTION   Given the current audit settings, can you use Security logs to detect intrusion attempts?

3. Click Start, select Run, type **runas /user:Contoso\adminx "mmc secpol.msc"** in the Open box, click OK, type your password at the command prompt, and then press ENTER.

4. In the Local Security Settings console, browse to Security Settings\Local Policies, and then select Audit Policy.

5. In the details pane, double-click Audit Account Logon Events, select the Failure check box, and then click OK.

6. Click Start, select Run, type **runas /user:Contoso\adminx "mmc secpol.msc"** in the Open box, click OK, type **badpassword** at the command prompt, and then press ENTER.

7. Switch to Event Viewer, right-click the Security log, and then select Refresh.

   QUESTION   Why is there no record of the failed logon attempt?

8. Switch to the Local Security Settings console, browse to Security Settings\Local Policies, and then click Audit Policy.

9. In the details pane, double-click Audit Logon Events, select the Failure check box, and then click OK.

10. Click Start, select Run, type **runas /user:Contoso\adminx "mmc secpol.msc"** in the Open box, click OK, type **badpassword** at the command prompt, and then press ENTER.

11. Switch to Event Viewer, right-click the Security log, and then select Refresh.

    QUESTION   Is there a record in the Security log that indicates a failed logon attempt?

12. Close Event Viewer and the Local Security Settings console.

EXERCISE 13-4: AUDITING FILE SYSTEM EVENTS

Estimated completion time: 30 minutes
In this exercise, you will configure auditing so that the Security log records attempts to access, modify, or delete files. You want to ensure that you record only the information necessary to detect inappropriate access to sensitive files. You will first create a folder for testing purposes, and then you will configure auditing to record all access attempts to that folder. You will then refine those settings to ensure that the Security log records only relevant information related to inappropriate access of files.

Configuring Audit Settings on a Folder

1. While still logged on as Contoso\User.x, click Start, select Run, type **explorer** in the Open box, and then click OK.

2. In Windows Explorer, expand My Computer, and then select Local Disk (C:).

3. From the File menu, select New, select Folder, type **SACL-Test** for the folder name, and then press ENTER.

    NOTE   SACL is an acronym that stands for System Access Control List.

4. Right-click the SACL-Test folder, and then select Properties.

5. On the SACL-Test Properties page, select the Security tab, click Advanced, and then examine the permission settings on the Advanced Security Settings For SACL-Test page.

    QUESTION *What permissions are listed in the Permissions column for the Userx account and the Administrators and Users groups?*

    QUESTION *Can the Userx account configure auditing on folders or files?*

6. Click Cancel to exit the Advanced Security Settings For SACL-Test page, and then click Cancel again to exit the SACL-Test Properties dialog box.

7. In Windows Explorer, in the left pane, select SACL-Test, select New from the File menu, click Text Document, type **AuditTest** for the filename, and then press ENTER.

    Because of the folder view settings, you do not see the .txt file extension. If you want to view the file extension, you can select Folder Options from the Tools menu, select the View tab in the Folder Options dialog box, and clear the check box option Hide Extensions For Known File Types.

8. Double-click the AuditTest file, type a few characters, and then save and close the file.

    NOTE *Because you cannot use the Run As command with Windows Explorer, and to avoid having to log off and log on using an administrative account, you are going to launch Microsoft Internet Explorer with the Run As command to access the file system in the context of an administrative account.*

9. On the taskbar, right-click the Internet Explorer icon, and then select Run As.

10. In the Run As dialog box, select the The Following User option, type **Contoso\Admin***x* (where *x* is your student number) in the User Name box, type your password in the Password box, and then click OK.

11. In the Address box of Internet Explorer, type **C:** and then press ENTER.

    The file system appears in the browser window.

12. In the Internet Explorer browser window, right-click SACL-Test, select Properties, select Security, and then click Advanced

    QUESTION *What is the difference between the Advanced Security Settings For SACL-Test page you see when you are logged on as an administrative account vs. the page you see when you are logged on as a user account?*

13. In the Advanced Security Setting For SACL-Test dialog box, select the Auditing tab.

14. In the Auditing tab of the Advanced Security Setting For SACL-Test dialog box, click Add.

15. In the Select User, Computer, Or Group dialog box, type **everyone** in the Enter The Object Name To Select box, and then click OK.

16. In the Auditing Entry For SACL-Test page, select the Full Control check boxes in both the Successful and Failed columns, as shown below, and then click OK.

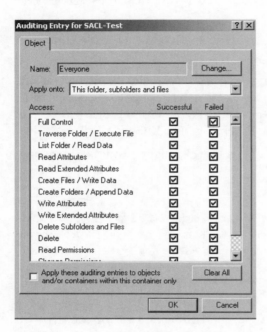

17. Click OK on the Auditing Entry For SACL-Test, click OK on the Advanced Security Setting For SACL-Test dialog box, click OK on the SACL-Test Properties page, and then close Internet Explorer.

Testing Audit Settings

In this section, you will test the audit settings you configured in the previous section and then determine which additional steps you have to take to record audit events for file and folder access. To determine if auditing is working properly, you will access the SACL-Test folder in the context of another user account, attempt to delete the AuditTest file you created earlier, and then examine the contents of the Security log.

1. On the taskbar, right-click the Internet Explorer icon, and select Run As.

2. In the Run As dialog box, select the The Following User option, type **Contoso\Student*x*** (where *x* is your student number) in the User Name box, type your password in the Password box, and then click OK.

3. In the Address box of Internet Explorer, type **C:\SACL-Test** and then press ENTER.

   The contents of the SACL-Test folder appear.

4. Right-click the AuditTest file you created in the previous section, click Delete, and then click Yes when prompted to send the file to the Recycle Bin.

   A message box appears, stating that the file cannot be deleted and that access is denied.

5. Click OK to close the message box, and then close Internet Explorer.

6. Click Start, select Run, type **runas /user:contoso\admin*x* eventvwr** in the Open box, click OK, type your password at the command prompt, and then press ENTER.

7. In Event Viewer, select the Security log, and review the audit events in the details pane.

   Leave Event Viewer open.

   QUESTION   Do you see any audit events indicating an attempt to delete the AuditTest file?

8. Click Start, select Run, type **runas /user:Contoso\admin*x* "mmc secpol.msc"** in the Open box, click OK, type your password at the command prompt, and then press ENTER.

9. In the Local Security Settings console, browse to Audit Policy, right-click Audit Object Access, select Help, and then read the description.

   QUESTION   When you define success or failure settings on Audit Object Access, what kind of access is audited?

10. Close the Microsoft Management Console help window.

11. In the Local Security Settings console, double-click Audit Object Access, select the Success and Failure check boxes, and then click OK.

12. On the taskbar, right-click the Internet Explorer icon, and then select Run As.

13. In the Run As dialog box, select the The Following User option, type
Contoso\Student*x* in the User Name box, type your password in the
Password box, and then click OK.

14. In the Address box of Internet Explorer, type **C:** and then press ENTER.

    The contents of the C drive appear.

15. In Internet Explorer, double-click the SACL-Test folder, right-click the
AuditTest file you created in the previous section, select Delete, and then
click Yes when prompted to send the file to the Recycle Bin.

    A message box appears, stating that the file cannot be deleted and that
access is denied.

16. Click OK to close the warning message, and then close Internet Explorer.

17. Switch to Event Viewer.

18. Right-click the Security log, select Refresh, and then examine the audit
entries in the details pane.

    QUESTION   How many failure audit events do you see in the Security log that are
    related to the action of attempting to delete the file?

19. Double-click the topmost failure audit event related to the attempt to
delete the AuditTest file, and then read the description of the audit entry.

    QUESTION   What is listed in the Accesses field of the description of the failed
    audit event?

20. On the Event Properties page, click the down arrow to examine the
descriptions of the audit failures related to the attempted deletion of the
file. Pay attention to the Accesses field in each entry. Click Cancel on the
Event Properties page when you reach the end of the Failure Audit events.

    QUESTION   What three kinds of access are listed in the Accesses field for all the
    entries related to the failed attempt to delete the file?

21. In Event Viewer, from the View Menu, select Filter.

22. On the Security Properties page, in the Event Types area, clear all the
check boxes except for Success Audit, type **Student*x*** in the User box, as
shown below, and then click OK.

    Event Viewer displays only Success Audit events for the Student*x* account.

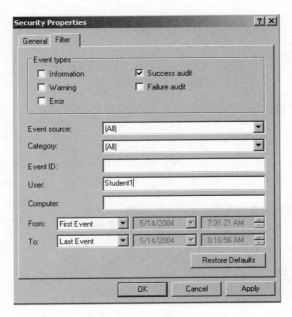

23. In Event Viewer, select the Category column to sort the entries by category, locate the first entry that displays Object Access in the Category column, and then scroll down to the final entry that displays Object Access in the Category column.

    QUESTION   What potential problems for audit log analysis and system resources are indicated by the number of Success Audit entries?

24. In Event Viewer, select Newest First from the View menu, and then select All Records from the View menu.

    Leave Event Viewer open for the next section.

Refining File Audit Settings

1. On the taskbar, right-click the Internet Explorer icon, and then select Run As.

2. In the Run As dialog box, select the The Following User option, type **Contoso\Admin*x*** (where *x* is your student number) in the User Name box, type your password in the Password box, and then click OK.

3. In the Address box of Internet Explorer, type **C:** and press ENTER.

   The file system appears in the browser window.

4. In the Internet Explorer browser window, right-click SACL-Test, select Properties, select Security, and then click Advanced.

5. In the Advanced Security Settings For SACL-Test dialog box, select the Auditing tab.

6. In the Auditing tab of the Advanced Security Settings For SACL-Test dialog box, ensure that the audit entry you created earlier is selected, as shown below, and then click Edit.

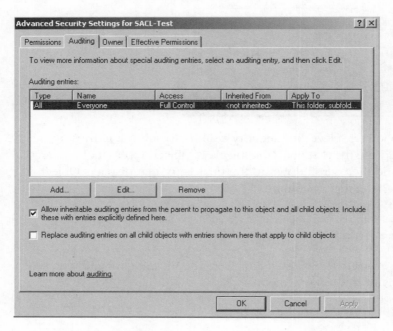

7. In the Auditing Entry For SACL-Test dialog box, select the Clear All option, select the Delete Subfolders And Files and the Delete check boxes (both Successful and Failed) as shown below, and then click OK.

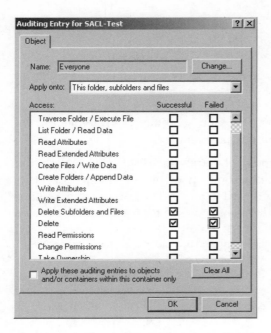

8. Click OK in the Advanced Security Settings For SACL-Test dialog box, click OK in the SACL-Test Properties dialog box, and then close Internet Explorer.

9. On the taskbar, right-click the Internet Explorer icon, and then select Run As.

10. In the Run As dialog box, select the The Following User option, type **Contoso\Student***x* (where *x* is your student number) in the User Name box, type your password in the Password box, and then click OK.

11. In the Address box of Internet Explorer, type **C:** and then press ENTER.

    The contents of the C drive appear.

12. In Internet Explorer, double-click the SACL-Test folder, right-click the AuditTest file you created in the previous section, click Delete, and then click Yes when prompted to send the file to the Recycle Bin.

    A message box appears, stating that the file cannot be deleted and that access is denied.

13. Click OK to close the message box, and then close Internet Explorer.

14. Switch to Event Viewer.

15. Right-click the Security log, and then select Refresh.

> **NOTE**   If you do not see the failed audit records for the most recent attempt to delete the file, click Newest First from the View menu.

16. Examine the recent audit entries that were generated for the file and folder access activity of the Student*x* account.

In Event Viewer, look for the group of entries that display Student*x* in the User column. You should see approximately eight Failure Audit events and two Success Audit events grouped together. The current audit settings have limited the number of audit events you see for folder and file access.

> **QUESTION**   Do you see any entries indicating that the Student*x* account was able to view the contents of the SACL-Test folder?

> **QUESTION**   If the SACL-Test folder contained highly sensitive information, would the current audit settings be sufficient?

17. Close all windows and log off.

EXERCISE 13-5: EXAMINING ISA SERVER WEB PROXY LOGS

Estimated completion time: 20 minutes

In this exercise, you will examine a sample Internet Security and Acceleration (ISA) Server Web Proxy log to determine if it has recorded any events that should cause concern. Your instructor will provide specific instructions on completing the exercise, including whether the exercise will be completed individually, in groups, or as an instructor-led discussion.

You are the administrator of an ISA Server used in a small branch office of Contoso Pharmaceuticals. The ISA Server logs traffic to and from the Internet in a number of log files. The Web Proxy log records all the traffic handled by the Web Proxy Service of the ISA Server. Every Monday morning, you examine the ISA Server logs that were generated over the weekend. Normally, no one is in the office over the weekend. Before reviewing the logs, you verify that only one employee was in the office during the weekend to complete work on a special project, and he did not open Internet Explorer or access the Internet from his computer. However, a number of computers in the office were left on during the weekend.

1. Log on to Contoso as **Admin.*x*** (where *x* is your student number).

2. Click Start, select Run, type **explorer** in the Open box, and then click OK.

3. In Windows Explorer, browse to C:\Lab Manual\Lab 13, and then double-click IsaWebPrx040306.log.

The sample ISA Web Proxy log file opens in Notepad.

NOTE This log file is based on events recorded in an actual ISA Server log file. However, the domain names and IP addresses have been changed. The internal network is represented by the address range 192.168.100.1–192.168.100.255. All other IP addresses, including those that use the private address ranges of 10.x.y.z and 172.16.x.y, represent external hosts. The external IP address of the ISA Server is represented by the IP address 172.16.25.239. All domain names that use examplex.com represent external domains.

To help you read the log files, note the meaning of the various prefixes used to describe the fields in the log file: "c" indicates client actions, "s" indicates server actions, "cs" indicates client to server actions, "sc" indicates server to client actions, and "r" indicates remote.

4. In the log file, toward the top, locate the entry that represents a GET request for a file named Default.ida from the ISA Server, and answer the following questions.

   Throughout this exercise, you might find it helpful to use the Find feature of Notepad from the Edit menu to quickly locate the entries of interest.

   QUESTION Does this entry look like a legitimate request? If not, why not? Hint: look at the length of the request.

   QUESTION Why would an attacker send an excessively long Uniform Resource Locator (URL) to a Web server?

   QUESTION Was the request successful? Hint: look at the HTTP status code in the sc-status column (the last entry on the line); an HTTP status code of 200 would indicate a successful request.

5. In the log file, locate the group of entries that display the IP address of 10.12.209.34 in the C-IP field (the left-most entry on each of the lines), and answer the following questions.

   QUESTION What kinds of files do the requests attempt to invoke?

   QUESTION What features of these requests lead you to believe that they represent an attempt to compromise a Web server?

   QUESTION A directory traversal attack attempts to invoke executable files that are found on the local hard drive outside of the virtual directories used by the Web site. Does this group of requests represent an attempted directory traversal attack?

   QUESTION Was the attempt to compromise the server successful? Hint: an HTTP status code of 200 indicates a successful request.

6. In the log file, locate the group of entries that displays the internal IP address of 192.168.100.222 in the C-IP field (the left-most entry on each of the lines), and answer the following questions.

QUESTION Based on the scenario that begins this lab exercise, what features of these requests might cause you to believe that an internal computer might have been compromised? Hint: look at the times the requests are being made.

QUESTION Were the requests from the internal computer to the Example2.net Web site successful?

QUESTION What information in the log file can you use to do research on the Internet to determine whether the internal computer has in fact been compromised?

7. Close Notepad and all open windows.

Stay logged on for the next exercise.

EXERCISE 13-6: COLLECTING INITIAL EVIDENCE AFTER A SECURITY INCIDENT

Estimated completion time: 25 minutes

Your daily review of the firewall logs shows that there is a Trojan horse program on an internal file server used by Contoso Pharmaceuticals researchers. You inform your manager, who tells you that she just received an e-mail from a researcher who believes the data he works with has been inexplicably altered. Your manager suspects that the two events are related and wants you to go immediately to the affected computer and take a snapshot of volatile system data and the contents of the security, system, and application logs as a preliminary, evidence-gathering step. For the time being, the CSIRT, of which you are a member, has decided to leave the computer running and connected to the network. Depending on an initial analysis of the system data you collect and a real-time analysis of network traffic and firewall activity, the CSIRT will determine the next step to take, such as quarantining the system from the network or powering it off.

For this exercise, assume that the user is currently logged on, the computer has not been restarted, and you have access to a command prompt. Your goal is to collect as much evidence as possible from the volatile memory of the computer without compromising that evidence.

Using Default Operating System Tools to Collect Evidence

In this section, you will use a number of commands to perform an initial collection of volatile system data. These commands are included as part of the default installation of the Microsoft Windows operating system.

1. If you are not logged into your computer, log on to Contoso as **Admin***x* (where *x* is your student number).

   NOTE In performing a forensic investigation of a computer, you want to leave as light a footprint as possible and avoid taking any actions that might possibly trigger events that could destroy data. One of the goals of doing a forensic analysis is to analyze the data without modifying it. You should always consider this before taking any action. Logging on to a computer could trigger undesirable changes to data that could compromise evidence. For example, logging on to a computer could cause a program to execute that would destroy evidence. If the user account is still logged on, you need to balance the possible limitations of using a nonadministrative account to collect information versus the risk of logging the user off and logging on with an administrative account. Also, you should never force an administrative password change on the user's account to gain access to his files. Doing so would, for example, make his Encrypting File System (EFS)–encrypted files inaccessible, unless you have access to an EFS recovery agent. If you have a faithful bit-level copy of the user's hard drive that you can use for analysis, you have access to the Security Accounts Management (SAM) database and can use forensic cracking tools to recover the user's password. But, note that in this case you are working with a copy of data, not the original.

2. Click Start, select Run, type **cmd** in the Open box, and then press ENTER.

3. At the command prompt, type **netstat -a**, press ENTER, and then review the contents of the screen output.

   QUESTION Why is it a good idea to collect information on the open ports of a suspect computer?

4. At the command prompt, type **netstat –a > "C:\Lab Manual\ Lab 13\Labwork\OpenPorts.txt"** (with the quotation marks) and then press ENTER.

   When you use the ">" sign in a command, you are instructing the operating system to redirect the output of the command. In this, and other instances that follow, you are redirecting the output to a text file that is created when you execute the command. In subsequent steps, you will first examine the screen output of various commands, and then run the commands again to redirect the output to text files that will form a record of the contents of volatile memory.

NOTE   In a real-life situation where you had to collect evidence that might need to be presented in a court of law, you would avoid writing any data to the hard drive of the affected system. If you write data to the hard drive, you risk overwriting sectors on the hard drive that could potentially contain evidence of malfeasance. Instead, you should use a floppy drive or some other writeable media other than the hard drive. You should also be aware that the system could be compromised at the kernel level, making any data you collect suspect.

5. At the command prompt, type **ipconfig /all**, press ENTER, and then review the contents of the screen output.

6. Type **ipconfig /all > "C:\Lab Manual\Lab 13\Labwork\Ipconfig.txt"** and then press ENTER.

7. Type **route print**, press ENTER, and then review the contents of the screen output.

8. Type **route print > "C:\Lab Manual\Lab 13\Labwork\ RoutingTable.txt"** and then press ENTER.

QUESTION   In steps 5–8, you collected information on the TCP/IP configuration of the target computer. Why is it a good idea to collect this information?

9. Type **ipconfig /displaydns**, press ENTER, and then review the contents of the screen output.

10. Type **ipconfig /displaydns > "C:\Lab Manual\Lab 13\Labwork\ DNSCache.txt"** and then press ENTER.

11. Type **nbtstat -c**, press ENTER, and then review the contents of the screen output.

12. Type **nbtstat -c > "C:\Lab Manual\Lab 13\Labwork\NBTCache.txt"** and then press ENTER.

13. Type **arp -a**, press ENTER, and then review the contents of the screen output.

14. Type **arp -a "C:\Lab Manual\Lab 13\Labwork\ArpCache.txt"** and then press ENTER.

   QUESTION In steps 9–11, you examined volatile data related to name resolution and IP–to–media access control (MAC) address resolution. What is the purpose of recording this kind of evidence?

15. Type **net start**, press ENTER, and then review the contents of the screen output.

16. Type **net start > "C:\Lab Manual\Lab 13\Labwork\ RunningServices.txt"** and then press ENTER.

17. Type **tasklist**, press ENTER, and then review the contents of the screen output.

18. Type **tasklist "C:\Lab Manual\Lab 13\Labwork\Tasklist.txt"** and then press ENTER.

   QUESTION Why is it a good idea to collect data on the tasks and the services currently running on the suspect computer?

19. Open Windows Explorer, and navigate to C:\Lab Manual\Lab 13\ Labwork.

   You should see a number of text files that you created in the previous steps.

20. Double-click the text files to open them in Notepad to verify that they contain the information you viewed on the screen in the previous steps.

   You should keep in mind that normally you would not create these files on the hard drive of a computer you were investigating.

21. Leave the command prompt open for the next section.

Using Windows Resource Kit and Support Kit Tools to Collect Evidence

In this section, you will use a variety of tools extracted from the Microsoft Windows 2000 Resource Kit, the Microsoft Windows 2003 Resource Kit, and the Microsoft Windows 2003 Support Tools. You can get the Resource Kit utilities either by downloading them from the Microsoft Web site at *http://www.microsoft.com/ windows/reskits/default.asp* or by buying the Windows Resource Kit. The Support Tools utilities are included on the Windows 2003 installation CD.

1. At the command prompt, type **cd\lab manual\lab 13** and then
   press ENTER.

2. Type **memsnap "c:\lab manual\lab 13\labwork\memsnap.log"**
   (with the quotation marks) and then press ENTER.

3. Type **"c:\lab manual\lab 13\labwork\memsnap.log"** (with the
   quotation marks), press ENTER, and then review the information displayed
   in Notepad.

   QUESTION   Both Tasklist.exe and Memsnap.exe display information on running
   tasks. What advantages does Memsnap.exe have over Tasklist.exe?

4. Close Notepad.

   NOTE   One of the goals of collecting evidence from a computer is to disrupt the
   system as little as possible while gathering information. If you can collect
   information from the suspect computer remotely, you should consider doing so if
   it is safe to not quarantine the affected computer from the network. So far, you
   have been collecting evidence by running tools on the local computer. In the next
   series of steps, you will use two Resource Kit utilities, Srvinfo.exe and
   Srvcheck.exe, that can collect evidence from remote computers.

5. At the command prompt, type **srvinfo -d**, press ENTER, and then review
   the contents of the screen output.

6. Type **srvinfo -d \\computeryy** (where *yy* is the two-digit version of
   your lab partner's student number), press ENTER, and then review the
   contents of the screen output.

   QUESTION   The output of the command issued against the local computer and
   the remote computer differs slightly: the command issued against the local
   computer shows detailed information related to the network interface adapter
   and installed protocols. What might account for this difference? Hint: the reason
   has nothing to do with the fact that one command is issued against a local
   computer and the other against a remote computer.

7. Type **srvinfo -d > "C:\Lab Manual\Lab 13\Labwork\Srvinfo.txt"** and
   then press ENTER.

   QUESTION   Both the Net Start and the Srvinfo.exe commands display
   information on running services. What advantages does the Srvinfo.exe command
   have over the Net Start command?

8. Type **srvcheck \\computer*xx*** (where *xx* is the two-digit version of your student number), press ENTER, and then review the contents of the screen output.

   QUESTION The Srvcheck.exe command enumerates shares and share permissions on local and remote computers. It can be useful to determine, for example, if an attacker has modified share permissions or created new shares. However, Srvcheck.exe does not display all shares on the computer. What shares does it not display?

9. Type **srvcheck \\computerxx > "C:\Lab Manual\Lab 13\Labwork\ Srvcheck.txt"** and then press ENTER.

   NOTE So far, you have been examining volatile system data that is destroyed when you shut down the computer. In the next steps, you will use Dumple.exe, a Windows 2000 Resource Kit command-line utility to export Event log information to a text file. You can also use this utility to export Event logs from a remote computer.

10. Type **cd Dumpel** and then press ENTER.

11. Type **dumpel /?**, press ENTER, and then note the capabilities of the command.

   QUESTION Can you use the command to filter events that occurred within the past 24 hours and pass them to a text file? If so, why would you want to perform this kind of filtering when investigating an incident?

12. Type **dumpel -f security.log -l security** and then press ENTER.

13. Type **security.log**, examine the contents of the file containing the audit events, and then close Notepad.

   QUESTION The results generated by the command-line utilities could also be generated using GUI-based tools found in Windows operating systems. For example, you could use Event Viewer on one computer to connect to the logs on a remote computer and then export those logs to another computer. Why might you use a command-line tool instead of a GUI-based tool?

14. Close all open Windows and log off.

LAB REVIEW QUESTIONS

Estimated completion time: 20 minutes

1. Why is it important to pay attention to the settings governing the size of log files and when they will overwrite data?

2. Every day, an automated process exports log files from computers on your network and places them in a central location. What special considerations should you give to the locations where the log files are stored?

3. Why is it a good idea to audit successful and failed attempts to read the Security audit log?

4. In reviewing your audit logs, you notice a number of account lockout events (Event ID 539). However, the users whose accounts have been locked out have not made requests to the Help Desk to have the lockout removed. Why haven't the users contacted the Help Desk, and what other information should you be paying attention to in analyzing the account lockout audit entries?

5. Why is it often advisable to selectively limit the audit information that is generated for successful or failed attempts to access a file or folder?

6. You are responsible for making the initial response to a computer security incident. In addition to executing commands to record system information stored in volatile memory, what other activities should you perform to ensure the potential admissibility of evidence you collect in a court of law?

7. You are responding to a computer security incident involving an employee who was abruptly asked to report to Human Resources after it was discovered she was using her computer in violation of company policies. You have been asked to collect evidence from the computer. When you arrive at the user's workstation, you discover that the employee's manager powered off the computer and then restarted it in order to log in with his own credentials to discover more details of the employee's activities. How has the manager potentially jeopardized the evidence available on the computer and increased the risk for the company?

8. You are responding to a security incident involving an employee's computer after it was discovered that the employee was using his computer for activities prohibited by company policies. You have recorded information stored in volatile memory. Based on your initial investigation, it is likely the employee will be terminated. Before you shut down the employee's computer, what additional actions should you take?

9. You are the network administrator for Contoso Pharmaceuticals. While performing a daily review of Web Proxy logs on your ISA Server, you notice a suspicious entry that indicates the presence of a Trojan horse program on an internal computer. How should you respond to this incident?

   To answer this question, select the possible responses from the following list, and put them in the correct order.

   a. Disconnect the computer from the network.

   b. Call the CSIRT.

   c. Power off the computer.

   d. Start a written journal of your actions.

   e. Continue reading the log files.

   f. Consult the company's Incident Response Procedure Guidelines.

LAB CHALLENGE 13-1: CONFIGURING AUDIT POLICIES FOR HIGH SECURITY SERVERS AND WORKSTATIONS

Estimated completion time: 25 minutes

You are a network administrator for Constoso Pharmaceuticals. Among your many duties, you are responsible for monitoring a group of servers used by researchers at the company. Much of the data stored on the servers is highly sensitive. You and your manager have been reviewing the audit settings on this group of computers. You have come to the conclusion that, given the sensitive nature of the data, you need to do extensive auditing on these computers to detect any attempts to compromise the computers or the files they contain. Your manager wants you to audit for the following kinds of activity:

- Any activity related to logging on and off from the workstations using both domain and local accounts

- Any attempts to modify and delete files or registry settings

- Use of printers connected to workstations

- Any attempt to add or modify user or group objects on the local computers

- Any attempt to modify user rights or audit policies

- Any attempt by users to exercise user rights

- Any attempt to shut down or restart computers

Because of the critical nature of the data and the importance of the Security logs on these computers, your manager wants you to provide the following configuration for Security logs:

■ Older events in the Security log should never be overwritten by newer events.

■ If the Security log fills up, the computers should shut down automatically.

■ Ensure that the computer does not shut down prematurely as a result of logging many entries to the Security log. Ideally, the maximum size of the log file should be at least twice the default size for the log file.

To complete this lab challenge, create a new group policy object named Audit Policies on your Employees*x* organizational unit (where *x* is your student number). Configure the policy settings, take the appropriate screen shots of the policy settings (you will need more than one screen shot), and save the screen shots as C:\Lab Manual\Lab 13\Labwork\LC13-1-*x_LastName*.bmp (where *x* is a sequential number starting with 1 representing each of your screen shots and *LastName* is your last name). Your instructor might want you to submit your screen shots for evaluation. If so, you will be given specific instructions for submitting your screen shots.

The figure below shows a sample screen shot (without the policy settings) similar to one of the screen shots you will have to create.

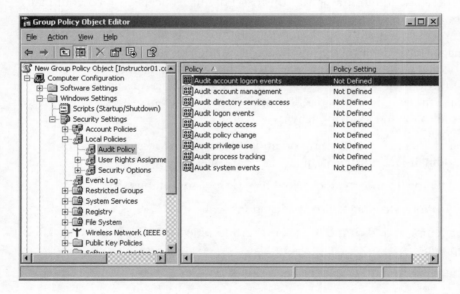

To take a screen shot and save it as a file, do the following:

1. Make sure that the window you want to take a screen shot of is in the foreground, and then press ALT+PRINTSCREEN to copy the screen image to the clipboard.

2. Open the Paint application, press CTRL+V to paste the image into the Paint application, then save the file with the appropriate name.

3. Open the Paint application by entering **pbrush** in the Open box of the Run menu.

TROUBLESHOOTING LAB B
ANALYZING A SECURITY INCIDENT

PART 1: REVIEW

You are a member of Contoso Pharmaceutical's Computer Security Incident Response Team (CSIRT) and are designated as the chief contact. At 8:30 A.M., Dr. Frank Lee, who is one of the company's top researchers and is generally regarded worldwide as a leading expert in his field, phones you to report that some of his research is missing from the RDFL004 file server he uses to store his top secret research data. He is convinced that his research has been deleted by an unauthorized third party, possibly an industrial spy. The RDFL004 file server on which the files were stored is closely monitored, and only Dr. Lee and a handful of other user accounts were able to access the research that was deleted.

At 8:35 A.M., you contact Max Benson, the network administrator and team lead who is responsible for the server containing the deleted files. You ask him to perform an immediate but cursory review of the Security logs that were copied by an automated process from RDFL004 to another server that is used to store audit files. The audit files are copied at 6:00 A.M. every morning. You tell Max not to log on to RDFL004 or perform any activity on it until notified.

At 8:45 A.M., Max confirms part of Dr. Lee's suspicions and reports to you that the Contoso\Sandram user account deleted the files at approximately 2:55 A.M. The user account belongs to Sandra Martinez, a high-profile employee who often acts as a spokesperson for the company. Max also tells you that he observed some unusual entries in the Event log related to failed logons for both the Contoso\Frankle and Contoso\Sandram accounts just before the files were deleted.

Although the CSIRT will not rule out the possibility that Sandra Martinez (or any employee of the company, for that matter) did in fact delete the files, the CSIRT believes this is not a very likely possibility. Currently, Ms. Martinez is attending a conference in Europe. Furthermore, the Contoso\Sandram account has, according to your documentation, no administrative permissions on the server that contained the deleted files. Also, the team believes that Ms. Martinez lacks the in-depth knowledge required to elevate the permissions for her account so that it could delete the files.

The CSIRT team has put you in charge of investigating whether a security breach has occurred. At 9:00 A.M., you begin your investigation by interviewing Max Benson, who provides you with the following information:

- Late yesterday, a Web server named CPSRV006 had to be rebuilt. This server is used as a Web server for business-to-business (B2B) transactions. Max notes that Amy Rusko, who is a member of his team and is responsible for performing security audits and applying patches, had to leave work suddenly this morning to deal with a family emergency. She was supposed to ensure that the rebuilt server passed a Microsoft Baseline Security Analyzer (MBSA) audit. Max has just received an e-mail from Amy regarding the MBSA audit she performed just before she had to leave the office. The e-mail contained the most recent change log for CPSRV006, which also showed the results of the MBSA audit. Because Max had to provide an initial response to Dr. Lee's incident report this morning, he hasn't had time to read the e-mail or look at the change log.

- Max reports that he might have lost an old network diagram of the Contoso head office. A couple of days ago, he was working on a new network diagram. He placed the old network diagram among the papers stacked on his desk. When it occurred to him to shred the old diagram, he couldn't find it. At the time, he assumed he had just misplaced it and that it would turn up eventually. But now he wonders whether he threw it out or if someone took it from his desk. Given the events of this morning, he is quite concerned that he doesn't know what happened to the network diagram.

Because of this initial information from Max, you decide to widen your investigation to include the recently rebuilt Web server (CPSRV006) in addition to the Internet Acceleration and Security (ISA) Server firewall, the domain controller, and the server where the files disappeared.

PART 2: TROUBLESHOOTING SETUP

Because this is not a hands-on lab, no troubleshooting setup is required.

PART 3: TROUBLESHOOTING

This lab requires you to analyze a number of log files to determine the cause and extent of the attack that occurred against the Contoso network and computer systems. After analyzing the log files, you will formulate an appropriate response to the attack and answer a series of questions related to the lab. You will record your findings and respond to the lab questions in a file named Troubleshooting Lab B Worksheet.doc, which is found in the C:\Lab Manual\TroubleshootingLabB folder.

Depending on your instructor, this lab can be performed individually, in small groups, or as the basis for a classroom discussion.

To view the log files for this lab, open Windows Explorer and browse to C:\Lab Manual\TroubleshootingLabB. You will see a number of folders that contain log files relating to the incident described in the scenario above. The names and descriptions of the log files are listed in Table B-1.

Table B-1   Log File Content Matrix

Log Filename	Content
Cpsrv006_changelog.rtf	Manually maintained change log
Mbsa-cpsrv006.rtf	MBSA log for CPSRV006
Cpsrv006-20020214.txt	Security log for CPSRV006
Dc-chi-01-20020214.txt	Security log for DC-CHI-01
Rdfl004-20020214.txt	Security log for RDFL004
IPPEXTD20020214.log	ISA Server log
Netstat-cpsrv006-020214.log	Netstat log
Tw-rdfl004-20020214.txt	File integrity checker log for RDFL004

In the C:\Lab Manual\TroubleshootingLabB folder, you will also find a number of other files to help you complete the lab. These files are listed in Table B-2.

Table B-2   Supporting Files

Filename	Content
Contoso Network Diagram.gif	Contoso network diagram
How Assets Are Attacked.doc	A summary of exploits that can be used against computer systems
Security Log Review Procedure.doc	A document that explains Contoso's official procedures for reviewing log files
Things To Look For In Log Files.doc	A document that provides information on useful strategies for analyzing log files
Troubleshooting Lab B Worksheet	A worksheet containing forms and questions that you complete as part of this lab

To complete this lab, use WordPad to open the file named Troubleshooting Lab B Worksheet.doc. (Because you will need to make entries in a Microsoft Word table, a better alternative is to use Word if it is available. Your instructor can tell you if either application is available.) Troubleshooting Lab B Worksheet.doc consists of four parts, with the first three parts representing typical kinds of documentation you would create when responding to a computer security incident.

- The first part consists of a table representing journal entries you would make while investigating and responding to an incident.

- The second part is a table that you complete to show a summary of the log entries that are relevant to the incident. The purpose of this table is to provide a kind of index to the entries in the log files and to show the relationship between events in different log files by grouping the related events together.

- The third part is an incident response form that you fill in once you have investigated and responded to the incident. To complete this form, you will need to formulate a hypothetical response to the scenario incident. Because this is a scenario-based exercise, you might not be able to fill in all the fields in the form. However, you should provide as much accurate detail as you can, according to the scenario. For example, the form should accurately list the type of attack and the classification of data involved.

- The fourth part consists of a series of questions that you answer after completing your investigation. Please answer the questions in the worksheet itself. The questions in the worksheet are listed in Part 4, "Troubleshooting Lab B Questions," to provide you with some additional guidance in completing this lab. In fact, you might want to consider the questions as you examine the logs, because the questions might help you in your analysis.

When you have completed the worksheet, save it as C:\Lab Manual\ TroubleshootingLabB\Labwork\TBLB_*YourLastName*.doc. If your instructor wants you to submit this worksheet for evaluation, he or she will explain how to do so. Documentation is crucial. You will be evaluated not only on your ability to correctly identify the problems that were introduced and their solutions, but also on the process you used to identify the problems and the solutions.

PART 4: TROUBLESHOOTING LAB B QUESTIONS

1. How did the attacker first gain entry to the network?

2. Did the missing network diagram play a role in the attack?

3. According to the Security log file for CPSRV006, what executable files were run by the attacker? Hint: search the file for the ".exe" text string.

4. According to the Security log file for CPSRV006, what two text files were created by the attacker? Hint: search the file for the ".txt" text string.

5. What protocol did the attacker use to transfer files? What log files show evidence of the protocol that was used? Hint: knowing the Transmission Control Protocol (TCP) ports for common protocols will help you answer this question.

6. According to the tripwire log for RDFL004, what files were modified or added?

7. According to the Security log file for RDFL004, what executable files did the attacker run?

8. Considering your response to question 7, are there entries in other log files that correspond to the running of one of these executable files?

9. What lapses in procedure allowed the attack to occur?

10. What format is used to generate user names at Contoso pharmaceuticals? That is, how is a person's name used to create a user name? Are user names easy to guess?

11. Should Contoso review its password complexity requirements?

12. What should Contoso's responses be to the intrusion? For example, should they power off the servers, contact other individuals, or discipline employees?

13. What should Contoso do to enhance security and prevent similar attacks from taking place in the future?